P9-CJZ-969

POWER OF THE CROSS

Power of the *Cross*

REAL STORIES ✚ REAL PEOPLE ✚ A REAL GOD

TIM LAHAYE

Multnomah Books *Sisters, Oregon*

POWER OF THE CROSS
Copyright © 1998 by Tim LaHaye
published by Multnomah Books

and published in association with the literary agency of
Alive Communications, Inc., 1465 Kelly Johnson Blvd.,
Suite 320, Colorado Springs, CO 80920

International Standard Book Number: 1-57673-212-6
Printed in the United States of America
Cover photograph by: Lisa Taft
Cover design by: Kevin Keller

Unless otherwise indicated, Scripture quotations used in this book are from

The Holy Bible, New King James Version (NKJV) © 1984
by Thomas Nelson, Inc.

Scripture references indicated NIV are from
The Holy Bible, New International Version (NIV) © 1973, 1984 by
International Bible Society, used by permission of
Zondervan Publishing House.

Library of Congress Cataloging–in–Publication Data
LaHaye, Tim F.
  Power of the Cross/by Tim LaHaye.
    p.cm.   Includes bibliographical references.
  ISBN 1-57673-212-6 (paper)
  1. Crosses. 2. Conversion. 3. Christian biography–United States.
4. Christian life. 5. LaHaye, Tim F. I. Title.
BT453.L25   1998   97-45539
232.96'3--dc21   CIP

98 99 00 01 02 03 04 — 10 9 8 7 6 5 4 3 2 1

Everyone is influenced by someone else. It has been said that the people with whom we associate and the books we read influence us all. As we work our way through life, we often find that most people are influenced by several people. I certainly fit that profile. So I would like to dedicate this book to the eight people who have most influenced my life.

Margaret LaHaye, my godly mother

Dr. Beverly LaHaye, my best friend and devoted wife of fifty years

Dr. Bob Jones Sr., who gave me a passion for lost souls

Dr. Wilbur Smith, who taught me Bible doctrine at Moody Bible Institute

Dr. David L. Cooper, under whom I studied prophecy for eight years

Dr. Henry Brandt, who taught me to test humanistic psychology by the Scriptures, and who showed me how to overcome anger by the power of the Holy Spirit

Dr. Francis Schaeffer, who convinced me secular humanism was a religious philosophy that should be opposed vigorously by all Christians

Dr. Henrietta C. Mears, who taught me as a young minister the importance of the Sunday school and the need to reach our generation of children for Christ before the devil gets to them.

All but two of these folks are in heaven today with their Lord. I look forward to meeting them soon and will thank them personally for all they have done to help mold my life. In addition, there are thousands of authors of good books who similarly have contributed to my thinking, to whom I am also indebted. For as the Bible says, "as a man thinks in his heart, so is he" and "out of the abundance of the heart, the mouth speaks" (or in my case, as the pen writes).

ACKNOWLEDGMENTS

It was not difficult to find individuals whose lives were dramatically and enduringly changed upon bending their knees at the cross of Christ. There are millions of such stories. The difficult challenge was to select from the many incredible stories I received only those I thought best illustrated my point, that is, that the power of God is revealed today in the lives of real people whom He enables to overcome all kinds of obsessions and addictions. The true significance of their transformation is seen when we contrast it with the prominent but impotent forces of secularism to do the same.

I am indebted to the following friends, many of them well-known Christian leaders, for allowing me to tell their stories or the story of a personal transformation they have witnessed themselves. I am also indebted to those transformed men and women who were willing to let their story be told, in the hope that it will glorify the One who changed their lives so dramatically—Jesus Christ, their Lord and Savior.

Sara Trollinger and the House of Hope Girls
Chuck Colson and Prison Fellowship
John and Linda Willet
Bob Vernon
Josh McDowell
Dave Hunt
Jim and Lenora Woodall
Frank Pastore
Bill Glass and Bill Glass Prison Ministry
Bill Kennedy
Jay Strack
Dr. Adrian Rogers
Luis Palau
Dave Wilkerson and Teen Challenge
Dr. Larry Lewis
Anthony Falzarano
Joe Dallas

Jack W. Hayford
Dr. Richard Lee
Carmen Pate
Pastor Gareld Murphy
Dr. Henry Brandt
Dr. Bill Bright
...and many others who have given permission to tell their stories!

TABLE OF CONTENTS

Introduction: At the Foot of the Cross 11

1. Making Broken People Whole 17

2. Just a Piece of Jewelry? 29

3. The Cross as a Symbol 37

4. The Message of the Cross 51

5. Homegrown Hostility to the Cross 65

6. Is the Cross Really Foolishness? 75

7. The Conversion of the Apostle Paul 91

8. From Haight-Ashbury and Vietnam to the Cross . . .117

9. A Big-League Skeptic Finds Faith at the Cross 127

10. The Cross Triumphs Over Crime and Violence 139

11. Alcoholics Changed at the Cross 151

12. The Power of the Cross over Drugs 165

13. The Cross Overcomes Depression 187

14. The Only Remedy for Homosexuality 199

15. Even Guilt Falls before the Cross 215

16. A Multicultural Phenomenon 231

17. The Foolishness of Man's Wisdom 243

Epilogue: Room at the Cross 267

Notes 271

AT THE FOOT OF THE CROSS

Many times I have wished that God would bare His almighty arm and demonstrate His supernatural power to this skeptical generation in such an overwhelming fashion that all would have to admit there is an omnipotent God in heaven. Nothing harmful, you understand, for I would not want Him to scare people. That isn't His style anyway. When He performs miracles, like the miracles of Jesus, they are always helpful to someone. God has performed many miracles in the past, from the saving of four families from the universal flood in the days of Noah, to the parting of the Red Sea so the children of Israel could walk safely on dry ground, to the resurrection of His Son Jesus from the tomb.

Just once I would love to see our living God demonstrate His existence in such obvious terms that all the world would know that He is THE LORD. No doubt you have entertained the same thought, just so God could vindicate Himself to a skeptical world. If you are not a Christian, it would prove once and for all that He does exist and that you should trust in Him.

Today we have an educational system, media, and entertainment industry that do not believe God exists largely because they can neither see Him nor recognize irrefutable evidence that He is very much alive. I sometimes think the underlying reason that many modernists will not accept the reality of an Almighty God is that they would be forced to acknowledge their accountability to that God for the way they live. That is why I have yearned for and prayed for one awesomely powerful act on the part of God that would settle the question once and for all—at least for all honest, objective people.

I don't think that yearning is unique to me. Probably all Christians share my belief that the God of heaven is the uncaused cause of all things, just as the Bible teaches. And they, like me, would love to have Him demonstrate His power and existence once and for all. Many of the Hebrew prophets felt the same yearning and said so. Even the rich man Jesus mentioned in Luke 16 meant the same thing when he begged Abraham to send Lazarus back to his father and brothers' house to warn them, lest they come to this "place of torment." He thought that a man brought back from the dead would be able to convince them. Many people are like that: they think a man who returns from the dead would convince any unbeliever. We all yearn for that, or some supernatural sign that would prove unmistakably that God does exist. But that is not His plan. He could easily stop the sun in its orbit, suspend the law of gravity without harmful consequences, or do any number of things to prove His existence—if He chose to do so. But He does not so choose. Instead, we are left with the words of Abraham to Lazarus: "If they do not listen to Moses and the Prophets, they will not be convinced even if someone rises from the dead" (Luke 16:31, NIV).

FOUR SIGNS GOD LIVES

God has chosen not to prove Himself by supernatural signs at this time in history because He has already given mankind four distinct signs to prove His existence. He refuses to give us more until "the end of the age." These four should be enough to spark faith in the heart of any objective individual. Consider:

1. CREATION

The first evidence that cries out for the existence of a Creator is the intricate design of the earth and the universe. The psalmist said, "The heavens declare the glory of God" (Psalm 19:1). I don't see how any astronomer can peer into the vast expanse of space, set his timepiece by the accuracy of the planets, and not believe in a God of design. In fact, those who reject the Creator have yet to come up with a satisfying explanation for the existence of man or the universe without Him.

2. THE BIBLE

For more than thirty-five hundred years, billions of people have found the Bible (or parts of the Bible) more than adequate to convince them of the existence of a supernatural God. Its very design is more than convincing to most people. It was written over a period of sixteen hundred years by at least forty different people from all walks of life. Some writers were well educated, like Moses and Paul. Others had little education, former shepherd boys like David who became king, or fishermen like the apostles John and Peter. Yet there is an incredible consistency from Genesis to Revelation that defies human authorship. There are also signs of the supernatural in its many fulfilled prophecies about nations, individuals, and the Messiah. I mentioned at least twenty-eight specific prophecies about Jesus the Messiah in the forerunner of this book, *Jesus: Who Is He?* All of them were fulfilled in His life and death. That in itself offers compelling evidence that the Bible is of supernatural origin, for no other book in the world comes close to such prophetic accuracy. It may surprise you to learn that there are over one hundred such prophecies of the Messiah. I had room for only twenty-eight—but all one hundred have been fulfilled in the life and death of Jesus Christ.

The adequacy of the Bible to reveal the hand of God is apparent to anyone willing to examine the hundreds of other prophecies in the Bible that have been fulfilled in history. For example, there are prophecies concerning Egypt, Sodom and Gomorrah, Babylon, the Jews, the rise of four succeeding world empires—only four until the end times—is uncannily accurate. Too accurate for them to be coincidental. Only the hand of the supernatural God can explain such accuracy. No wonder Jesus held the Jews of His day accountable to know God (John 5:39).

Jesus meant that the Bible is fully adequate to inform mankind about God, eternity, and how to get there. And that was before the New Testament was written! If the thirty-nine books of the Old Testament were considered by Jesus to be ample evidence about God, just imagine how much more responsible are people today to believe, for we have the twenty-seven books of the New Testament, containing the very words of Jesus and His apostles. And that brings us to the third powerful revelation of God.

3. THE LIFE OF JESUS CHRIST

The greatest of all evidences for the supernatural is found in the life and activities of the most incredible person who ever lived. The skeptic who rejects Him is faced with the impossible dilemma of explaining how He became the most important person who ever lived. He is acknowledged by almost everyone as the one human who most influenced the world's billions of people, culture, art, education, and every other meaningful area of life—and all without a formal education, fame, fortune or anything that most regard as essential to produce greatness. And He did it all in three years! There is no merely human explanation that can account for what He did. His life necessitates the supernatural.

This greatest of all persons was in His day a special spokesman for God (Hebrews 1:1–3). Jesus taught many things about God that were either barely mentioned by the prophets or not mentioned at all. In every case, He has given mankind the most complete revelation of the God of the universe that can be found anywhere. Anyone who reads the words of Jesus Christ about God as they appear in the four Gospels will have more than enough information to believe in Him. In fact, the best way to know about God is through studying His Son, Jesus. As the apostle John said, "No one has seen God at any time. The only begotten Son, who is in the bosom of the Father, He has declared Him" (John 1:18).

With these three witnesses to the existence of the supernatural God who controls our destiny, man can know all he needs to about Him. But in addition, God has chosen to reveal Himself in these last days by still one more significant means, and it is that one that this book is all about.

4. THE POWER OF THE CROSS

The apostle Paul called the message of the cross, "The power of God" (1 Corinthians 1:18). He meant that the cross, the most famous symbol in the world, is more than just a symbol. It is literally "the power of God" to "save those who believe" (v. 21). And they demonstrate that salvation by their changed lives.

For almost two thousand years billions of people have come to that cross with their sins and weaknesses, kneeled before it, and asked God to forgive their sins and save their souls. When they leave that cross, they begin to live differently. Thieves stop stealing; liars begin telling the truth; prostitutes find a new profession; drunkards and drug addicts throw off their lifetime addictions to substance abuse and become models of transformed behavior. And that transformation of life becomes the fourth witness of the existence and power of God. To properly understand the extent of that you must compare it with the impotence of man-made schemes or plans to enable mankind to overcome those same addictions.

For example, homosexuality often becomes such an entrenched way of life that most non-Christian counselors do not even try to extricate the victims from that lifestyle. (Besides, most of them today believe it's perfectly natural and legitimate.) Yet as I will show, hundreds of Christians, many of them former homosexuals, are leading men and women to the cross of Christ before whom they bow, and they rise with the power to live a new and transformed life. To date I have personally met forty-eight individuals who have undergone such a life-changing transformation. Now, that is power! The power to transform lives.

God is content during this period of history to confine Himself to revealing His presence largely through this consistent pattern of life transformation. Not just in overcoming homosexuality, but in enabling people to conquer anger, depression, violence that leads to criminality, and every addiction known to man. We ignore this expression of God's power in our generation at our peril, for it is real, tangible, and provable. No other source of power on earth compares with the power of the cross!

THE POWER GENERATION

This generation, more than all others, should understand the significance of the power of the cross, for we are a power-obsessed generation. Sports lovers are used to "power runners" in football or "power forwards" in basketball, or "power hitters" in baseball.

We have "power engines" and "power rockets"—the list is endless. If it doesn't have "power," we aren't interested. Well, there is power in Christianity—the power of the cross, or more fully explained, the power to transform lives.

In my youth, I was impressed with the power of the transformation of Mel Trotter. He was a derelict from Chicago whose addiction to alcohol had so destroyed his self-respect and sense of honor that he stole the booties off the feet of his own dead infant daughter to buy his next drink. Somehow God brought him to the foot of the cross of Christ where he bent his knees and cried out for forgiveness and mercy. Not only was he saved from his sins, he was also transformed by the new Spirit within him and he became what the Bible calls "a new creature in Christ." He then gained victory over the addiction of alcohol and became a responsible husband and father. Eventually he became the director of the Union City Rescue Mission in downtown Chicago, where thousands of other derelicts have been pointed to the cross and have seen their lives transformed.

God is in the life-transformation business, even in this present generation. But it always begins at the foot of the cross, in an act of repentance and humility that begins the process of change. When the addicted individual recognizes he has come to the end of his own resources and in faith turns to the Christ of the cross—or as Paul said, "Accepts the message of the cross"—and humbly receives Him as his Savior and Lord, then the process begins. As far as I have been able to discover, there is no addiction that cannot be changed by the power of the cross. It is my intention to prove that claim by telling the stories of real people who are living proof that God is in the life-transformation business.

And it always begins at the foot of the cross.

CHAPTER ONE

MAKING BROKEN
PEOPLE WHOLE

Twelve hundred people attended a special banquet in the grand ballroom of the Swan Hotel in Orlando, Florida. Everyone was dressed in their finest, ladies in long gowns and men in tuxedos. It was an unforgettable night as guests came from all over the state and other parts of the world to pay tribute to the power of the cross of Jesus Christ.

A highlight of the program was the introduction of the beautiful young soloist, Katrina. Dressed in a floor-length, white dress shining with sequins, she stepped into the spotlight as the house lights dimmed. All eyes were on her. I don't remember what she sang, but the performance was so beautiful the audience gave her a standing ovation. When everyone was seated, this twenty-three-year-old woman—whom every mother present would be proud to call "daughter"—began to tell her story.

"When I was fourteen years old," she began, "I rebelled against my parents, ran away from home, became addicted to drugs, and had to sell my body for sex to get enough money to buy my next fix." Many in the audience gasped, for she stood before us looking every bit the model of virtue and wholesome living. Then she told how for two years she lived a literal hell on earth, much like the prodigal son, wallowing in the moral pigpen of the drop-out, drug-crazed culture of our day.

After countless arrests she was judged hopeless by juvenile authorities and was admitted to the House of Hope, a home for throwaway girls in Orlando founded and directed by Sara Trollinger. The first thing Sara did was to give Katrina her love, a gift which Katrina found difficult to accept. She did not love anyone, herself included. Then Sara introduced Katrina to the love of God in the person of Jesus Christ, who died for her sins on the cross and rose again. Katrina was particularly interested in the offer, not only of forgiveness for her sins, but also in the *power* to overcome her two-year nightmare of addiction and prostitution. She longed for the power to permanently live a new lifestyle.

Katrina accepted Jesus Christ at the House of Hope and was carefully discipled by Sara and her staff. For two years she remained in the home, where she learned to be a godly woman with a forgiven past wiped clean of all guilt and shame. I will never forget how she stood in regal innocence and beauty, an obvious witness to the power of the cross and God's amazing ability to transform the lives of those who invite Him to save them.

With a smile on her radiant face Katrina said, "Ladies and gentlemen, I have someone here I want you to meet." Suddenly another spotlight appeared at the other end of the ballroom where a handsome young man in a white tuxedo stood holding an infant. "My husband and our six-month-old baby girl," Katrina announced to a chorus of sniffles. There wasn't a dry eye in the house or a throat without a big lump as her little family joined her on the platform. The crowd stood as one, men and women wildly applauding their approval and praising God for this walking illustration of the power of the cross. A once hopelessly fallen girl, now changed 180 degrees from her former lifestyle, undeniably demonstrated a supernatural transformation—a transformation that lifted her not only to a beautiful Christian life and family, but also to a concert ministry singing the praises of Him who made it all possible, Jesus Christ her Lord and Savior.

HOUSE OF HOPE IS FULL OF KATRINAS

If Katrina were the only illustration of the power of the cross to transform the lives of men and women for the better, we might find it less than overwhelming evidence that Jesus Christ is still in the people-changing business two thousand years after His death and resurrection. But Katrina is far from the only example of a throwaway girl now living a chaste life, dedicated to Jesus Christ.

Drug-crazed girls who can't be controlled by their parents, the authorities, or even a judge, come to House of Hope as a last resort—and often become models of virtuous behavior. There must be a reason.

After Sara had been ministering to girls for four years, a local judge called to say, "Mrs. Trollinger, we have a fifteen-year old girl who our best juvenile authorities cannot control. Our last recourse is to put her in prison and I am reluctant to do that; you know she will be destroyed if we do. Can you make room for her at House of Hope?" Sara prayed and felt the leading of God to give this girl one last chance—a chance for something different, a touch from God. Within weeks that rebellious teen on the verge of self-destruction responded to the loving presentation of the gospel, knelt at the cross, and experienced the life-transforming power God promises. Today this girl is a whole new person.

When I first met her, I had a hard time believing that this gracious, happy girl was ever the drug-crazed, suicidal young woman who had been described to me. She smiled and said, "That was the former me; today I am a different person!" No wonder former President Ronald Reagan, during a 1985 visit to the Epcot Center, was so impressed by an *Orlando Sentinel* article about the House of Hope that he wrote out a personal check for $1,000 to the ministry. (A copy of that check now hangs on an office wall.) Sometime after President Reagan left office, he and his wife, Nancy, came to Orlando where he was the featured speaker at a fund-raising banquet for the House of Hope—a clear indication that he believed in the life-transforming work that was occurring in girls' lives there. What made this special to the former president, and to all of us who like him serve on the ministry's Honorary Board of Advisors, is that the girls who pass through the doors of the House of Hope are never again the same.

THE POWER OF THE CROSS

What God is doing at the House of Hope powerfully illustrates the power of the cross to heal broken lives. It is a place of last resort. Everyone else has given up on these girls; if they aren't helped at House of Hope, the next step is the street, drugs, crime, prostitution, violent abuse, and in some cases, suicide. They are that desperate.

Yet very few girls leave by their own volition. There is something about the place—the love, the obvious power of God in the lives of the others—that makes them stay. Eventually many of them come to the cross, bend their knees and their will to the Savior, and sense the power of His cross for themselves. They begin a whole new way of life.

Sara's latest venture is a House of Hope for boys. I can remember when she first asked me to pray about its possibility; today it is a reality. Just as hundreds of girls have been transformed at House of Hope, so too there will soon be a House of Hope for throwaway boys who come to know the transforming power of Jesus Christ.

And notice: The House of Hope is doing what no government agency can duplicate, even with all their money, programs, and professionals. Sara and her staff take the impossible cases and, without medication or so-called "professional treatment," see many of them miraculously transformed. And always the source is the same: *the power of the cross.*

THE BLUE LEWIS CONVERSION

Blue Lewis was serving a life sentence for murder. A big boy at sixteen, he killed a man in a street fight. Blue got his nickname because one inmate had described him as so black that he looked blue. In prison he took up boxing and eventually became champion of the entire federal prison boxing system. Like many young men his age, he was angry, powerful, and violent. Everyone gave him a wide berth and even prison guards tried not to make him angry.

One person who wasn't afraid of him was my mother. At twenty-eight years of age she was widowed and left with three children—I was nine, my sister five, and my brother only seven weeks old at the time. My dad died right after the Great Depression, and our financial situation was so grim that my mother realized God was her only hope. She worked in a factory, hospital, and machine shop. Not only did she raise us all, but by the time my brother went into the Air Force at age eighteen, she herself had graduated from the Detroit Bible College. With her family responsibilities completed, she resigned her secure job and became the Child Evangelism Director for Lansing, Michigan, serving in that capacity for the next twenty-three years.

Her love for and dedication to Jesus Christ left her with two major passions: winning children and black people to Jesus Christ. Everywhere she went she attracted both. Her genuine love for them was so obvious they both thought of her as one of their own. Somehow the liberal chaplain of the Ionia, Michigan, prison allowed her to go inside to tell the Easter story on a Good Friday evening. Can you visualize this little five-foot woman, the smallest person in the group, in a prison chapel with violent criminals? After the singing, she set up a flannelgraph board she used in presenting the gospel to her many children's groups. By arranging the cutout figures of Pilate, Jesus, the Jews, and other characters, she described the crucifixion, burial, and resurrection of Jesus Christ. Several prisoners became Christians the first night. Suddenly she became the most popular outside teacher among the prisoners, and attendance began to grow.

The chaplain didn't agree with her gospel or her theology, but the big attendance looked good on his proficiency reports, so with his blessing she became a regular Friday night Bible teacher. During the succeeding years she taught the entire Bible, from Genesis to Revelation. One prisoner told Blue what was going on, so he visited, got hooked on the message of "the little lady," and was marvelously converted to Christ.

It didn't take his peers, the guards, and his family long to realize that Blue Lewis was a changed man. Soon everyone detected a new spirit of love and cooperation in this once-frightening man. Most of the prisoners watched to see if his temper and conversation changed. It did. Many came to the Friday night Bible studies at his invitation and many of them received Christ. In the process Blue grew to love my mother, calling her his "spiritual mother." Blue always made time for the Friday night Bible studies, even though he spent much time in the gym training for his next fight. Eventually he brought the heavyweight championship trophy home to the prison.

During this time I was pastoring two thousand miles away in California, and I asked my mother if she was safe with all those prisoners. "The Lord and Blue take good care of me," she said with a laugh. "The other prisoners are so afraid of Blue they wouldn't dare hurt me."

Blue showed his commitment to my mother's safety one strange night when, in the middle of her presentation, a severe storm caused an electrical short and plunged the chapel into darkness. Mom admitted she was terrified during the few minutes between the blackout and when the auxiliary lighting kicked in. As usual, Blue had been in the back of the auditorium where he could "keep order." Mom was on the platform and knew there were only two guards, a chaplain, and a room full of restive prisoners. Before she realized it, she took two steps backward and ran into a body. Suddenly she heard Blue's deep voice whisper, "Don't be afraid, Margaret, I'm here." How he got there so quickly no one knew, but he showed his love and concern for the woman who introduced him to the One who gave him spiritual life.

The story doesn't end there. Blue was transferred to the federal prison in Jackson, about fifty miles away, and soon he arranged for my mother to hold Bible studies there too. One day a riot broke out in the prison and thirteen guards were captured by some of the most violent prisoners in the facility. After a standoff of several days, the warden sent for Blue, who was still active in his boxing career and a hero to the other prisoners. The warden asked him if he would volunteer to serve as a negotiator to visit the hostages and see if he could negotiate a peaceful settlement. Naturally Blue asked, "Why me? Can't you find someone experienced in such things?" The warden replied, "Blue, you're the one man in this prison who both the prisoners and the staff respect. You have the reputation that you keep your word." Neither man made any promises and Blue said he would give it his best shot. After several trips between the rebels and the warden, they negotiated a deal "with the Lord's help" that resulted in the safe release of all the hostages. In return, the inmates received several improvements in living conditions which they had demanded.

After order was restored and prison life returned to normal (or as normal as prison life can ever be), the warden recommended that Blue Lewis be paroled. Such action was not as common back then as it is today, but after months of examination of his fifteen years in prison—considering that the crime was committed in his youth, his conversion to Christ, the transformation in his life and behavior, his excellent prison record and his assistance in quelling the riot—he was released before his thirty-second birthday.

One of the first things he did upon his release and return home to Detroit was to become active in a Bible-teaching church. He tried to make it as a professional boxer and was able to become the fourth-seeded heavyweight, but Father Time had taken a toll even on his superb body. He found a regular job and gained the respect of the brothers and sisters in his church, where he became a leader. About two years after his release, my mother received a wedding invitation for Blue Lewis and his wife-to-be, a fine young Christian woman in his church.

My mother talked a friend into driving to Detroit with her to attend the wedding. Neither woman ever forgot it! They were the only two whites in attendance, and after the wedding Blue spotted her and disrupted the reception with a vigorous greeting. He then proudly took Mom around and introduced her as "my spiritual mother," first to his wife, then to his parents and many of his family and friends. Think of it—two people of different races with an obvious love for each other, made possible because both bent their knee before the cross of Jesus and received Him into their hearts.

God later blessed the Lewis family with several children and a life filled with blessings. Blue is now in his sixties, and like so many millions of others, his life illustrates the astonishing transformation made possible through the power of the cross.

EVEN IN DEATH THE CROSS REACHES OUT

Assistant Police Chief Bob Vernon, a longtime friend, worked his way up from being a patrolman to Assistant Chief of the Los Angeles Police Department. During his thirty-eight years of impeccable service, he led many men to experience the power of the cross in their lives. In fact, the *Los Angeles Times* criticized him for being the reason there were at least eight hundred Christian police officers in the LAPD. Because the department had eight thousand police officers at that time and 40 percent of the country's population professes to be "born again," I am surprised it was not more. But the paper had heard of only eight hundred.

When Bob was a sergeant he had a partner named Pierre to whom he had witnessed many times. One Saturday night they were involved in a drug bust in which Bob came within seconds of having to shoot a man. Fortunately, on his command, the man lowered his gun, and Bob was able to arrest him peacefully. But as he described it, "The adrenaline rush had left me completely exhausted." When he drove up to Pierre's house that night, he was anxious to get home and crawl into bed. But instead of getting out of the car, Pierre, who had been part of that spine-tingling drug bust, said, "Bob, would you tell me one more time what I must do to be saved?"

Bob's first inclination was to ask him to wait until Monday when they could go over it in detail, but fortunately he went through the plan of salvation one more time. When Bob finished he said, "Pierre, do you know any reason why you cannot invite Christ into your heart right now?" He replied, "No, Bob, I'd like to do that!" So after midnight, Sunday morning, he bent his knees before the cross of Jesus and said an eternal, "Yes, I will have you take over my life and become my Lord and Savior."

When Bob got to work on Monday morning, he discovered that Pierre had been transferred to another department and both were assigned new partners. The next Thursday night Pierre was tragically shot and killed. Bob and many of the LAPD officers were devastated. He had been a well-liked and respected officer. But Bob comforted himself with the fact that at least he was in heaven.

Almost eighteen years later Bob took his wife, Esther, to Hawaii, where they enjoyed a delightful vacation. On Sunday evening they visited a small church on the island. After the service, a bubbly woman came up and welcomed them to her church. She asked where they were from and what Bob did, and as soon as he said he was an officer of the LAPD, she asked if he knew her brother Pierre and gave his last name. It was Bob's slain partner! She was so elated when she found they had worked together that she asked if Bob could tell her how Pierre prayed to receive Christ. Then she told Bob and Esther how Pierre had led her to Christ *after* his death. It seems that in the wee hours of Monday morning he had written a letter to his sister describing how he had just received Christ. He gave his sister the plan of salvation and she accepted Christ as a result of that letter. She then led Bob and Esther around that church and introduced them to thirteen other family members who had also come to Christ because of Pierre's witness. All because one police sergeant put serving his Lord above his own creature comfort when his exhausted body cried out for rest!

That is what Peter evidently meant when he said, "always be ready to give a defense to everyone who asks you a reason for the hope that is in you" (1 Peter 3:15). That reason is the same for all Christians, for we have been introduced to the power of the cross and we dare not keep it to ourselves.

ICEM SNOW, ONE TOUGH HOMBRE

Who would name their son *Icem?* That was my question on my first Sunday as pastor of the Oolenoy Baptist Church in Pumpkintown, South Carolina. But there he stood, a hulking man of six foot four inches and at least 240 pounds. Today he would be every football coach's dream. Not only was he big, he had been one tough hombre in his day. An ugly scar ran down his face from the corner of his eye to his chin, earned in a drunken brawl when the man he was fighting slashed him with a knife. He would be one scary looking dude in a dark alley or if he got angry (as old-timers in the area said he often was) in the days before he got saved. But there he was, smiling at me with a mouth full of pearly white teeth and the love of Jesus all over his face, offering his huge hand for me to shake. "Welcome to our church, Pastor LaHaye," he said. "If I can ever be of service to you and the Lord, don't hesitate to call on me."

I soon found Icem to be a man of his word. Not only was this once-scary man an active deacon in the church, he was also deeply concerned about winning others to Christ. I was a twenty-two-year-old pastor working my way through college, and every Saturday afternoon that I was free at school I asked church members to join me for three hours to go into the community to win people to Christ. "Snow," as everyone called him, was the only one who ever came.

Pumpkintown boasted many Christian homes, but it also had its share of Christ rejecters, moonshiners, and others who needed Christ. Obviously, we went to the tough cases. I always felt safe when Snow was with me. I would teach the Bible's plan of salvation and Snow would give his personal testimony. With tears he would plead with those sometimes rough and rude men to receive his Savior.

I loved to hear this gentle giant tell how he had been a cruel First Sergeant in the Civilian Conservation Corps, an enlistment for which he "volunteered" at an early age rather than take a prison sentence for an episode of drunkenness and brawling in which a man was killed. He had a rough background; no one in his family was religious, and he was almost an adult before he realized that Jesus was not merely a term of profanity. One of his neighbors who knew him "back when" told me, "He was the meanest man I ever knew." Once Snow's commanding officer found a man on the street, unconscious with a broken jaw and writhing in agony. "What happened to this man?" the officer demanded of a nearby private. "He refused an order from the First Sergeant, sir," the private replied. It was Snow's simple method of keeping the 250 men under his command in order.

Several times I heard Snow tell unsaved men, "You know me, you know what kind of man I was. I would be dead today if I had not received Jesus Christ ten years ago." No one ever protested; they knew what he had been before kneeling at the cross of Jesus, and they knew he was a changed man today. I often heard them say "Snow, I'm just not ready yet." But several added, "But when I am, I'd like you to pray with me!" And some did.

I don't know the details of how Snow accepted the Savior; I do know he fell in love with a young woman in the community, and after they married and had their second child, he began to take parenthood seriously. That little church, which on Easter Sunday could barely crowd 125 people into its auditorium, held a revival meeting every third week in August. About ten years before I became the pastor, someone in the church invited the Snow family to the meeting. They surprised everyone by coming—not just one night, but several—and both Snow and his wife were marvelously saved. Snow told me that when he kneeled at the altar just below a cross, he not only repented of his sins and received the Savior, but said, "Lord, I have never done anything halfway in my life. I have been a terrible sinner. Tonight I give you all of my life and will serve you as long as I live."

The man was true to his word and he began to grow spiritually. He hungered for the Word of God and was in church every time the doors were open. I visited his home and saw his well-worn and much-used Bible. There is no question he got up off his knees a different man than when he got down.

I had the joy of pastoring that congregation for two years. If Snow missed a service, he was either out of town or someone in his family was sick. Even some of my youthful sermons caused him to weep. Nothing moved him more than the price Jesus paid for his sins on Calvary's cross. Many times he would say through tears, "There are two things I don't understand: why He would die such a terrible death for my sins, and how anyone who hears that message can reject the Savior?" Frankly, those questions still mystify me too.

Almost fifty years have passed since those days and Snow has gone to be with the Lord he loved so dearly. Last year my wife and I were scheduled to speak in Greenville, just thirty-five miles from our old church. We rented a car and drove to the area, and though the community had changed very little, the old church building that dated back to 1794 had been torn down and a beautiful new facility erected in its place. When we went inside, the sun was just beginning to set and streams of light blazed through a beautiful stained-glass window. I caught my breath as I read at the bottom, "In memory of Icem Snow, saved sinner and dedicated servant of God."

Tears of joy welled up in my eyes as I remembered "the meanest man in town" who had been transformed into a loving, gentle giant by the power of the cross. I still think Icem is a pretty strange name to give your son, but strange or not it's a name written in large letters and permanent ink in the Lamb's Book of Life. I wonder: is your name written in that same book?

CHAPTER TWO

JUST A PIECE
OF JEWELRY?

The cross is the most popular symbol worn by the public today, more common than anything representing sports, music, the arts, or any other system of belief. Why is that?

To Christians, the cross is a visible symbol of that which is invisible—the power of God. The cross has no power in and of itself, yet what it represents has awesome, world-shaking power— the power to transform the life of any individual willing to put it to the test. Yet not everyone who wears a cross knows this or believes it.

In the past year, whenever I saw someone wearing a cross as a piece of jewelry, I asked him or her about it. I explained that I was writing a book on the cross and that I was taking a survey consisting of just two questions:

1. Why do you wear that cross?
2. What does it mean to you?

Surprisingly enough, no one took offense at my questions. I had expected to be occasionally rebuffed with "That's none of your business!" But so far, after more than one hundred such encounters, no one has objected. (Although one waitress made a point to avoid me after she heard the questions.)

I have found that "born again" Christians are quick to identify themselves, usually with enthusiasm. Religious Christians were more deliberative, particularly those who had never considered the question.

One woman waiting to enter a restaurant said of her cross, "I saw it in the display case of a shop and thought it was attractive. Because it was on sale for 50 percent off, I bought it." And what did it mean to her? "It means I am a religious person who respects all religions."

Another woman said, "I have never gone to church much, except on Easter and Christmas, but I consider myself a Christian. I wear it to identify myself—besides, I think it is a beautiful piece of jewelry."

A young clerk wearing a beautiful gold cross on a gold chain around her neck said, "My boyfriend gave it to me for Christmas, and I love him very much. I wear it because it reminds me of him."

WEARING THE CROSS FOR "PROTECTION"

The receptionist at a computer shop where I had my laptop repaired held her cross as it hung around her neck and said, "I wouldn't be without this cross; it goes with me everywhere I go. It brings me good luck." And why did she wear it? "My girlfriend gave it to me, and ever since I have been wearing it, good things have happened to me." She denied that she wore it as a good-luck charm, but admitted, "I am afraid something bad would happen to me if I didn't wear it."

Protection is not an uncommon reason some give for wearing the cross. One thirty-something professional said, "I live in a somewhat dangerous neighborhood. I am terrified of being raped, beaten, and even murdered. I read about a woman who was attacked and when the man saw her cross, he stopped and let her go. I wear it for protection."

I suppose we shouldn't be surprised that many people wear the cross for protection. I even met a truck driver who said, "I drive late into the night. My biggest fear is that I will fall asleep. I wear it to keep me awake. Many times I hold it when I am sleepy and pray to God to help me stay awake." When I asked, "What does it mean to you?" he replied, "It reminds me that the Man Upstairs is always ready to help when I need Him."

TO SOME IT'S MEANINGLESS

One young man I met while waiting to board an airplane was particularly candid. He was dressed in a gray athletic sweatshirt and pants and wore the biggest silver cross I have ever seen hanging around a person's neck. When I asked why he wore it, he replied, "My grandmother gave it to me for Christmas, and I am going to visit her this weekend. I knew she would expect me to wear it." And what did it mean to him? "Absolutely nothing!" End of conversation.

THE CROSS AS CRUCIFIX

Contrast this man's response with that of the obviously devoted young Radio Shack receptionist who wore a medium-sized and rather expensive-looking crucifix on a chain around her neck. "I want to remind myself daily of the price Jesus paid for my sins, and I want my friends to know it too," she said. "I wear it to help me remember to pray daily, and when I have to make decisions, I look to Him and He guides me. I am a Roman Catholic and am not ashamed of it; by wearing this cross I let everyone else know that." And had she personally received Jesus as her Lord and Savior? "Yes, several years ago," she replied quickly. Somehow I was not surprised.

I met another young woman obviously being led by the Spirit who wore a crucifix around her neck; on each of her earlobes hung empty crosses. I spoke with her shortly after Easter. "I have worn the crucifix for a long time, but over Easter I read the story of the resurrection and decided I wanted to include something that spoke of that important event," she said. "So when I saw these cross earrings, I bought them. I want people to know that I am a Christian."

JUST ONE SYMBOL AMONG MANY

One man in his midfifties had more jewelry around his neck, fingers, and wrists than anyone I have ever seen. He looked like a walking jewelry salesman. There among his pendants and baubles was a cross. When I asked him the two questions he said, "I love jewelry, and this cross is one of my most beautiful pieces. I don't wear it for religious reasons; I just like to wear it."

He reminded me of the Athenians described in Acts 17. Paul witnessed to them by mentioning the idols in their city that represented every god in the world, including one to "the unknown god" (just in case they had missed one). Somehow, I don't think Jesus Christ, who died on the cross, was impressed with the man's answer.

On another flight a devoted woman in her late sixties was seated next to me. I saw a cross pendant on a chain around her neck and asked her about it. She claimed she used it when she confessed her sin and talked to God. "It makes me more conscious of His presence in my life," she said. "Religion is very important to me." A short time afterward when we hit bumpy air, and then later again when we landed, she held the cross in her hand and bowed her head.

During our conversation I told her that my new book, *Jesus: Who Is He?* had just come off the press. She said she would like to read it, so I asked for her address and sent her a copy when I got home. About ten days later I received a thank-you letter and the welcome words, "Your book changed my life. I have a whole new perspective on who Jesus really is." I praised the Lord, for her response represents why I wrote the book.

A REMINDER FOR A CHRISTIAN FLIGHT ATTENDANT

A middle-aged flight attendant wore a cross pendant around her neck, not long enough to interfere with her work, but an obvious expression of her faith. When I asked her my questions, she said, "I wear this cross to remind me to be patient with some of the difficult people I meet. Most people are real easy to work with, but every now and then I get an unreasonable person, and I use the cross to remind me that, as a Christian, I should love them and be kind to them. After all, God loves me. It means that I am a Christian, I have put my faith in what Jesus did on that cross, and I expect to thank Him personally in heaven someday." For a 30 second testimony, I would have to score that a 9.99 on a scale of 10.

DISPLAYING THE CROSS MAKES A STATEMENT

One evening I saw two young women in a restaurant, both of whom were wearing crosses. One tenderly held her cross and with tear-filled eyes said, "This cross means everything to me. Jesus Christ has saved me and changed my life." She mentioned her terrible past and said, "Had I not become a Christian, I probably wouldn't be alive today." The other woman declared, "I have just come through a terrible divorce. My husband left me for another woman, and I know I could not have made it without the Lord." They agreed why they both wore the cross: "We want everyone to know we are Christians and that Jesus changed our lives."

Many Christians echoed what one young man told me: "Jesus Christ cleansed my sin because of what He did on the cross—and the resurrection made salvation possible. I want the world to know that I am a Christian." I myself have worn a gold cross on my ring finger for over forty years, essentially for the same reason.

The testimonies of these cross-wearing men and women typify the one hundred or more I interviewed. In all probability they represent the general population. Some who wear a cross are non-Christians who know little about the meaning behind the symbol. To many it is merely a piece of jewelry, a religious relic or good luck-charm one step ahead of a rabbit's foot. Recently I talked to a prominent jeweler in our city who told me the cross is the one piece of jewelry consistently in demand at his store.

Some wearers of the cross know the gospel story but disbelieve its power. Others are openly hostile to it. And, of course, there are the passionate believers who wear a cross to declare their allegiance to Christ, to announce that they believe in the life-changing event of Calvary.

THE IDEAL MEANING OF THE CROSS

The cross is the heart of the gospel message. The symbol, whether carved from wood, silver, gold, or costly stone, should symbolize the very heart of that gospel. It should say to the world, "I was a sinner. I knelt at the cross of Jesus where He was crucified for my sin, and I have accepted Him as my Lord and Savior. Because He rose from the dead, symbolized by the empty cross, He came into my life in the person of His Holy Spirit and has transformed my life."

Ideally the wearing of a cross should be like baptism or communion, a commemoration of our identification with the work of salvation which Jesus purchased on that cross. It should never be worn merely as a piece of jewelry. It should always have a spiritual meaning.

LIVING UNDER THE SIGN OF THE CROSS

The most coveted possession in all of sports is a championship ring. In the National Football League, it is a Super Bowl ring. A number of times in NFL history a veteran superstar has taken a lesser salary so that he could be traded to a team he thought had a good chance to win the Super Bowl, all because he wanted to own one of those rings. A Super Bowl ring would cap off his career and be a visible symbol of his achievement.

Much more than that, the cross as a symbol should be won in the game of both life and death. The cross signifies that we are prepared to live a Christian life. And when it comes to death, we win the *true* Super Bowl, just as Jesus promised: "In my Father's house...forever."

Since we are considering ideals, one more thing must be mentioned about the cross as a symbol. Jesus didn't come only to save us, He also came to challenge us to be His followers and to live our entire lives under His cross. "If anyone desires to come after me, let him deny himself, and take up his cross, and follow me," He said in Matthew 16:24. On another occasion He added, "Anyone who does not take his cross and follow me is not worthy of me" (Matthew 10:38, NIV).

In this day of "easy believism," many are tempted to want Jesus Christ as their Savior as fire insurance from hell but are not willing to give Him control over their lives. Somehow they fear that serving Jesus is too much of a sacrifice. They want to go to heaven when they die, but they don't want Him to run their lives now. Such believers, in Jesus' own words, are not *worthy* of Him. Frankly, I wonder whether such secret believers have really had a conversion experience.

This is no day to be a secret believer. It is a day to answer Jesus' call to be "followers of the way" of the gospel of Christ, just as it was in the first century and in all centuries since. A *bearer* of the cross should be a *follower* of the Christ of the cross.

And how can we tell if we are following Him? Very simply, if we are a follower of Jesus Christ, we will obey Him. Obedient followers are wonderfully entitled to openly wear the cross.

DOES IT MEAN NOTHING TO YOU?

One day just before Easter, I was driving down a busy street past a Lutheran church. On the lawn members had erected a large, hand-hewn wooden cross. Under it they had printed the words of the prophet, "All you that pass by, does it mean nothing to you?"

That is the supreme question of the ages, a question every person must answer for himself.

What does the cross mean to you?

CHAPTER THREE

THE CROSS
AS A SYMBOL

For almost two thousand years the cross has served as the universal symbol of Christianity. These days it is the most famous symbol in the world. This was vividly illustrated to me in Beijing, China, while walking on the Great Wall in 1995.

As we returned from our guided tour of the Wall, I heard a siren in the distance. Some tourist had suffered a heart attack and needed medical attention. To my amazement, the ambulance that came roaring up to the site featured a red cross painted on both side doors and on the back. When we returned to the hotel and took a seat in its restaurant, I struck up a conversation with a waiter who wanted to practice his English. I asked him why the ambulance was painted with a red cross. He had never thought about it, and he answered momentarily, "It is so people will clear a way for it to pass. You know, the cross is a universal symbol of humanitarianism." But why was that? I persisted. He didn't know. Then I asked, "Why is it always red?" He still had no answer. So I told him the story of the cross on which Jesus Christ was crucified, adding that it was painted red because of the blood He shed on that cross for the sins of the whole world.

The young man had never heard that story, which is understandable since his country has been a communist prison for fifty years. Yet officially, even though its leaders reject the story of the Son of God, they use His symbol to convey humanitarianism.

You know, there has never been a greater love story than that. The Bible says, "For God so loved the world He gave His only begotten Son, that whoever believes in Him should not perish but have everlasting life" (John 3:16). China is not unique in its use of the cross to express mercy (or humanitarianism if you please). It is found in Europe, South America, Russia, even the Orient. It's a universal symbol.[1]

THE HISTORY OF THE CROSS

Even during the Dark Ages when the Bible was kept from the common people in the mistaken belief that they could not understand it for lack of proper theological training, the cross was the central symbol of the church. Later, when a number of pagan practices began to be introduced by the clergy—including the sign of the Tau that had played such a significant role in Babylon's mystical rituals for thousands of years before Christ—church teachings gradually became a composite of pagan mysticism mixed with Christian tradition. For example, it was common in the religion of Babylon for the priests to carry a symbol that looked like a large *T* on the end of a long pole in reverence for Taumuz the mother of Nimrod. The *T* was eventually replaced by a cross carried by the priests in regal procession. Kissing the cross—as practiced previously with the Tau—was introduced, and slowly the cross as symbol gave place to the cross as sacred relic. Some ascribed mystical powers of healing to the cross and placing the cross on a wound or on the forehead, as if it were a talisman or good-luck charm, became common. Many still think of the cross in these terms today. Such syncretism all but ruined the church until the Protestant Reformation.

It is a fact of history that many religious leaders used the cross as a symbol of power having nothing to do with the salvation of one's soul. Used as such a symbol, the cross no longer illustrates the transformation of one's life from sin and shame to one of holiness and blessing.

THE DIVIDING SYMBOL OF HISTORY

It is impossible to exaggerate the significance of the cross as a symbol of Christianity. The cross divides human history between B.C.

and A.D., before Christ and after Christ. Such prominence is justified because Calvary is without doubt the most important single event in the history of the world. The cross symbolizes the one event that offers hope to a hopeless world. The cross is the single solution to the great human dilemma. How can fallen man, who is an eternal creature, have his sins forgiven and be restored to the status God gave Adam and Eve? The cross is the only solution! Consequently, it deserves its status as the most popular symbol in the world.

Yet amazingly, the cross is also a symbol of execution. Crucifixion is usually considered the most cruel and inhumane form of capital punishment ever exercised by nations on their own citizens. It seems incredible that this emblem of shameful death is now worn by millions of Christians as a symbol of hope. We never see a gold electric chair or a platinum gas chamber hanging around someone's neck. Those symbols of painful death represent failure and defeat. But the cross is a symbol of triumph! It represents the one place in time when the Son of God, Jesus Christ, met all the requirements of a substitutionary sacrifice for man's sin, taking on Himself the sins of the whole world. And the symbolism doesn't end there, for He triumphed over that death through the resurrection. If the cross does not include the resurrection, it is an inadequate symbol. As we shall see, Christ's death *and* resurrection supply the true significance of the empty cross.

ALL RELIGIONS HAVE A SYMBOL

"Every religion and ideology has its visual symbol," says John Stott in *The Cross of Christ*.[2] Such a symbol illustrates some significant feature of each faith's history and beliefs. The lotus flower, for example, is now particularly associated with Buddhism (although it was also used by the ancient Chinese, Egyptians, and Indians). Sometimes the Buddha is portrayed as enthroned in a fully open lotus flower.

Ancient Judaism avoided visual signs and symbols for fear of violating the second commandment, which prohibits the manufacture of images. But modern Judaism has adopted the so-called shield or Star of David.

We are all familiar with the Marxist hammer and sickle adopted by the Russian government to symbolize the rise of the worker and farmer. In 1917 the communists rid themselves of the elitist monarchs who had ruled Russia for hundreds of years and replaced them with a group of elite gangsters and criminals who ruled until the economy of the nation lay in shambles. The hammer and sickle proved to be a hollow symbol which fell far short of its touted promise.

The repugnant Nazi swastika was not a new symbol; its history goes back six thousand years and was adopted by Hitler and the German government as a symbol of the Aryan race. Today it stands for the ultimate in man's inhumanity to man. Nazism and communism caused the deaths of almost 180 million people in this century alone, making this the most barbaric hundred years in the history of mankind. If nothing else, these governments have proven that evil people do evil things. Or as Lord Acton said, "Power corrupts and absolute power corrupts absolutely"—hard lessons illustrating the total depravity of the natural man.

The cross, however, the supreme symbol of Christianity, is an emblem of mercy and hope. It represents the greatest single event in the history of mankind since the fall of Adam and Eve. The following simple diagram, with the line between ages past and ages to come called the "time line of human history," covers the entire history of mankind. Billions of people have lived during that period and millions of events have taken place, many of monumental significance. If one symbol were to be placed on that time line representing the most important single event of all time, it would have to be the cross—for it and it alone represents the one event that makes possible the forgiveness of one's sin and offers all mankind eternal salvation.

The cross highlights the most important event in all of human history by reminding us that God sent His only Son—Jesus the Messiah, who was born of a virgin so that He could be human without ruining His divine holiness—to willingly become sin for us that He might taste death for every man, even the death of the cross. The cross signifies that at one time all men and women were hopelessly lost because of their sin, but God reached down and rescued us by allowing His own Son to pay the penalty for our sin on the cross. That sacrifice does indeed pay the debt for our sin, a debt none of us could ever pay out of our own paltry resources. And it was approved by God! How do we know that? By the resurrection, the most provable event of the ancient world!

The resurrection of Jesus Christ from the dead is the most significant event in history because it shows that God accepted the sacrifice of His Son on our behalf. Had there been anything deficient in the sacrifice of Christ, He would still be in the grave. Instead, the resurrection testifies to the perfect acceptability of the Son's death to God.

In short, the most popular symbol in the world, the cross, is a testimony to the most important event in human history: the willing sacrifice of God's own Son for the sins of the whole world, coupled with His resurrection three days later.

Ideally, those who wear the cross are Christians who proudly and unashamedly say to all who see them, "I am not a follower of Buddhism, Muhammadanism, Confucianism, or Hinduism; I am a Christian. I have received Jesus Christ as my Lord and Savior and have dedicated my life to Him." That is what the cross on my ring means to me. Sadly, many who wear that cross know nothing about its meaning.

THE CROSS WAS NOT USED
UNTIL THE SECOND CENTURY

It may surprise you to learn that the cross was not used as the universal symbol of Christianity during the first century. That may have been because the early Christians did not wish to further antagonize the Jews in and around Jerusalem, for Jews took literally the statement of Moses that "Cursed is anyone who hangs on a tree" (Deuteronomy 21:23, paraphrase). Of course, Moses was speaking of execution, since the only people who were hanged on a tree were criminals. (Incidentally, it is worth noting that the Jews did not practice crucifixion, yet Psalm 22 and Isaiah 53 give detailed prophecies of the death by crucifixion of the Messiah. In fact, the Romans began practicing that gruesome form of execution only about forty years before Jesus was born—just in time to fulfill prophecy!)

The Romans were among the most barbaric soldiers of their day; that may be why they adopted such an inhumane form of execution. Yet even they ultimately considered crucifixion so repugnant that it was declared illegal for Roman citizens to be so executed, although they continued to employ it for others until the fourth century A.D. This ignominious form of execution carried with it enormous shame, for only the worst criminals, murderers, and enemies of the state were executed by crucifixion.

The death of the Son of God by crucifixion has received its own share of ridicule by scoffers, skeptics, and antagonists. Gandhi, the founder of modern India who while working in South Africa as a young lawyer was attracted to Christianity, yet wrote in 1894, "I could accept Jesus as a martyr, and embodiment of sacrifice, and a divine teacher, but not as the most perfect man ever born. His death on the cross was a great example to the world, but that there was anything like a mysterious or miraculous virtue in it, my heart could not accept."[3]

A more defiant rejection of Christ could be expected of Friedrich Nietzsche, a contemporary of Gandhi, who died in 1900. He hated all religions, but saved special venom for Christianity. He dismissed the deity of Jesus contemptuously as "God on the Cross."[4] His opinion should be evaluated in the light of his contributions to humanity—he did as much to promote atheism, socialism, and Nazism as any other person.

Probably another reason the early Christians did not use the cross as a symbol was that they were so persecuted their attention was focused more on staying alive to fulfill the great commission.

Persecution gave them little time for evaluating symbols. Yet they did use subtle symbols during the first century as a clandestine means of identifying each other. Finally they settled on the fish, or the Ichthus, an acronym in Greek for "Jesus Christ, Son of God, Savior." Although the symbol can still be found inscribed on walls in the catacombs of Rome, the fish did not remain the central symbol of the early Church, for the cross is really the central message of Christianity.

That conviction was spread abroad as portions of the New Testament began to circulate throughout the churches. Now everyone could see that the cross was truly at the core of their faith. "Without the shedding of blood there was no remission of sin," said the Old Testament, and the Holy Spirit confirmed through Paul, Peter, and others that the cross of Christ provided a perfect sacrifice. In fact, it was the final sacrifice. The writer of Hebrews summed it up best: "But Christ came as High Priest of the good things to come, with the greater and more perfect tabernacle not made with hands, that is, not of this creation. Not with the blood of goats and calves, but with His own blood He entered the Most Holy Place *once for all*, having obtained eternal redemption. For if the blood of bulls and goats and the ashes of a heifer, sprinkling the unclean, sanctifies for the purifying of the flesh, how much more shall the blood of Christ, who through the eternal Spirit offered Himself without spot to God, purge your conscience from dead works to serve the living God?" (Hebrews 9:11–14, italics mine). No wonder he concluded we have a *better* sacrifice—it was God's own Son. Peter, near the end of his life, wrote, "Knowing that you were not redeemed with corruptible things, like silver or gold...but with the precious blood of Christ, as of a lamb without blemish and without spot" (1 Peter 1:18–19).

The early Church did not need to be reminded of Christ's death and resurrection; that was at the very core of their belief and experience. What they needed and received from the writings of the apostles was an understanding of the significance of that historic event to them and to all Christianity. Gradually, the significance of the cross became so clear that all other symbols, even those used to protect themselves, were superseded by the cross. The empty cross is the one encompassing symbol that clearly portrays the true message of Christianity. In its beautiful simplicity it signifies Jesus' death, according to the Scriptures, His burial, and His resurrection.

Some thirty years after the ascension of Jesus to heaven and the subsequent founding of the church, Peter became a martyr during a period of Roman persecution. If tradition is to be believed (and there is good indication that it should be in this instance), he requested to be crucified upside down, saying, "I am not worthy to be crucified in the same manner as my Lord." The incident could not help but influence many in the church to recognize the importance of the crucifixion of our Lord, and to encourage them not to keep their faith secret.

THE CROSS AS A SYMBOL DURING THE DARK AGES

Near the end of the first century, Justin Martyr, the second century Christian apologist, acknowledged that everywhere he looked he saw the cross: "Neither the sea is crossed nor the earth is ploughed without it." As John Stott paraphrased him, "Diggers and mechanics do not work without cross-shaped tools, alluding presumably to a spade and its handle. Moreover, the human form differs from that of the irrational animals in nothing else than in its being erect and having the arms extended. And if the torso and arms of the human form proclaim the cross, so do the nose and eyebrows of the human face."[5]

"It seems certain that, at least from the second century onwards," writes Stott, "Christians not only drew, painted, and engraved the cross as a pictorial symbol of their faith, but also made the sign of the cross on themselves or others." One of the first witnesses to this practice was Tertullian, the North African lawyer/theologian who labored about A.D. 200. He wrote, "At every forward step and movement, at every going in and out, when we put on our clothes and shoes, when we bathe, when we sit at table, when we light the lamps, on couch, on seat in all the ordinary actions of daily life, we trace upon the forehead the sign [the cross]."[6]

He then goes on to quote Hippolytus, the scholar-presbyter of Rome, an authoritative witness on this subject, in expounding on the forms and traditions of the day. The sign of the cross was always used when anointing candidates' foreheads in ceremonies establishing them as bishops, and also when they confirmed individuals, describing the sign of the cross as "the sign of His passion." Then he admonished, "As a protection against evil: when tempted, always reverently seal thy forehead with the sign of the cross. For this sign of the passion is displayed and made manifest against the devil if thou makest it in faith, not in order that thou mayest be seen of men, but by thy knowledge putting it forth as a shield."[7]

These are but a few of the many quotations that could be marshalled to show that gradually the cross as a symbol began to supersede all others until it became the primary symbol of Christianity. Signing the cross, which had no place in the early church, was brought in from Northern Africa and was probably learned from a similar practice in pagan Babylonian religions.

The cross was never intended to be used as a symbol of terror, as Constantine used it in the fourth century to slay his enemies. Nor was it intended to be used on the shields of Crusader soldiers in their vain attempt to kill or expel the heathen for "mother church" in an effort to free the city of Jerusalem. Unfortunately, the meaning of the cross has been so diluted by centuries of misuse that when we see it, we do not know what the wearer means by it. As we saw in the previous chapter, many of those who wear it have no idea what it actually signifies.

To Solzhenitsyn It Meant Hope and Power

We are indebted to Chuck Colson, who in his book, *A Dangerous Grace,* gave us an incredible illustration of the power of the cross. "Like other prisoners in the Soviet gulag, Alexander Solzhenitsyn worked in the fields, his days a pattern of backbreaking labor and slow starvation," he wrote.

One day the hopelessness became too much to bear. Solzhenitsyn felt no purpose in fighting on; his life would make no ultimate difference. Laying his shovel down, he walked slowly to a crude work-site bench. He knew that at any moment a guard would order him up and, when he failed to respond, bludgeon him to death, probably with his own shovel. He had seen it happen many times.

As he sat waiting, head down, he felt a presence. Slowly he lifted his eyes. Next to him sat an old man with a wrinkled, utterly expressionless face. Hunched over, the man drew a stick through the sand at Solzhenitsyn's feet, deliberately tracing out the sign of the cross.

As Solzhenitsyn stared at the rough outline, his entire perspective shifted. He knew he was merely one man against the all-powerful Soviet empire. Yet in that moment, he also knew that the hope of all mankind was represented by that simple cross—and through its power, anything was possible. Solzhenitsyn slowly got up, picked up his shovel, and went back to work—not knowing that his writings on truth and freedom would one day enflame the whole world.

Colson rightly concludes, "Such is the power God's truth affords one man willing to stand against seemingly hopeless odds. Such is the power of the cross."[8]

True Christianity—that is, Christianity based on the Word of God—has never raised an army. Yet millions of Christians have gone to the uttermost parts of the earth to convey the message of the cross. It is the central message of the church and the only message of hope in this world for sinful men and women. It alone offers them undeserved hope in this life and for the life to come.

THE CENTRAL THEME OF THE CHURCH

Dr. Martyn Lloyd-Jones, an English minister who gained fame after World War II, was a medical doctor before answering his call to the ministry. For several decades after the war, he was the most significant Christian leader in the country. He admitted freely that "a change came in his preaching as a result of an experience he had in 1929, while still a young man." After preaching one night in Bridgend, South Wales, "a minister challenged him that the cross and the work of Christ appeared to have little place in his preaching."

He went at once to his favorite secondhand book shop and asked the proprietor for the two standard books on the Atonement. On returning home, "He gave himself to study, declining both lunch and tea and causing his wife such anxiety that she thought he needed a doctor. When he later emerged, he claimed to have found the real heart of the gospel and the key to the inner meaning of the Christian faith. So the content of his preaching changed, and with this its impact. As he himself put it, the basic question was not 'Why did God become man?' but 'Why did Christ die?'"[9] It is obvious to anyone familiar with his life that Lloyd-Jones was never again the same. Nor will any person or church be the same that concentrates on the preaching of the whole message of the cross. The faithful church will be full of it.

THE CROSS AS A SYMBOL TODAY

Years ago navy Lieutenant John Willet and his wife visited our church in San Diego. Linda was eight-and-a-half-months pregnant when John, an Annapolis graduate who intended to make a life-time career of the navy, began to realize the seriousness of becoming a new father. He had rarely, if ever, gone to church and knew nothing about Christianity. *Nothing* is the right word in this case, for he, like many Americans, had allowed no place for religion in his life. He wasn't opposed to Jesus Christ; he simply didn't know Him.

Linda was a bit different in that she had been raised in a religious home from the time she was a junior in high school. Her mother accepted Christ, and to Linda she seemed a religious fanatic. Linda's last years at home were not happy. A strong-willed young woman, Linda rejected her mother's faith, rules, and control. Her ideas of Christianity were not pleasant, but she loved John very much and she, too, was sensing the responsibility of imminent parenthood.

Perhaps you can imagine her feelings when John came home one night and said, "Honey, since we are about to become parents, I think we need some religion in our lives. Being a parent is serious business. What do you say to our going to church next Sunday?" They had lived in their house only a few weeks, so Linda asked, "Where should we go?" To which John replied, "There is a church down the block with a white steeple and a cross on the top that points to God."

Only a few years before we had moved into our new colonial-style church, and even I had not realized how the cross pervaded the entire church facility. The cross was everywhere, not just on top of the steeple. A cross was painted in black against a white sign out on the street. The Willets found a cross inscribed on the door handles as they came in. The usher gave them a bulletin featuring a beautiful drawing that included a cross. As he ushered them to their seats, they saw a cross on every other pew. They were barely seated when they looked up at the pulpit and there was an open Bible inscribed across the front of the lectern, a cross engraved on the pages. Behind the minister was the baptistry and on the wall above it, a brilliantly lighted cross. The communion table was laid with silver containers in preparation for the Lord's Supper, and the top cover was embellished with a cross. When they opened their hymn book they found these beautiful words:

> When I survey the wondrous cross
>   On which the Prince of glory died,
> My richest gain I count but loss,
>   And pour contempt on all my pride.
>
> Forbid it, Lord, that I should boast
>   Save in the cross of Christ my God;
> All the vain things that charm me most,
>   I sacrifice them to His blood.

I don't know what I preached that Sunday, but the Willets went home confident that if they were to find God, it would be in that church. There is something reassuring about the cross that gives even those who know little about Christ or His church the idea that it symbolizes the true message of salvation. By their third Sunday John and Linda were convinced to bend their knees at the cross and each say, "Yes, Jesus Christ, I will have you to reign over me, forgive my sin, come into my heart." Their first child came the day they received Christ!

It wasn't long before John felt the call of God on his life for the gospel ministry. In fact, in the evening of the day they were saved John attended a soul-winning training program and before the week was over he was instrumental in seeing his unsaved father-in-law, who was visiting along with his wife to see their first grand-child, pray to receive Christ. After his navy commitment expired, John enrolled in seminary and has served the Lord for over three decades as a pastor and evangelism leader.

Two years ago, I had the delightful privilege of bumping into John and Linda in the Holy Land. We met at the Mount of the Beatitudes, where we had only enough time to say hello. Yet it was enough time to witness that they were still serving the crucified One, evidence of the power of the cross to permanently transform lives.

As a pastor for forty years of my life, I know it is not wise to be a "Johnny one note" and preach only the gospel every Sunday. The fact is, we are commanded to preach "the whole counsel of God." But we *must* make the gospel clear every time we speak, because we never know who is in our audience and whether this might be the day of their salvation. The same is true of our personal witness. We never know when the person with whom we are speaking will ever have another chance to hear the message of the cross—the only "power of God unto salvation."

MORE THAN JUST A SYMBOL

That the cross is more than a mere symbol can be seen in Paul's classic statement that "the message of the cross is the power of God." It is that supernatural power that transforms a person's life when he bends his or her knee at the cross. And it is that transformation which is the tangible evidence that God is indeed alive and well and working in the affairs of men.

To make this possible on a permanent basis, God sends His Holy Spirit supernaturally into our lives at the moment we kneel at the cross and open our lives to Him. The Bible calls that being "born again." In that moment, the individual becomes a "new creature in Christ" and is thereafter empowered to live a whole new lifestyle, able to overcome what had been his or her greatest weaknesses. In some cases, the transformation is instantaneous. I have talked to alcoholics who claim they became instantly sober and never had another craving for alcohol. Others claimed they did not immediately lose that craving, but for the first time had the power to overcome it.

People are individuals and God treats them so, but all true believers eventually overcome their old sin habits and live a new life in Christ. Some don't struggle at all; others struggle constantly. In either case, the change in their lifestyle is a demonstration of the power of the cross.

This power is not found in the cross as a symbol; the cross is not some object we press against our forehead to get our thoughts to change. It is not an object we put up in the way of Satan or his demons to drive him away. It is not an icon that can be used as a magic charm. Rather, it is a message we accept and a historical fact we bow before in the name of the One who died on that cross. He then, through His Holy Spirit, empowers us to live a whole, new life. And it is that demonstration of life transformation that God uses to enlighten the faith of those who sincerely seek after truth.

Some of those life transformations are thrilling beyond description. Many are literally life saving; without them the individual would have died a premature death. And a large percentage of them occurred when all other avenues of seeking help had failed. But why shouldn't they? When we introduce the power of God into the equation, there really are no surprises. Just lots of celebration!

CHAPTER FOUR

THE MESSAGE
OF THE CROSS

Many of the sincere people who wear a cross as a symbol have no real understanding of its true meaning or message. As we saw in our survey, people have a variety of reasons for wearing a cross, but only true Christians seem able to explain why they do so and what it means to them. Millions of those Christians proudly wear the cross, not in memory of an execution, but in commemoration of the way their Lord and Savior, the Son of God, gave His life a ransom for their eternal soul.

Christians wear the cross proudly because only they can appreciate its full meaning. We have already seen that to the world it is a symbol of humanitarianism, but as Paul said, "To us who are saved, it is the power of God." The cross is the supreme symbol of power. It is greater than the crown or scepter, the paltry symbols of kings and rulers. It is greater than the symbol of space, atoms, and neutrons, for it has the power to save the soul for eternity.

Constantine was wrong in A.D. 312 when he adopted the "sign of the cross" and told his troops, "With this sign conquer," then bid them exterminate their enemies with the sword. The cross is a weapon of *spiritual* warfare and can do what no other power can do, save the soul and change the lifestyle of any individual who will believe its message and receive its Savior. In that sense it is the most powerful symbol on earth and the might of its message is able to trumpet the existence of God Himself.

But what is that message? Let us consider it now before we examine how it has miraculously transformed the lives of desperate men and women throughout history.

THE LOVE OF GOD

The first message conveyed by the cross was described by John in what has become the best known verse in the Bible: "For God so loved the world that He gave His only begotten Son, that whoever believes in Him should not perish but have everlasting life" (John 3:16). If you had an opportunity to give only one Scripture verse to a dying person, it should be that text, for it tells the extent of God's great love for mankind. And it is the cross that best illustrates that love.

Most people who don't know God are afraid of Him. Anyone familiar with the religions of the world will find a consistent thread running through them all: a fear and dread of God. Couple that with man's natural guilt complex and his universal penchant for sin, and you have a perfect formula for creating an unwholesome fear of God. This fear universally grips the heart of all who recognize His existence—except for the Christian who has confessed his sins at the foot of the cross and gained the forgiveness made possible through the blood of the Son of God.

In my early Christian life I did not know God well; consequently He frightened me. I was raised in a very legalistic church and heard much about the "justice of God" but very little about "the love of God." In fact, my confusion almost ruined my chances with the woman who is now my wife. On our first date I told her, "I am not really interested in going to heaven. Floating around on a cloud and playing a harp is not my idea of how I want to spend eternity."

She asked me, "Why then are you a Christian, and why are you in a Christian school studying for the ministry?"

To which I replied, "Frankly, I don't want to go to hell for eternity; and besides, I love Jesus. I am here because I love Him."

No wonder she went back to her dorm and told her room-mates, "I just dated the weirdest guy! I'll never date him again." (That is one vow I am glad she did not keep.)

Today I can honestly say that I truly love God, and of course, I love Jesus. After all, He was the one who died on the cross for my sins. But now I understand that God is not merely an awesome Judge to be feared, but a loving heavenly Father to be adored. The cross proves that. As Paul wrote, "God demonstrates his own love for us in this: While we were still sinners, Christ died for us" (Romans 5:8, NIV).

God has blessed Beverly and me with two daughters and two sons. I also have two best friends, both of whom are ministers of many years' standing. One day it dawned on me that if the need arose, I would give my life for either of my two friends. Don't mis-understand; I'm not volunteering for the assignment! But my love for them is sufficient that if there were no alternative, I think I could give my life in exchange for theirs. However, for neither of my friends would I be tempted (even a little) to give the life of one of my sons. Yet God loved us so much, "He gave His *only begotten* Son." The cross is the ultimate reminder of that love.

As a Christian counselor for many years, I have noticed that the happiest people in this world are those who know and accept the love of God their heavenly Father. I learned early that a per-son's attitude toward God often determines his attitude toward himself and others. The most secure individuals are those who enjoy a deep, abiding love for God, which in turn assures them that He loves them. As a counselor I enjoyed assuring the hearts of those who came to me with problems of fear, anger, or depression. Often I would explain that Jesus pictured God as the prodigal's father who so loved His son that he let him exercise his own free will by making some bad mistakes. Yet when the father saw his son coming at a distance, he ran to him, kissed him, and wel-comed him back into his home and life.

It was Jesus who knew God best and who described Him in such richly human terms, likening Him to a father who dearly loved His errant son. No religion in the world encourages its followers to address God, the Supreme Ruler of the universe, as "Our Father who is in heaven"—yet Jesus did just that.

Even this, however, is not the greatest proof that God loves us; what Jesus accomplished on the cross proves that. The apostle Paul asked, "He who did not spare His own Son, but delivered Him up for us all, how shall He not with Him also freely give us all things?" (Romans 8:32). The cross is a constant reminder of God's love. Whenever you see the cross, it should remind you of what no other power or symbol or person on earth can tell you: God loves you! A hymn writer caught that message when he wrote the words:

> The love of God is greater far
>   than tongue or pen could ever tell,
> It goes beyond the highest star
>   and reaches to the lowest Hell.
> The love of God, how rich and pure,
>   how measureless and strong;
> It shall forevermore endure
>   through saints' and angels' song.[1]

THE POWER OF GRACE

A brilliant scientist, a professor at San Diego State University, had attended our church with his wife for several weeks. When we had our first personal talk, he candidly said, "LaHaye, you make salvation too easy. I think more people would buy into what you are saying if you urged them to do something to receive it." Here was a typically "good" man. He was a model of self-discipline, he loved his Christian wife, and wouldn't think of being anything but faithful to her. Yet like so many in our day, he had no concept of the grace of God. He is not a God who sells His salvation to the highest bidder or the hardest worker; He is a God who gives His salvation to the undeserving, freely by His grace.

So I told this good man, "You do not understand two important factors in God's offer of salvation—it is not easy and it is not free. It seems that way to you because Jesus paid it all on Calvary's cross. He paid the redemption price for our sin by sacrificing His holiness and becoming sin, so that He could taste death for every man, even the death on the cross."

We had just come through the Easter holiday and I had preached on the suffering of Christ on the cross—not a pretty picture as it is presented in the Gospels. This man had been impressed with the price Jesus paid for humanity's sin, but it seemed too "easy" from his standpoint. He was not saved until he understood that we cannot add to salvation; it is not a matter of Jesus plus my own efforts. It is solely Jesus! The old hymn got it right: "Jesus paid it all, all to Him I owe, sin had left a crimson stain, He washed it white as snow."

That is grace—the unmerited favor of God. We have no right to salvation. Even if we could live a sinless life (which no man other than Jesus has ever managed), we would still fall short of the standard of God, which is righteousness. Instead, we have all come short of the glory of God. Yet by repenting of our sins and calling on the name of the Lord, we are promised salvation and eternal life—freely by His grace. Men and women can do nothing for their salvation. It is all of grace, the gift of God through the finished work of Christ on the cross.

Paul referred more to the grace of God than all the other writers of the New Testament put together. Many Bible scholars think that was because he was more conscious of what God had saved him from. He was not only a sinner, he was a persecutor of the church. He did all he could to destroy the church, even to consenting to the death of the first martyr, Stephen. Yet God saved him and gave him a calling to preach the gospel to millions, leading more to salvation than anyone on record through his voice and pen. To take such a despicable sinner, save him, turn his life around 180 degrees, and use him as a preacher of the Good News—now, that was grace! Perhaps that is why Paul refers to the gospel as the "gospel of the grace of God" (Acts 20:24). The Good News is that our merciful God has given us a Redeemer-Savior in the person of His Only Begotten Son, who was born of a virgin, lived a sinless life, died a sacrificial death, and then rose again for our justification. The resurrection was God's seal of approval that Jesus' sacrifice on the cross was adequate in His sight to atone for the sins of the whole world.

Every soul who has ever been saved was once an undeserving sinner, totally unable to save himself or herself. But by receiving God's gift of salvation through what His Son did on Calvary's cross, he or she was forgiven and saved for eternity. As another songwriter phrased it, "Nothing in my hand I bring, only to the cross I cling."

If Satan or any of his imps (some of whom are in human garb) came to you and said, "But you don't deserve salvation!" they would be right. For you don't, and neither do I! None of us do. Yet we are saved by faith alone in what Jesus did on the cross. That is the measure of the power of the cross, which is the grace of God in action whereby He gives salvation to those who do not deserve it.

THE JUSTICE OF GOD

The best known characteristic of God is His justice. There are two reasons for this. First, the Bible makes it clear He is a "just God;" the other is man's conscience that either accuses or excuses him. That is why normal human beings feel guilty when they have violated God's laws. They intuitively know they will meet Him at the Day of Judgment, where they will be held accountable for their deeds. That is all many people know about God, that He is just and as such holds them accountable for their deeds. Many Scriptures emphasize that God punishes sin.

God set a path for His chosen people, Israel, in the Old Testament, set His rules for personal behavior before them, and said, "If you obey Me I will bless you, but if you disobey Me I will punish you." The enormous trials that have befallen the children of Israel through the centuries came because they first rejected God's rules for living, then rejected the warnings of His prophets, and finally rejected His promised Messiah, even though He gave them at least one hundred prophecies in advance of His coming to earth so they would recognize Him.

The cross is a testimony to God's judgment on sin. Even more than He warned Israel, God has warned all humankind that He will judge all who sinned against His law. He gave an example of that in the first two human beings in the Garden of Eden. They were tested for all mankind by being forbidden to eat of the Tree of the Knowledge of Good and Evil. They could eat from any of the other trees, but they desired the forbidden fruit, ate it, and in doing so defied the will of God. That act of defiance is called *sin.* For that sin they were cast out of the Garden and cursed: hard work for Adam, pain in childbirth for Eve. The point is, God is a just God who keeps His word.

Unlike human beings, God does not have to *try* to keep His word. He cannot do otherwise. That is why the penalty of sin, which is death, had to be paid. Otherwise, no man or woman could ever enjoy the blessings God has prepared in heaven for those who love Him. It is also why Jesus, who had never committed a single sin, had to die on the cross for our sins. "The just for the unjust," the Bible calls it. But it is more than that; it is God in human flesh dying for the sins of the whole world.

Suppose one human being in history had lived a sinless life and was crucified as a sacrifice for the sins of mankind. At best, his blood could cover or atone only for the sins of one man. The blood of even a perfect man is not enough to cover the sins of all the billions of humans who have ever lived.

But Jesus "was made a little lower than the angels" (Hebrews 2:9) and "became obedient to the point of death, even the death of the cross" (Philippians 2:8). The cross speaks to us as the symbol of God's judgment meeting God's mercy, wherein the blood of God was shed for the sins of mankind. Now, we can escape death and go to heaven for eternity because someone eminently worthy paid the price for our sin on the cross. Jesus was a more than adequate sacrifice for our sin. The cross reveals God's mercy, while at the same time satisfying God's justice.

No story in the world compares to that of the cross. No religion on the planet teaches that the founder of its religion died to pay the price for their sins so they could be free of the consequences of their sin and enjoy God forever. There are many religions in this world, but none like Christianity. The Christian message is in a class by itself. Buddha did not die for his followers; nor did Confucius or Mohammed or any other religious leader. But Jesus did! And the cross testifies to that fact wherever it is seen.

Phil Donahue, the maverick Catholic, loved to ridicule Bible-believing Christians on his nationally televised talk shows. One of his favorite ploys was to mock those who believed Jesus is the only way to heaven. On one show he asked me, his guest, to explain how a person can be saved. I could see it coming. He whipped up his audience by asking a question, then let the audience respond their approval or disapproval. Of course, I told him what the Bible says, how a person must believe that Jesus died on the cross for our sins, was buried, and on the third day rose again (1 Corinthians 15:3–4), and that he should repent of his sins and that whosoever shall call on the name of the Lord shall be saved. He smiled because he knew he had me (and so did I). Then he asked, "Dr. LaHaye, what about the Jews who don't accept Jesus—is there any hope for their salvation?"

It was not easy to explain to that hostile audience that the Bible teaches "there is no other name under heaven given to men by which we must be saved" (Acts 4:12, NIV) and that anyone, Jew or Gentile, could be saved only by faith in and repentance toward Him. You can imagine the hooting and booing that greeted my "intolerance." Mr. Donahue then asked, "Are you saying that *yours* is the only way to heaven?" To which I responded, "It isn't *my* way. Jesus said, 'I am the way, the truth, and the life. No one comes to the Father except through Me'" (John 14:6). The crowd response indicated that if a vote had been taken, my position would have lost two hundred to two (my wife would have voted with me).

Admittedly, the Christian gospel is intolerant, narrow-minded, and exclusive. The one thing it has going for it is that it is true! Although there are many religions, all of which try to offer some way to heaven or the next life, there is only one God who has offered one way of salvation. It is the way of the cross, where His divine justice and mercy meet to offer mankind His great salvation.

The cross does not offer salvation through Buddha or anyone else. The message of the cross is simply this: Jesus paid the debt of our sin on His cross. If we repent of our sins, His blood shed on that cross will wash us as white as snow. The message of the cross is both just and merciful, in that it offers the only hope in the world for the human dilemma—that "all have sinned and come short of the glory of God." Jesus paid it all!

THE CROSS IS A SYMBOL OF MERCY

One of the least known truths of the Old Testament is that the God of the Bible is a merciful heavenly Father. The Jews seldom considered His mercy, for their disobedience seemed to constantly confront them with His justice. But the whole Garden of Eden scene is evidence of His mercy. Had I put two perfect people with a free will in the idyllic Garden of Eden and given them hundreds of trees to eat from and forbade them to eat from only one, and they ate from it anyway, I would have been tempted to give them a hot blast of my wrath. Not so God! He demonstrated His mercy by giving them Plan B, a blood sacrifice that culminated with the death of His own Son on a cross.

Perhaps you know the story of the prophet Jonah, who refused to go to Nineveh to warn its residents that they were about to be destroyed for their sins. Instead he rebelled and went to Tarshish, in the opposite direction. God sent a big storm on the sea where he was traveling, and when the sailors threw the rebellious prophet overboard, the Lord sent a great fish to swallow him. After three days and three nights he was thrown up on land by the fish, and the Lord ordered him the second time to go to Nineveh. This time he went. When the people heard the warning of the prophet, the whole city repented and God in His grace forgave them and stayed His hand of judgment. The story illustrates the mercy of God to those who repent.

Have you ever noticed why the prophet refused to go in the first place? He said, "For I know that You are a gracious and merciful God, slow to anger and abundant in lovingkindness, One who relents from doing harm" (Jonah 4:2). Obviously, God was more merciful toward the dwellers of Nineveh than was His prophet, for Jonah hated the Ninevites for all their crimes against Israel. God really is more gracious than mankind, for who of us would have responded differently than Jonah? Nowhere is that made clearer than on the cross. For at the cross God's justice and His mercy meet—and both are satisfied.

We tend to think that because God makes the rules, if He were *really* merciful, He would simply overlook our sins. But He could not do so and still maintain His perfect holiness! God's justice would not permit it. But in the cross, both are satisfied. His Son mercifully paid the penalty for our sin, satisfying God's justice which in turn maintains His holiness. How can a just and merciful God send man to hell for his sins or send him to heaven despite them, and still be holy? The answer is: the cross. The cross is the supreme symbol of divine mercy. God's eternal mercy is often called "compassion" in the New Testament, and it can be seen every time you look at the cross.

A middle-aged woman, wearing a gold cross around her neck, sat next to me on a plane. I asked her my two questions: What does that cross mean to you? And why do you wear it? Her eyes immediately filled with tears as she said, "I lived a very desperate life for over thirty years. There is no sin known I did not commit—drugs, robbery, deception, you name it, I did it. I was so bad I lost the custody of my two beautiful children. I tried to commit suicide three times, and during my darkest days a Christian woman told me about Jesus, that He died on the cross for my sins. I repented and accepted Him as my Lord and Savior and was instantly forgiven and saved. Now, twenty-one years later, I am a different woman. He saved both my life and my soul. And I wear this cross so that everyone will know I am a new person."

One more testimony to the power of the cross! That woman did not do one thing worthy of forgiveness, but she didn't have to; Jesus did everything for her on the cross. The cross she wears cries out to all who see it, "God is merciful!"

A SYMBOL OF FORGIVENESS AND SALVATION

Early in our marriage my wife gave me as an anniversary present a beautiful gold ring with a black onyx stone, on which is located a gold cross. For over forty years I have proudly worn that ring as a symbol that the most important event of my life took place when I knelt at the cross, confessed my sin, and found the forgiveness and salvation only God can give. I do not wear it to *become* a Christian, I wear it because I *am* a Christian.

Yet I do not deserve to be a Christian; that is true of all of us. Forgiveness and salvation are not the result of "works of righteousness which we have done, but according to His mercy He saved us" (Titus 3:5). Forgiveness is a merciful act of God in which He applies the shed blood of His Son, Jesus, to our sins and washes our slate as white as snow. Even though we have sinned grievously many times, we Christians have been forgiven of *all* unrighteousness. The cross speaks of forgiveness.

The Bible is filled with the message of forgiveness, and all of it is dependent on a blood sacrifice. The Bible teaches that "the life of the flesh is in the blood" and that "without the shedding of blood there is no forgiveness of sins." We see this message all through both the Old and New Testaments. The Jews earned the epitaph that theirs was a "bloody religion." At the heart of their sacrificial system in the wilderness was the Tabernacle and its required blood sacrifice offered by the priests, first for themselves and then for the people. A pure, white lamb, "without spot or blemish or any such thing," was the only acceptable sacrifice. Again, when God brought the children of Israel out of Egypt, it was a blood sacrifice He required. He told them to make a mark in blood over their doorposts, warning the death angel that this was a believing Jewish home. The blood instructed the angel, "Pass over this house."

All such animal blood sacrifices were little but promissory notes, statements of intent. The person of faith was expressing his repentance in faith, not in that animal's sacrifice, but in God's Word that promised eventual forgiveness. That permanent forgiveness was finally won on the cross when the Son of God died for the sins of the whole world, including all the sins past and all those that were to come. That could be accomplished only by the death of God. It was as though Jesus reached back and picked up

all the promissory notes of faith from Adam to the end of the mil-
lennium and marked them "paid in full"! As He hung on the cross,
shedding His divine blood for the sins of mankind, He cried out,
"It is finished!" What was finished? The sacrificial system! That is
why Christianity has no system of sacrifices today and why it
hasn't had one for two thousand years. Jesus paid it *all*—He paid it
all on the cross.

Nothing can be added to Peter's words when he said,
"Knowing that you were not redeemed with corruptible things,
like silver or gold…but with the precious blood of Christ, as of a
lamb without blemish and without spot" (1 Peter 1:18–19). Jesus'
precious blood was shed on the cross as the only adequate means
of our forgiveness. Without it, there would be no forgiveness of
sins.

Many gospel tracts graphically illustrate this truth by showing
lost humanity on the edge of a great divide, over which they cannot pass. On the other side, God in His holiness is standing. Often
something like this will be written on man's side: "Man is sinful
and separated from God." Another picture showing the cross as a
bridge covering the great divide depicts man walking to safety. It is
sometimes labeled, "God commended His love toward us in that
while we were yet sinners, Christ died for us."

For good reason, the cross is still the best symbol of forgiveness and salvation.

THE MESSAGE OF THE CROSS IS THE POWER OF GOD

Most people would like to see God reveal Himself in unmistakable
terms, so even our sophisticated age would be convinced that He
truly exists. I have confessed to such yearnings myself. But God in
His sovereign wisdom has chosen not to do so. If mankind will
not accept the obvious signs He exhibits through creation, His
incredible book, the Bible, and by the most incredible person who
has ever lived, His Son, then there remains only one other sign:
the power of the transformed life of a person who kneels at the
cross and cries, "Yes, Jesus Christ, I will have You reign over me. I
confess my sin and throw myself on Your mercy and ask for for-

giveness through the blood You shed on the cross." That cry of salvation has not only *saved* millions of people throughout history from all walks of life, it has also *transformed* them into what God wanted them to be.

Multiplied millions have been transformed by their experience at the cross. So many people have been transformed from myriad obsessive forms of behavior, that it can be no mere accident of history. It can be accounted for by only one thing: the astonishing power of the cross.

CHAPTER FIVE

HOMEGROWN
HOSTILITY TO
THE CROSS

There is no question that the cross has been the object of more love, affection, testimony, and even worship than any other symbol in the world. It has also been the most hated object on the planet. Whole religions dislike, ignore, despise or actively oppose it. And this is nothing new. "Roman historians and writers like Tacitus and Suetonius looked on the idea of a 'crucified God' with contempt."[1]

In America today the cross is probably the principal symbol to be targeted by an assortment of secularizers, atheists, humanists, and members of the American Civil Liberties Union. They seem determined in this free country, where free speech is supposed to be respected, to rid the nation of all religious symbols. And these symbols are indeed a form of speech; Christians call it *testimony*.

America's history is filled with crosses. Paintings of our nation's earliest events, from the Pilgrim's landing at Plymouth Rock to the first Thanksgiving Day celebrations, all include crosses. Crosses were placed on our earliest public buildings and on our official documents. In both North and South America it has been traditional for crosses to mark the site of someone's death. From Arlington Cemetery in the nation's capital to every military cemetery in the country, white crosses are used to commemorate those who died in the service of their country. The cross is a historic symbol of the price of freedom.

Yet though the cross is loved and respected by millions, it is hated by a few. And because many of the few happen to be influential lawyers and judges, they are able to impose their secularist will on the majority.

CROSSES: AN ACLU TARGET

While we lived in Crystal City, Virginia, near Washington, D.C., a sixteen-year-old girl was killed on the interstate highway. Her parents and friends wanted to erect a small white cross on the roadside in her memory. They were quickly informed by atheists and ACLU supporters that it was illegal to erect such symbols on government property. Had it not been for the generosity of a local farmer who permitted his land near the highway to be used for the purpose, no suitable spot could have been found near the site of the tragedy to commemorate the tragic loss.

The ACLU, with its warped view of the First Amendment and its nonhistoric claims of separation of church and state (a phrase not even mentioned in the Constitution), has sparked many legal decisions calling for the elimination of the cross from public places. Now that so many ACLU members have been appointed as federal judges (thanks to Jimmy Carter and Bill Clinton), it is not uncommon to see the cross ordered out of all official documents.

One such judge ordered a New Mexico city to change its 185-year-old official seal because it contained a cross. Another city in California was ordered to remove a cross from atop the local fire station because it was a religious symbol, in supposed violation of the separation of church and state. Forget that it was a memorial to a heroic fireman who lost his life in the line of duty. Most citizens can understand the anger of his firehouse comrades at having to comply with the mandate. Similar decisions have been handed down by equally hostile judges all over the country. We are becoming a secular nation by design of a minority of atheistic activists who are using their power as government agents to impose their will on the majority.

The ACLU probably has become the most harmful and detested organization in the United States because of its relentless attacks on Christianity and the way it has turned the First Amendment upside down. The group likely has done more to secularize America than any other organization in the country, except for its counterparts in education. And I doubt the situation will get better in the near future. The ACLU is only one or two votes away from controlling the Supreme Court and has one justice who is rumored to be next in line for Chief Justice, the first woman in history to serve in such a capacity. She is the first ACLU national board member ever appointed to the nation's highest court.

As unbelievable as it may seem, the Supreme Court decided that a cross in a prominent location in a cemetery must be removed because someone driving on a nearby highway might find it offensive. And as a result of recent court decisions and policies inspired by secularists in the Equal Employment Opportunity Commission, the cross is vanishing even as a piece of jewelry in the workplace. Many employers don't have the money or time to fight government bureaucrats who issue a mandate that outlaws the wearing of the cross in the workplace. What such an order has to do with equality of employment perplexes me, but such decisions are seized upon by atheists in public education to eliminate the wearing of the cross in the schoolroom. After all, as one principal told a Christian teacher, "Your students might interpret that cross as an expression of promotion of your religious preference." And that is illegal in America?

One Christian teacher of whom I asked my two-question survey mentioned in another chapter had a beautiful gold cross hanging on a chain around her neck. "I am forbidden by the principal to wear it in my classroom," she told me, "so I try to wear it whenever I am on my own time." I find it incomprehensible that such things now occur in a school system originally founded by Christians, the greatest such system in the world before many of its leaders became hostile to the Bible, traditional moral values, and symbols of Christianity like the cross. But it shows how far the secularists have taken America in the past fifty years. Unless our nation's Christian leaders stop trying to be noncontroversial and begin to lead their congregations to vote into office representatives who hold values amenable to their own, we will continue to be dominated by secularists who hate the cross and everything it stands for.

CROSSES ON THE ENDANGERED LIST

For twenty-five years I pastored one of the great churches of America, located in San Diego, California. It was there I came to appreciate the religious heritage of that city, as well as many others across the state. Father Sierra, a Catholic priest, established the first mission there almost three hundred years ago. The San Diego Mission, a historic landmark still open to the public, commands a prominent position that can be seen far down Mission Valley. It was the first of twenty-one such missions stretching from San Diego to San Francisco. Travelers in those early days found a welcome haven as they traversed the state. Several of these California cities still bear various marks of their religious heritage.

For many years the city of San Diego prominently displayed two giant crosses. One was on Mount Soledad near the ocean, the other on Mount Helix about eight miles east of Mission Valley. Both were lighted at night and provided beautiful landmarks. The thirty-six-foot Mount Helix cross was built by a devoted couple in 1936 and maintained by them until their death, when it was deeded to the city of La Mesa for a local park. An amphitheater was located there and was used annually for Easter sunrise services, as was the four-thousand-seat outdoor stadium at Mount Soledad. The forty-three-foot cross there, located on the highest point in San Diego, was also built by private citizens in 1954 as a memorial to those who died in World Wars I and II and the Korean War. It has been maintained by a nonprofit association ever since with the realization that it was "preserving the religious heritage of the city."

In 1992, however, an appeals judge decided in favor of an atheist professor from a local college that the cross must be torn down because it was residing on city property. In this instance, the judge's determination was so biased and wrongly motivated that the city fathers attempted to donate the land to a private association with the understanding that it continue to maintain the site. The issue is still in the courts.

Just to show their hostility, atheists filed an application to reserve the amphitheater on Easter, for the sole purpose of preventing local Christians from using the site of "their cross" as they have for the past forty-two years. Can you visualize seventy-five atheists gathering on Easter Sunday morning in a four-thousand-seat stadium to celebrate that Jesus *didn't* rise from the dead (even though they had no more idea of where His body is than skeptics have had for two thousand years)? It must have been an inspiring service!

One of the largest crosses in the country, a 103-foot concrete structure that stands alone atop Mount Davidson in San Francisco, is also under attack. Although local officials are trying to save the cross by deeding the property on which it stands to a nonprofit association, it will be difficult because that cross was built in 1934 with city funds and stands in a city park. An ACLU lawyer for the American Jewish Congress lost an appeal to remove the cross before the U.S. Supreme Court, but the case continues.[2]

Hawaii, an island settled by Polynesians, never has been a bastion of Christianity, although missionaries and churches have been active there for many years. In 1962 the U.S. Army constructed a huge cross and a two-hundred-foot stairway leading up to it with taxpayer dollars. The cross is located near Scaffold Barracks, an army base used extensively for training and as a staging area to Vietnam during the seventies. According to news reports, the American Atheists Inc., in February 1997, demanded the removal of the cross. Evidently the group was cheered by a court decision in 1988 that caused the demolition of a sixty-five-foot cross at nearby Camp Smith.

At last report, the Pentagon was reviewing a decision on whether to remove another thirty-seven-foot metal cross on an army base. Given the high percentage of secularists in the present administration—men and women who choose the leaders who serve at the Pentagon—it is a good bet that these and other crosses will fall to the hostility of a powerful minority of atheists who are attempting to remove all vestiges of Christianity from our country's military and public life.

HOLLYWOOD AND THE MEDIA JOIN THE FIGHT

The antagonism of Hollywood and the media to the cross is legendary. We're familiar with the Washington, D.C., battles over funding for the NEA (National Endowment of the Arts), an organization which has given taxpayer-funded grants to artists with blasphemous tastes, such as Andres Serano's infamous "Piss Christ." He and the NEA called it a work of "art." You be the judge. The piece is nothing more than a crucifix in a bucket of urine. They may call it *art* but Christians call it *blasphemy!*

The *Los Angeles Times,* so typical of the media, published a cartoon after the '96 election showing Senator Bob Dole impaled on a cross and wearing a crown of thorns arranged to read: "Christian Coalition." Evidently the cartoon was meant to imply that it was Dole's association with the Christian Coalition that caused him to lose the election and end his legislative career.

You don't have to be a Christian to conclude that a high percentage of people in the media, the entertainment industry, education, and the legal profession are hostile to Christianity in general and the cross in particular.

THE SMITHSONIAN FALSIFIES HISTORY
TO IGNORE THE CROSS

For twelve years my office was within two blocks of the mall in Washington, D.C., where the Smithsonian Institute is located. It is the largest museum in the world and the most expensive to maintain, costing taxpayers about 300 million dollars annually. Every year millions of tourists, including armies of schoolchildren, visit the Institute. Most Americans think of it as the authoritative museum on history, science, and many other subjects. They assume it provides an unbiased, factual account of everything it presents. It has never been that. It was founded by atheists to promote the evolutionary concept of history and science. To my knowledge the museum has never been positive toward Christianity.

Most people are unfamiliar with the ill-advised attempt by atheist/socialist Robert Owen to build the first socialist city in America in 1826, at New Harmony, Indiana. Even though he attracted a colony of atheists, freethinkers, academics, and others who shared his views, the experiment failed miserably in 1828. Owen decided the American people were not ready for socialism, so he organized what he called "the Friends of Education" in 1830. The stated purpose of the group was threefold: (1) to make public education mandatory; (2) to control the teachers' colleges; and (3) to train socialists to produce the curriculum and thus prepare for future generations. Today's liberal one-world philosophy that dominates the majority of graduates is a constant reminder that he was quite successful in attaining his objective.

What few people realize is that after the failure of that first socialistic experiment, many academics remained in New Harmony, where they founded the U.S. Geological Society. American citizens tend to think of it as a scientific organization, but in truth it was started by atheistic scientists who saw the new study of geology as a means of driving a spike into the heart of Christianity by scientifically disproving the creation story of the Bible.

In 1845, the socialist son of Robert Owen, Robert Dale Owen, ran for office and was elected to congress, where in 1847 he introduced on the floor of the U.S. Congress the bill that established the Smithsonian Institute "for the increase and diffusion of knowledge." He saw to it that it would eventually tap into perpetual support by taxpayers. Just eleven years later, in 1856, the U.S. Geological Society moved from New Harmony to the Smithsonian in Washington, D.C., where it has been ever since. Now you may understand why both of these organizations have been so evolutionary and anti-Christian.

The story doesn't end there, however. Fast-forward to 1994 and the publication by the Smithsonian of an expensive ($49.95) coffee-table chart book on history titled, *Smithsonian Time Lines of the Ancient World*. This book purports to date human history from the supposed origins of life to A.D. 1500. Of course, it begins with the assumption that evolution continued for millions of years, despite much scientific evidence that the earth is a young planet. After presenting the Ice Age in chapter 2, it goes to "the first modern humans, 35,000 years ago." Then in chapter 4, it talks about pre-Christopher Columbus visits to America. It uses the designation "B.C." when referring to dates throughout the book, until page 162, where it describes events from one hundred years before Christ to A.D. 1.

Unbelievably, it does not show a symbol of the cross on the time line of man's history on this earth! Nor does it mention a single word about Jesus Christ, the most significant person who ever lived. How is it possible to write an honest, factual history of mankind and omit the most influential person who ever lived? Nor does it include the cross to mark the most important event in history. Christ is the only one in history whose life provided the watershed date for our calendars. Why? Because He is undoubtedly the most important person who ever lived. And as I proved in my book *Jesus: Who Is He?* He did all that in only three years! No one has ever achieved what Jesus did, yet the Smithsonian does not even mention Him; it is as if He never existed. No other world historian to date has totally ignored Jesus Christ and His cross.

That is not academically honest, but it does advance the secularist agenda of the Smithsonian and the U.S. Geological Society. It also shows the not-so-hidden hostility of secularists in education. Like their counterparts in media, entertainment, and law, they refuse to face the fact that Jesus lived, died on the cross, and rose again.

CHRISTIANS BEGIN TO FIGHT BACK

Let's face it, there is a noisy but powerful group which is hostile to all crosses today. To many others it is just "not a big deal." Fortunately, there are some to whom it has deep meaning. To them it is important to wear or display a cross for all to see. Not for the gold or wood it's made from, but for the message it conveys.

Wauconda, Illinois, is a community of about seven thousand

people which for the past forty years has maintained two water towers that feature lighted crosses at night. "A gadfly atheist," as he was described by the local media (and backed, he said, by the ACLU), threatened to sue the city if it didn't take down the crosses. Not wanting to spend time or money in an expensive defense, the city fathers caved in and ordered the crosses removed.

The community reaction was intense and spontaneous! Suddenly crosses appeared on lawns, fields, windows, yards, TV antennae, just about everywhere. One man climbed a 110-foot telephone tower near his place of business to place a cross there which could be seen throughout the area. Local reports indicated this campaign in support of the cross was not organized but spontaneous. Maybe—just maybe—Christians have had enough of cowering and back-pedaling before the ACLU and other assorted secularizers.

ETERNAL LIFE AT STAKE

Hostility adversely affects a person's thinking and judgment. That is why those who feel hostility toward the cross (the world's most famous symbol of love and humanitarianism) have a difficult time accepting the awesome evidence for the divine nature of Jesus Christ.

If they don't change their minds someday, it will cost them eternal life.

CHAPTER SIX

IS THE CROSS
REALLY FOOLISHNESS?

S everal university students were elated when their philosophy professor finally agreed to go to church with them.
Their brilliant new pastor was creating quite a stir in the
community with his hard-hitting but interesting Bible-based sermons. He was well educated, holding a Ph.D. in the history of
religion and an equally advanced theological degree. He was a
spellbinding preacher and the students were convinced if they
could just get their brilliant-but-skeptical professor to hear him, he
would accept Christ.

That morning the pastor preached a powerful message from 1
Corinthians 15:1–4 on "The Meaning of the Gospel," showing that
the central message of Christianity was that Christ died for our
sins according to the Scriptures, was buried, and on the third day
rose again. In his conclusion he pointed to the cross as the primary
illustration of the gospel. It was a powerful sermon and at its conclusion several people came forward to receive Christ.

You can imagine the students' disappointment after the service
when they took their professor to lunch and asked him, "What did
you think of the message?" He replied, "It was well delivered, carefully thought out, and interesting, but for me, the whole idea of
the cross is just plain foolishness! The idea that a Holy God would

be so rigid as to demand penalty for sin to such a degree that He would sacrifice His own Son—seems foolish to me." He then added, "offering salvation free, without expecting anything on the part of the recipient, seems ludicrous."

Little did he realize that he was expressing exactly what Paul predicted would be the reaction to the message of the cross by those who did not believe in God—"foolishness," or as the apostle Peter called them, "willfully ignorant" (2 Peter 3:5). In that sense, the message of the cross becomes a stumbling block to those who already reject God's revelations of Himself in creation, revelation, and Jesus Christ. They see no need for the cross. As one said, "When I tried to explain that Jesus was not forced to die on the cross, but gave Himself freely that He might taste death for every man, the reply came, 'What a waste of a brilliant man.'"

The problem with both of these men is they could not receive the gospel message of the cross because they did not believe in a supernatural God, much less one who held them accountable for their conduct. Paul described such individuals as "those who are perishing." What an apt description! They are perishing even as they live. They are perishing in this life because they reject God's precepts for happy living, and more importantly, they are already perishing in the next life since their attitude toward the cross (unless it changes before they die), will keep their immortal soul from enjoying the blessings of the heaven which God has in store for them.

The main purpose of man on this earth is to prepare for the eternity to follow. That is why Christ came into this world "to seek and to save that which was lost" (Luke 19:10). Jesus called them "lost", while Paul calls them "perishing"; the meaning is the same. Once someone has heard the message of the cross, the heart of the gospel, they have to make a decision. If they say God's plan of redemption is foolishness, they are perishing. If, however, they bend their knee at the foot of the cross and say, "Yes, Jesus Christ, You died on that cross for my sins and I accept You as my Lord and Savior," they receive and are changed by the power of God.

The Wisdom of God vs. the Wisdom of Man

Paul, the closest thing the early church had to a brilliant philosopher, put it all in perspective in 1 Corinthians 1:17–31. He pointed out there are basically only two points of view regarding God, the world, man, and the purpose of life. One of those philosophies of life he calls "the wisdom of God," the other he calls "the wisdom of man." Today we call them *world-views* or *philosophies of life.* Be sure of this—your world-view or your basic attitude toward God will affect every important decision you make in life. As we shall see, the two views Paul names are 180 degrees in opposition to each other. One is described as *perishing,* the other as *being saved.* And they both call the other *foolishness!*

Paul was probably the first to codify these two opposing viewpoints, for they had not been fully developed at that point in history. It is not coincidental that Paul gave this message to the church of Corinth, comprised largely of Greeks. The Corinthians were within walking distance of Athens, Greece, the intellectual capital of the ancient world. In fact, Paul had just been to Athens before he established the church in Corinth. He found the Athenians antagonistic to the gospel, particularly his teaching on the resurrection of the dead.

Today the philosophy of Greece, in the form of secular humanism, has become the dominant philosophy of academia in the western world. Descartes, Voltaire, Rousseau, Nietzsche and others have added to it as French skepticism and German rationalism entered the mix, but it is still founded on the writings of Aristotle, Socrates, Plato, and many others from before the first century. Today it is the foundation of all that is considered academically acceptable throughout the western world.

Paul lumps all this philosophy together and calls it "man's wisdom" or "the wisdom of this age" or "the wisdom of this world." We know it today as secular humanism, a godless, man-centered philosophy that attempts to solve the problems of man, the universe, and eternity, independent of God. The apostle sums it up in verse 20: "Has not God made foolish the wisdom of this world?"

Calling the wisdom of man *foolishness* aggravates those who spend nine to twelve years in college and graduate school in a valiant attempt to become educated. They may become highly proficient as doctors, architects, engineers, or professionals in many other fields, but the moment they begin to use their "man's wisdom" worldview to consider the great questions of life (Why am I here? Where did I come from? Where will I spend eternity? How can I prepare for it?), they come up with *foolishness.*

Whenever a modern academician (unless he is a biblical Christian) ponders matters of the soul or eternity, his concepts are just plain *foolishness.* That is seen most clearly when they are confronted with the message of the cross. If their response is *foolishness,* as is so often the case, their answers to those most important questions are themselves *foolishness* from a biblical point of view. In many cases they just don't have *any* answers, good or bad.

The Greek word translated *foolishness* also means "futility." That is essentially what results from "man's wisdom," because it lacks divine wisdom. Consider the subject of evolution, the mantra before which all followers of "man's wisdom" or worldview worship. It is not scientifically provable, but it is presented dogmatically by many who reject the creation story because they reject the God of creation. They attach millions of years to the age of the earth without sufficient scientific evidence, because their theory of explaining man's origin without God requires such eons of time. I well remember the huge pods attached to the feet of the Apollo lunar landing vehicle to keep the ship from sinking deep into the dust scientists were sure covered the surface of the moon. They reasoned that inasmuch as dust particles settle on hard surfaces in space, and because the moon has existed for millions of years, their mooncraft would naturally sink into the siltlike dust they expected to find there. Imagine their embarrassment when the landing craft settled in about one and one-half inches of dust—a finding more in keeping with a young earth theory of creation. But, of course, that exercise in futility was swept under the dust and they rushed on in their foolishness rather than acknowledge the God of the Bible. Our efforts in space exploration would be greatly advanced if we acknowledged God as did the many inventive scientists of the seventeenth and eighteenth centuries, who paved the way for the Industrial Revolution. Cooperating with a Creator God who designed His universe with built-in fixed laws would help scientific discovery today far more than our current insistence on operating according to the evolutionary addiction to random chance.

Sir Isaac Newton, considered by many to be the most brilliant scientist who ever lived and the man who discovered the law of gravity and many other principles of science, was not addicted to the futility of "man's wisdom" thinking. He was a devoted Christian who began every scientific subject with the presupposition that there is a God of creation who has set changeless laws into motion. By accepting "the wisdom of God" by faith, including bending his knee before the cross of Christ, Newton was wise in this world *and* the one to come. By contrast, those who wholly accepted the wisdom of the world lived a futile life and went into a Christless eternity without hope. Some indeed went out screaming.

A "Futile" College Professor

A forty-year tenured philosophy professor at UCLA agreed to debate me for two hours at the annual meeting of The American Humanist Association when it was held in San Diego where I was pastoring. He was the secretary/treasurer for the group and a favorite board member. This man had made a lifetime vocation of attacking Christianity and had written several books on the myths of religion. During the break, he told me one of his greatest joys was "changing the beliefs of students from fundamentalist homes." He then exulted about how that year he had convinced a young man to abandon his dream of attending Dallas Theological Seminary and becoming a minister after finishing UCLA. His "man's wisdom" may have been sufficient to temporarily derail the faith of a young man obviously not grounded sufficiently in the Word of God, but it offered him no personal hope beyond the grave.

That was obvious from an article he wrote in the *American Humanist Magazine* in which he told about the tragic loss of his grandson, whose birth defect had taken his life before he reached three months of age. The professor told how he stood at the crib where the dead boy lay and emotionally told him, "My son, you shall live as long as I live, for you shall live in my mind!" *That* is hope? Sadly it is the only hope for a humanist whose "wisdom of this world" is limited to this world. No wonder Paul called it foolishness or futility. I couldn't help but contrast that incident with what I could have said, were I to attend one of my seven grandsons at death. I could honestly say in the words of David, "My son, you cannot come to me, but I can come to you, and we will forever be together and with the Lord for eternity." Now that is *hope!* A hope beyond the grave based on the unshakeable promises of Almighty God. But then, I accept the wisdom of God from which I derive this confident view of a future life.

It has long fascinated me that except for blatant atheists whose lives are spent in endless attacks on Christianity, almost everyone who dies resorts to Christian ministers to conduct the funeral of their loved ones. I have seen presidents, world leaders, Hollywood stars, and many others—even those who have totally ignored Jesus Christ during their lives—try to apply His teachings of life after death in the funeral parlor. Why? Because there is no real alternative! The emptiness of humanistic answers at that point are exposed for all to see. Can you imagine a widow being comforted at such a time by such foolish statements of humanism as "When you're dead you're dead," or "There is no God to save us," or "There is no life after death"?

The Christian message of life after death is a beautiful message of hope, because it is contained in the wisdom of God. The secularizers, who reject God and limit their knowledge to the wisdom of man or the wisdom of this age, have no hope because they reject Him who died for them and rose again the third day.[1]

EVERY PREMISE OF MAN'S WISDOM IS FALSE

Secular education today, from kindergarten through doctoral studies, is based on secular humanism, even though all five of its basic premises are wrong. Yet they are held tenaciously by those who reject the wisdom of God. I have maintained in several of my other books that the philosophy of secular humanism is really a religion, for all five of those tenets must be accepted by blind faith. In fact, there is substantial evidence that contradicts them, yet their advocates cling to them and reject the truths of Scripture. Unfortunately for them, it is not until death that they awaken to the truth they have rejected in their life on earth. As the writer of Proverbs said, "There is a way which seems right to a man, but its end is the way of death" (Prov. 14:12; 16:25).

The foundation of this wisdom of the world is laid out in many books. "The wisdom of this age" thinkers are influenced by the atheists, skeptics, and secularist writers before them—just as we Christians are influenced by the Bible and Christian writings before us. Therefore the diagram below, showing the five basic premises of man's wisdom, are shown on the foundation of some of the writings of world-respected thinkers, for it is from their writings the wisdom of man arises. Take special note of their five basic premises:

THE WISDOM OF MAN

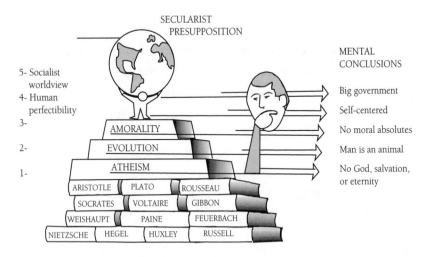

The chart above shows the secularist's five "futile" presuppositions based on the writings of God-rejecting men whose writings and *theories* mold their thinking. It also explains why they came to the "foolish" conclusions that are having such a harmful effect on our nation's cultural values—which in turn have produced the drastic rise in crime, drugs, alcohol, perversion, promiscuity, divorce, fatherless children, poverty, and other human miseries.

1. ATHEISM

Man's wisdom rejects the personal God of the Bible. Most do not even believe He exists. Some whom we would call deists accept a "God force" because the evidence for a supernatural God is so strong, but they do not think He gets personally involved with man or this world. Others are religious polytheists who believe "God is everywhere"—but all reject the personal God of the Bible.

To hold this atheistic and foundational belief as a "wisdom of man" thinker, one must blind himself to the obvious design of the world, nature, and man. Such unbelief is viewed by Christians as foolishness, for it requires that you look at the heavens in all their splendor and precision and say, "It originated by blind chance." Even though the stars and constellations are so perfectly located and coordinated that we set our timepieces by them for accuracy, God rejectors must say it originated *by chance*. The well-known "Big Bang" theory of origins flies in the face of the fact of design—that is, anything that has design must have a designer. It also contradicts the universal concept that order never comes from disorder. If the "Big Bang" explosion accounts for everything, then why isn't the universe a heavenly junkyard of chaos? Instead, the more we learn of it, the more it illustrates order and design. To believe otherwise, Paul calls *foolishness*. So also does the wise man who said, "The fool has said in his heart, 'There is no God'" (Psalm 14:1). Why is he called a fool? Because the signs of a divine Creator are so obvious only a fool can miss them.

2. EVOLUTION

The second premise of the wisdom of this age is that man *evolved* over millions of years until he reached his present condition. There is no scientific proof for evolution beyond the given "species" God originally created. There still are no transitional life forms that show animals becoming men, yet theorists try desperately to explain such evidence exists to convince us that it really happened. The fossils in the rocks and the fish shells at high altitude cry out against them, yet so anxious are they to explain man's origin without a creator God that they readily adopt this foolishness.

3. Amorality

Since the wisdom-of-this-age thinkers reject a Creator but believe man evolved, they conclude man is merely an animal, the highest form of primate. Consequently, they do not accept a fixed moral standard of behavior that produces happy living. Instead, they prefer that man lives to satisfy his urges.

The problem, of course, is what results from that kind of undisciplined and selfish living—sexually transmitted diseases, AIDS, and premature death. Such a philosophy is not new; Jesus addressed the "eat, drink, and be merry" crowd who advocated that man should grab all the gusto he can get. It is a futile (and brief) lifestyle. They forget how the famous phrase ends: "...for tomorrow we die." Death is inevitable! The Bible calls all who ignore it foolish. Even today those who disregard the laws or "wisdom of God" do so at their peril, for they possess the highest mortality rate in the world. Homosexuality, for example, bears a life expectancy rate of 39–42 years while the rest of the population lives an average of 73–77 years.

4. Human Perfectibility

Since man's wisdom is confused about God, origins, and fixed moral values, it follows that it would have a confused view of human nature. Humanists believe man is, at his core, very good and only needs the right environment to improve his quality of life.

The problem is: it is not true and does not work. Consider welfare, the most expensive test ever made by mortal man. It has proven to be a gigantic exercise in foolishness. Over thirty years ago the Great Society program of welfare was launched "to eliminate poverty." Today, after six trillion dollars spent (more than the national debt), it has proven to be a total failure. Its humanist sponsors assumed that if people had enough food, money, security, and a good environment, the good in them would surface and improve their lifestyle. Any inner-city ghetto will prove that theory to be foolishness, for welfare has created several generations dependent on government handouts who have little or no initiative for self-improvement. They live in worse conditions than existed before the program was launched. Instead of being a temporary aid in cases of emergency hardship, it has become a way of life that has destroyed the hopes and dreams of millions.

What do the liberal secularizers have to show for their efforts? Children bearing children, fatherless children, immorality run rampant, drugs, crime, fraud, human misery, and a national debt that borders on insanity. But that is not the most foolish part. They ridicule any biblical solutions to the dilemma that might involve a work ethic or personal responsibility or accountability and persistently try to improve an inherently flawed system. This is pernicious foolishness in action. Many other similar illustrations could be named, like the greater concern for criminals than for victims.

5. WORLD SOCIALISM

Since man has rejected God and His laws to govern him, history has been a drearily consistent study of the abuses of the alternative—human government. Man always has feared the anarchy that follows the fall of government, even though the atrocities of government are often far worse. Whether it is a monarchy or dictatorship, human government has always produced human misery. As we have seen, our own century has proven to be the most barbaric in human history, having perpetrated over 180 million deaths, more than in any preceding century. Yet the "wisdom of man" thinkers have for the most part continued a running romance with socialism as a form of government—even though socialism has been the primary cause of most of those deaths!

For over two hundred years, "the wisdom of this world" thinkers have caused, as one historian called it, "a fire in the minds of men." That fire is socialism. It has taken many forms, from Marxism, communism, Nazism, fascism, to liberalism, but they all amount to basically the same thing: to have world peace, man must create a one world government that has total control of individuals and all institutions and agencies. In Russia, communism dictated that the government should own all industry. This proved such a total failure that now, this once-upon-a-time superpower is teetering on the verge of bankruptcy. In America, liberalism doesn't see the need for government to *own* everything; total *control* will suffice. And as our government has grown, personal and corporate freedoms have shriveled.

Currently these liberal thinkers are trying desperately to salvage the United Nations, which was set up to facilitate world control. Yet its record of impotence and futility is the only consistency in its fifty-year history. It is worldwide foolishness in action. But instead of abandoning this futile plan, they demand more money to increase their bureaucratic control over the people of the world, including Americans.

The Bible says, "'My thoughts are not your thoughts, nor are your ways My ways,' says the LORD" (Isaiah 55:8). By now that truth should be apparent to everyone! Instead of solving the problems of man, human philosophy only makes them worse—but the leaders of this world refuse to acknowledge that the wisdom of this age is foolishness with God. But in time, its foolishness will be revealed to all.

THE WISDOM OF GOD

The sixty-six books of the Bible contain the wisdom of God. His wisdom is 180 degrees in opposition to the wisdom of man. The Old and New Testaments together reveal to us the foundation of God's wisdom. Man ignores them at his peril. Note how different the five fundamental principles of God's wisdom are compared to man's wisdom:

1. GOD

The first words of the Bible make clear that there is indeed a personal God, "In the beginning God created the heavens and the earth" (Genesis 1:1).

2. MAN'S ORIGIN—CREATION

Man was not the result of a long evolutionary process (even theistically guided). God Himself created man a special being, above all living creatures, with a living, eternal soul.

3. MORAL ABSOLUTES

Moral absolutes were established early by God, and mankind was expected to obey His laws, statutes, and commandments. We function better and longer when we obey these laws, and so do our fellow human beings.

4. HUMAN NATURE—FALLEN

As a result of the bad choice of Adam and Eve in the Garden, we are born with a fallen nature that cannot be trusted. The best antidote to the Fall is the teaching of the commandments of God and the realization that we are responsible in this life and the one to come for our behavior. Unfortunately, man in his "wisdom" today has eliminated the laws of God from the educational system, and in the process has destroyed optimum learning opportunities for millions of children and youth. Instead, mankind has created an environment of violence and chaos that is wasting billions of dollars and millions of lives each year.

It is more than interesting that the fifty-five founding fathers of America, who were predominantly Christians of Calvinist persuasion, designed the constitution of this country with an understanding of the fallen nature of man. That is why they established the famous "checks and balance system," so that when one branch of government proved untrustworthy, two other branches could counter the imbalance. That constitution, the greatest in the history of the world, has produced more freedom for more people for a longer period of time than any other in history—all because the founders understood the fallen nature of man and made allowances for it.

5. WORLD FREEDOM WITH RESPONSIBILITY

God designed man to be free, but also to obey His rules for successful living and to be his brother's keeper. That is why the happiest people today are those who obey God's principles and serve their fellowmen. Christians do not have the luxury of living only for themselves; historically that produces misery. The happiest people are those who have given themselves in the service of others and seek to glorify God by the way they live. As the Scripture teaches, "You are not your own? For you were bought at a price" (1 Corinthians 6:19–20). Or as Paul said of himself many times, "I am a bondservant of Jesus Christ." There is freedom and success in being that kind of bondservant.

One thing about Christians: they never run out of something to do! We have the Great Commission ever challenging us to convey the gospel message to lost men and women. *Nothing* is more rewarding in life. As this book will demonstrate, the power of God directed by the wisdom of God has transformed millions of lives. I have seen miserable individuals on the verge of suicide bend their knee at the cross and say "Yes, Jesus Christ, I want You to rule over me." They were transformed by His power and today live as effective, happy, and productive people.

Unfortunately those who are addicted to the wisdom of this age look at these miraculous conversions and say, "Foolishness!" In so doing they cheat themselves in this life and in the one to come.

THE WISDOM OF GOD

The above Christian presuppositions, based on the written Word of God produced the above five conclusions that influence everything a Christian does. When these conclusions dominated the American political, educational, and religious systems, this country enjoyed safe streets, low crime, good education, little governmental interference in our lives, high moral values, few illegitimate children, low divorce rates, concern for our fellow man, and the greatest personal freedom of any country on earth.

THE CROSS IS THE DECIDING FACTOR

Nothing is so decisive as the cross. Nothing illustrates more clearly what you are—a person committed to the wisdom of man or to the wisdom of God—than the cross. What you think of the cross will determine where you are in the game of life and will determine almost everything about you. If you say "Foolishness!" you are perishing. If you say "The power of God!" you are saved. It is that clear-cut. Consider the following two diagrams.

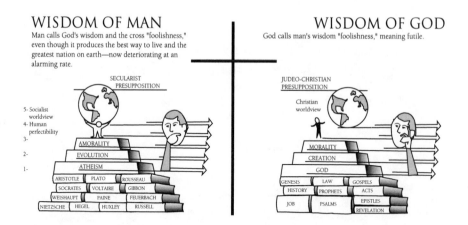

Your view of the cross will affect your attitude toward your fellowman, God, life, eternity, and will determine how you live your life. If you say "Foolishness!" you will live to satisfy yourself, independently of God. If you say "Truth!", "The power of God!" or "The wisdom of God!" you will live to please the One who died on the cross. The world may look at you and say you are foolish, but God calls you wise. The choice is yours.

A Ph.D. Changed His Mind

Dr. Fred K. is a highly respected university professor who specializes in training physical-fitness educators on the graduate-school
level. He once had 150 more requests for the graduates of his program than he had graduates. Like many "wisdom of this world"
advocates, he went to church with his wife and children but never
made a personal commitment to Christ. Then one day when he
was about fifty years old the truth of the message of the cross
gripped his heart, he bent his knee to the Savior, and said, "Yes, I
am a sinner. I want Christ to come into my heart and life."

Rarely have I seen a man his age manifest such a hunger for
the Word of God. He and his wife were on the front row every
time the church doors opened. They studied the Bible together
and individually. Two years after his salvation, he was commenting
on how much of the wisdom of God he had learned in such a
short time. Then he said, "I can't believe I could have been so
dumb for so many years. The Bible has changed my whole way of
thinking."

The wisdom of God does that to people. It exposes the foolishness of man's wisdom and introduces them to the truth of God.
And in the process, it transforms the person's life. Such is the
power of the cross!

CHAPTER SEVEN

THE CONVERSION OF
THE APOSTLE PAUL

The apostle Paul is easily the most significant of all the first-century Christians and may well be the most effective servant of Christ in the history of the church. He stands as the all-time model of Christian conversion, as well as the one person (other than Jesus Christ Himself) who impacted Christianity the most in the past two thousand years. Not only in his own generation, but also through the thirteen epistles he wrote that wound up in the New Testament. Doubtless, his writings have changed the courses of millions of lives.

One reason for his influence is that his exploits were given such extensive coverage in the Book of Acts, written by the scholarly Dr. Luke, his traveling companion and Greek convert. Another reason is the call of God on his life. Even before his salvation, God had a plan to use him in laying the doctrinal and evangelistic foundation for the young churches. At a time when the leaders of the church did not see much beyond their Jewish environs of "Judea and Samaria," Paul saw and went to "the uttermost parts of the earth." It was Paul and Barnabas who launched the first missionary journey, in which they saw thousands of Gentiles and some Jews come to faith. But more importantly, they founded indigenous churches in each community where God blessed their efforts with the transformation of souls. Later it was Paul and Silas who journeyed out to the mission field, always preaching the gospel "for the Jew first and also for the Gentiles" (Romans 1:16). In the process he founded many churches that outlived him by centuries. It is doubtful that anyone led more people to Christ than Paul until the twentieth century, when rapid means of travel and communication, high-speed computerization, printing, and telecommunications emerged.

Even John, who outlived Paul by some three decades, did not impact the early Church as Paul did. John, who is probably loved and revered by Christians today more than any of the other disciples, would not be a close second to Paul in his impact on the church. At best he might be the next most significant leader of the early Church. It should be noted that he also wrote five books of the Bible, a fact which suggests that writing is an incredibly significant way to impact your own and succeeding generations for Christ. In fairness to John, Peter, and some of the other lesser-known disciples, we should recognize that we simply have no substantial record of their ministries. One of the neat things about heaven is that we will know even as we are known (1 Corinthians 13:12, paraphrase). So don't be surprised when you hear "the rest of the story" to find there were men like Thomas, Andrew, Bartholomew, and others who mightily contributed to the cause of Christ.

SAUL OF TARSUS, THE MODEL CONVERT

The conversion of Saul of Tarsus—the Jewish-trained Pharisee, expert on the Old Testament, and zealous persecutor of the church whose transformation made him the leading convert, believer, and exponent of this new faith—is nothing short of a miracle. That he, "one born out of due time" (1 Corinthians 15:8), would identify with and lead this small band of believers stands as a model of religious conversion to this day. Although it is not mentioned frequently in the halls of academia, all conversions that demonstrate a transformation are still measured against the conversion of Saul of Tarsus. To get the full impact of his conversion, we must examine the account written by his friend, Dr. Luke.

The New Testament begins the story after Paul was an adult, having been trained as a Pharisee in the "school of Gamaliel." He may have been a young member of the Sanhedrin in charge of persecuting the church. He comes on the scene in Jerusalem at the stoning of Stephen, where he had to listen to that first martyr's brilliant last sermon. Some think that was instrumental in leading him to Christ.

Now Saul was consenting to his death. At that time a great persecution arose against the church which was at Jerusalem; and they were all scattered throughout the regions of Judea and Samaria, except the apostles. And devout men carried Stephen to his burial, and made great lamentation over him. As for Saul, he made havoc of the church, entering every house, and dragging off men and women, committing them to prison. Therefore those who were scattered went everywhere preaching the word. (Acts 8:1–4)

Then Saul, still breathing threats and murder against the disciples of the Lord, went to the high priest and asked letters from him to the synagogues of Damascus, so that if he found any who were of the Way, whether men or women, he might bring them bound to Jerusalem. And as he journeyed he came near Damascus, and suddenly a light shone around him from heaven. Then he fell to the ground, and heard a voice saying to him, "Saul, Saul, why are you persecuting Me?"

And he said, "Who are You, Lord?"

And the Lord said, "I am Jesus, whom you are persecuting. It is hard for you to kick against the goads [pricks of the Holy Spirit]." So he, trembling and astonished, said, "Lord, what do You want me to do?" And the Lord said to him, "Arise and go into the city, and you will be told what you must do."

And the men who journeyed with him stood speechless, hearing a voice but seeing no one. Then Saul arose from the ground, and when his eyes were opened he saw no one. But they led him by the hand and brought him into Damascus. And he was three days without sight, and neither ate nor drank.

Now there was a certain disciple at Damascus named Ananias; and to him the Lord said in a vision, "Ananias."

And he said, "Here I am, Lord."

So the Lord said to him, "Arise and go to the street called Straight, and inquire at the house of Judas for one called Saul of Tarsus, for behold, he is praying. And in a vision he has seen a man named Ananias coming in and putting his hand on him, so that he might receive his sight."

Then Ananias answered, "Lord, I have heard from many about this man, how much harm he has done to Your saints in Jerusalem. And here he has authority from the chief priests to bind all who call on Your name."

But the Lord said to him, "Go, for he is a chosen vessel of Mine to bear My name before Gentiles, kings, and the children of Israel. For I will show him how many things he must suffer for My name's sake."

And Ananias went his way and entered the house; and laying his hands on him he said, "Brother Saul, the Lord Jesus, who appeared to you on the road as you came, has sent me that you may receive your sight and be filled with the Holy Spirit." Immediately there fell from his eyes something like scales, and he received his sight at once; and he arose and was baptized. And when he had received food, he was strengthened.

Then Saul spent some days with the disciples at Damascus. Immediately he preached the Christ in the synagogues, that He is the Son of God. Then all who heard were amazed, and said, "Is this not he who destroyed those who called on this name in Jerusalem, and has come here for that purpose, so that he might bring them bound to the chief priests?" But Saul increased all the more in strength, and confounded the Jews who dwelt in Damascus, proving that this Jesus is the Christ.

Now after many days were past, the Jews plotted to kill him. But their plot became known to Saul. And they watched the gates day and night, to kill him. Then the disciples took him by night and let him down through the wall in a large basket. And when Saul had come to Jerusalem, he tried to join the disciples; but they were all afraid of him, and did not believe that he was a disciple. But Barnabas took him and brought him to the apostles. And he declared to them how he had seen the Lord on the road, and that He had spoken to him, and how he had preached boldly at Damascus in the name of Jesus. So he was with them at Jerusalem, coming in and going out. And he spoke boldly in the name of the Lord Jesus and disputed against the Hellenists [or Greeks], but they attempted to kill him. (Acts 9:1–29)

This incredible conversion story cannot be explained on a purely human level. How could a man who obviously hates Jesus Christ, who thinks He is an impostor, who totally rejects His bodily resurrection, and who even persecutes and kills believers who believe in Jesus as their Messiah, turn 180 degrees around, become a believer himself, and become the outstanding evangelist of his generation for the next thirty years? The story demands an explanation! A few skeptics have claimed he had a sunstroke which changed him. But 180 degrees? Impossible! Besides, someone suffering from sunstroke doesn't act like Paul did. "Madness," others have declared. But can madness turn a man from the desire to murder and persecute believers into a man of compassion, personal sacrifice, and suffering? As someone has said, "Oh, blessed madness!" Nothing even close to such madness has ever been recorded in history. It is easier to believe that the events occurred just as eyewitnesses and historical data say they ocurred. In fact, the newly named Paul lived consistently as an apostle for more than thirty years, then died willingly as a martyr, gladly testifying to the genuineness of his conversion until the sword severed his head from his body.

WHAT SOME SKEPTICS HAVE CLAIMED

Christianity has never lacked for detractors. As I detailed in *Jesus: Who Is He?*, only a few heretics appeared in the first century, and from then on each new attempt to destroy faith in the deity of Jesus (and particularly in His resurrection) was convincingly answered, which only added credence to the faith. It took seventeen hundred years for skepticism to become a science, for most men of letters were educated in religious schools and started their philosophical inquiries with the assumption of a supreme being and the supernatural. Descartes and his followers changed all that. Gradually the anti-God philosophy of French skepticism and German rationalism merged into The Enlightenment, which together with Unitarianism and socialism produced secular humanism. During the last three hundred years, these atheist-based *isms* began to seriously question the Christian faith. They were far from objective, for they started with the false premise that there is no God; therefore, they concluded there is no supernatural. Thus they disbelieved the miracles of Jesus and His bodily resurrection, not because they had proof, but because such well-established historical facts contradicted their rejection of the supernatural. For them it was enough to say that Jesus' deity and resurrection were impossible because they were supernatural, "and we know the supernatural does not exist."

It is not surprising, then, to find these seventeenth-century thinkers and their modern disciples attacking the conversion of the apostle Paul. Not because they have found new historical or archeological evidence to support their antagonism, but because his transformation conflicts with their preconceived bias. In fact, the science of archeology and further study of the details of history have only confirmed that the events of early Christianity occurred exactly as they were described in the Bible. But that does not deter skeptics from trying to find alternative suggestions for the supernatural power of the cross in transforming the celebrated convert Saul of Tarsus.

One current scholar describes the problem well.

Negative readings of Paul's Damascus experience flourished under the sway of rationalism and the emergence of the historical-critical method. Paul was an ecstatic, a crank driven by some physiological or psychological weakness. On the one side stood the opponents of Christianity, who joined with Nietzsche in declaring Paul to be the lawbreaker—"violent, sensual, melancholy, and malicious in his hatred"—who single-handedly invented Christianity and deceived the world. On the other side, however, so-called proponents of Christianity did little better for the apostle. Nineteenth century explanations, in fact, commonly delved into mythic projections of guilt, hallucinations and apparitions, epileptic seizures, or the power of a thunderstorm (cf. Pfaff, *Bekehrung*, 3–97).

What may be called "the ecstatic hypothesis"—that is, that Paul was in a state beyond reason—was constructed in various ways. But it rested on three assumptions, as summarized in 1845 by F. C. Baur: 1) the narratives of Acts are contradictory and not reliable; 2) a miracle on the Damascus road is no longer tenable; and 3) Paul's vision of the risen Christ was a mythic objectification of a subjective impression (*Paul, the Apostle of Jesus Christ*, 2 vols., trans, E. Zeller [London: Williams & Norgate, 1876, from 1846 German edition] 1.63–75). Others supplied explanations for the various details, often more absurd than they had imagined Paul to be. For example, while fighting off a pernicious fever in the region of Damascus, Paul encountered a thunderstorm of great violence on the slopes of Mt. Hermon; he mistook a flash of lightning for an apparition of the "sweet master" (E. Renan). Or again, Paul's epilepsy was the culprit, transforming "an immanent, psychological act of his own spirit" into a vision of Christ (H. J. Holtzmann).[1]

As we read over these inventive reasons (or excuses) not to believe, I am reminded that Paul's life—of which we know more about than anyone else in the early Church except our Lord Himself—contains no signs of their suggestions. For example, a man with a severe sunstroke is left weakened for life. That hardly sounds like Paul, whose body was capable of the rigors of three missionary journeys and many beatings and floggings. The same could be said of the epilepsy theory. No record of his life and travels suggests he ever had a seizure—and no one in the first few centuries ever offered such a ridiculous suggestion.

Either way, the skeptic is stuck with the supernatural. That a man could suffer what they suggest and yet be robust enough to be stoned and left for dead, then get up the next day and walk twelve miles to preach the gospel, taxes credibility. It is easier to believe he really did have a supernatural confrontation with the risen Christ on the Damascus road, just as the Scripture records and his companions and the early Church believed and taught. The truth is that most secular historians present the events of Paul's life and his incredible contributions to Christianity just as they are narrated in the New Testament, for there really is no other plausible explanation.

Some have considered the dramatic conversion of Saul of Tarsus to be second only in importance to the bodily resurrection of Jesus Christ as a convincing proof of Christianity. Now, almost twenty centuries removed from the events, the big question is, Is it believable?

IS THE STORY BELIEVABLE?

Those who have studied the case for accepting the reliability of the New Testament have no trouble accepting the facts concerning the conversion of Saul of Tarsus. Others want additional reasons for so believing. I think there are many. Consider the following:

1. The physical phenomena attending his conversion were testified by many eyewitnesses.

- A supernatural light, brighter than the sun, appeared in daylight (see Acts 9:3 and 26:13). It was already broad daylight in the desert at midday outside Damascus, when another, brighter light was seen around Saul the persecutor. It was so bright that it blinded Saul and was seen by all those with him.

- The audible voice of Jesus was heard. Paul later indicated that those with him did not understand the words, either because they were not spiritually prepared or because they were not close to him, but they knew a supernatural voice had sounded (Acts 9:7).

- Saul was supernaturally blinded. For three days he was blind because of the supernatural light that had shown around him. It was clear to those traveling with Saul that something supernatural had happened, for they had to lead him by the hand. It is highly probable that many witnesses saw Saul, the well-known persecutor, being led blind into Damascus. And he remained that way for three days.

- Saul's sight was miraculously restored. That Ananias was too frightened to go to Saul as God directed him fits the facts well; Saul had earned their terror. Yet Ananias went as directed and, just as was promised, when he prayed for Saul's sight to be restored, it was. That in itself was a physical miracle confirmed by witnesses.

- Something like scales fell from his eyes (Acts 9:18). While the restoration of sight from sun blindness is gradual, Saul's healing was distinct and immediate. Whatever the scales were, they were physically perceptible by Ananias and any others who were in the room. They saw a miracle and reported it to the church.

- Saul immediately stopped persecuting the church. Though he still had the documents of authority to arrest and imprison any followers of this new "way," he did not utilize them. In fact, his failure to do so incurred the wrath of his former friends, the religious leaders of Jerusalem. That wrath is clearly portrayed in Acts 21–23 as almost obsessive hatred.

- Saul's conversion was witnessed by many. Consider the

many people who witnessed all or parts of his conversion story. These were not arranged participants set up to confirm an alibi, but historical people who happened to be in the right place at the right time.

- There are no reports of anyone refuting the testimony. The events of Saul's conversion were seen by many witnesses, many of whom would have been alive when the account was written some twenty-five years later. To date, no evidence has ever been discovered that would deny the accuracy of the details. No one ever recanted, and history does not indicate that anyone ever claimed that any of the witnesses denied the events.

It is safe to conclude that the physical events of Saul's conversion happened precisely as the Scripture describes them. Luke, the narrator of most of the events, is considered by scholars to be one of the most accurate writers of history in the ancient world. In fact, he is so identified even by some who are not believers.

2. Saul's life was totally transformed.

No one in the history of the world has transformed more people than has Jesus Christ. Christians commonly use an expression to describe how bending their knees before Christ enabled them to triumph over some self-destructive obsession that once had dominated them: "He changed my life," they say. Many use it because it is the most succinct description of what happened to them after receiving the Savior. As a minister, I can attest to many such experiences, some of which are included in this book. But it is safe to say that neither I nor anyone living today has ever seen a more graphic change in a person's life than the one that occurred to Saul of Tarsus, who became the apostle Paul. Consider some of the following graphic changes in his life, all of which point to a supernatural conversion, not merely modifications of behavior.

- He quit persecuting the church and immediately became its promoter.

- He embraced the very belief in Christ that he once vehemently rejected.
- He immediately began preaching Christ. Acts 9:20–21 says, "Immediately he preached the Christ in the synagogues, that He is the Son of God. Then all who heard were amazed, and said, 'Is this not he who destroyed those who called on this name in Jerusalem, and has come here for that purpose, so that he might bring them bound to the chief priests?'"
- He began defending the faith he once persecuted. "But Saul increased all the more in strength, and confounded the Jews who dwelt in Damascus, proving that this Jesus is the Christ" (Acts 9:22).
- He stopped being a hate-filled, angry man motivated by self-will and personal ambition and became a gracious, loving, and self-sacrificing individual.
- He stopped trusting God's law to save him and became the premier exponent of God's grace.
- He abandoned a lifetime quest of seeking a Jewish-only means of salvation and became the exponent of Gentile evangelism, something totally at odds with his Jewish background. He gave his life sacrificially to reach millions of Gentiles.
- He never wavered from the faith after his conversion, right up to and including the time of his decapitation.

This Pharisee from the Greek city of Tarsus, schooled in both Jewish and Greek learning, was totally transformed on that Damascus road. For the most part, that transformation was immediate. Suddenly, all the Messianic prophecies made sense to him. How could he deny them? He had met the risen Christ and the encounter changed him forever.

3. Common sense demands the acceptance of Saul's dramatic conversion.

God challenges us to "come now, and let us reason together" (Isaiah 1:18), which implies that faith is not some blind leap into the dark, but a reasoned and logical acceptance of a divine offer. Paul carefully considered the offer given to him on the Damascus Road and eagerly accepted it—even though it cost him everything, even his very life. Consider:

- He had nothing to gain materially or socially. We have already seen that he was a "celebrity" on the scene in Jerusalem. He had the right genes, right education, right background, and much earlier than most was rushing up the ladder of success. He was a leader in Israel and the sky was the limit. By accepting Christ, he turned his back on everything he held dear. He knowingly gave it all up. For what? Christianity was not an admired religion respected by his friends; they hated it. By receiving Christ he knew he would lose all his old friends, except any who would join him in receiving the Savior. His future, instead of being secure and promising, would become doubtful and precarious.

One thing Paul never has been accused of is abandoning Judaism for an easier, richer, or more pampered way of life. He gave up everything he previously held dear for the sake of Christ Jesus his Lord and the spread of the gospel. He lost everything: position, status, rank, respect by his peers. It was all lost the day Saul kneeled before the cross and became Paul, the new Christian. The very people who once had admired and promoted him became his deadly enemies and even clamored for his death. Some plotted to have him killed and one group of assassins took a blood oath not to eat or drink until they had killed him (Acts 23:21). Why would Paul create such a reaction just two decades or less after his conversion? Because he was so effective for the cause of Christ and the spread of the gospel. Thousands all over that part of the world were receiving Christ through his ministry.

- He suffered more for his faith than most. He went from Saul the persecutor to Paul the persecuted. While many

Christians have suffered for their faith, it has always intrigued me that the man God used most to write encouragement to those who suffer, himself suffered more than almost anyone else on record. Consider his own description of his sufferings:

From the Jews five times I received forty stripes minus one. Three time I was beaten with rods; once I was stoned; three times I was shipwrecked; a night and a day I have been in the deep; in journeys often, in perils of waters, in perils of robbers, in perils of my own countrymen, in perils of the Gentiles, in perils in the city, in perils in the wilderness, in perils in the sea, in perils among false brethren; in weariness and toil, in sleeplessness often, in hunger and thirst, in fastings often, in cold and nakedness—besides the other things, what comes upon me daily: my deep concern for all the churches. (2 Corinthians 11:24–28)

Keep in mind that this list includes only Paul's sufferings that occurred before he wrote this book. Later he was imprisoned again and suffered the persecutions of Nero, the mad Caesar, for four or five years. He may have gone to Spain to preach the gospel, where little is known of his reception. Finally he was reimprisoned in the last big purge of Christians by Nero and then beheaded. Such suffering would have broken lesser men; yet through it all he never wavered, never flinched, "but counted it all joy that he could suffer for His name's sake." In fact, his commitment to Christ in the face of suffering is a source of encouragement to the many followers of Christ today who are also forced to suffer for His sake.

No one in his right mind would ever leave a life of ease for a life of suffering and persecution, unless he was utterly convinced of the truth that gripped his heart. Anyone who reads the writings of Paul, the sermons he preached as recorded in Acts, and examines the impact he had on the early Church is forced to admit that this man was in his right (and very brilliant) mind.

- His acceptance by the other apostles as "an apostle born out of due time." Anyone who understands human nature must be struck with the miracle of acceptance extended to this former persecutor of the church. The church already had decreed that an apostle had to be one of those who saw the Lord and who was familiar with His deeds while on this earth. Paul is a ready exception! Through his meetings with the other apostles in Jerusalem after his first missionary journey, he had a mighty impact on the policies of the early church. Acts 15 shows how the church began ministering to the Gentiles, accepting them as equals in the Body.

Even more amazing is that he rebuked face-to-face some of the elders of the church for what he considered hypocrisy (see Galatians 2:1–17). Yet Peter, one of those whom he rebuked, later paid a tribute to Paul when near the end of his life he wrote in 2 Peter 3:15–16, "Our beloved brother Paul, according to the wisdom given to him, *has written to you, as also in all his epistles,* speaking in them of these things, in which are some things hard to understand, which those who are untaught and unstable twist to their own destruction, as they do also *the rest of the Scriptures.*" Notice that Peter is aware of Paul's "epistles" and that he equates them with "the other Scriptures." In addition, he calls him "our beloved brother Paul." This letter was written during the days of Nero's persecution, when tradition tells us both men were martyred for their faith—Paul by the sword and Peter at his own request by inverted crucifixion. (He felt he was not worthy to die in the same manner as his Lord.)

- Paul's extensive teaching was fully embraced by the church. Anyone familiar with basic Bible doctrine knows that God used Paul to build on the teachings of Jesus and the Old Testament by further explaining salvation by grace through faith, "not by works, so that no one can boast" (Ephesians 2:9, NIV). He never received a single word of disapproval from a single apostle (not even John, who wrote long after

Paul was dead) or any of the early Church fathers, some of whom were avid writers. Instead, his writings were immediately recognized as Scripture and were accepted and used in the churches. Paul really was inspired by the Holy Spirit to write them, as he and the early Church claimed.

I find it incredible that this former persecutor of the church, who terrified believers for a short time even after his conversion, became a highly respected leader in and molder of the church. Never has an aspersion been cast against him, except from the enemies of the church. We could hardly ask for more believable evidence for the genuineness of the conversion of Paul.

4. More compelling evidence from a popular author.

Dave Hunt, a veteran conference speaker and author of many books, has some excellent thoughts on this subject in his latest book, *In Defense of the Faith.*

Saul of Tarsus had been the chief enemy of the church at its very beginning, arresting and imprisoning many believers and persecuting some even to death. This course so diligently pursued must have made him very popular among the religious Jews. As a young rabbi, Saul was already a hero well known for his zeal against Christians. He had everything to live for in remaining true to Judaism. That he would forfeit a brilliant future and become one of those whom he had persecuted, knowing that the same beatings, imprisonment, and eventual martyrdom would befall him as well, is indeed powerful evidence that he was convinced beyond doubt that Jesus Christ was alive and that he had personally met Him. Hallucination simply doesn't fit the known facts.

Even more convincing is the leading role which Paul quickly assumed in the explosive growth of early Christianity. He had inside knowledge and taught new doctrines completely at odds with his years of training and practice in Judaism, doctrines which he couldn't possibly have acquired except from Christ Himself. Yet Paul had never met Him prior to His crucifixion. He claimed to have learned all he knew of this new faith directly from the risen Christ.

> I have *received of the Lord* that which also I delivered unto you, that the Lord Jesus the same night in which he was betrayed took bread; and when he had given thanks, he broke it and said, Take, eat; this is my body which is broken for you; this do in remembrance of me. After the same manner also he took the cup, when he had supped, saying, This cup is the new testament in my blood; this do ye, as oft as ye drink it, in remembrance of me (1 Corinthians 11:23–25).

Paul wasn't present on that occasion, so how did he know what happened at that final intimate meeting between Christ and His 12 disciples? Why was it left to Paul to explain what happened at the Last Supper and its meaning? Why not Peter or James or John, who were there? Clearly the Holy Spirit had Paul write these words as part of the proof of Christ's resurrection. He testifies that he "received of the Lord" all that he is now teaching. We repeat: Everything that he knows about this new faith and now teaches with such authority Paul claims to have received personally and directly from the resurrected Lord Jesus Christ Himself. Nor is there any other explanation.

Unquestionably, Paul had never studied under Christ with the other disciples. He was a rabbi *opposed* to Christ during the latter's life. Yet suddenly he became not only the chief spokesman for Christianity but its chief authority. He even rebuked Peter to his face and Peter had to acknowledge that Paul was right and he was wrong. (Galatians 2:11–14) Whence this sudden authoritative knowledge?

Of course the skeptics suggest that Paul had hurriedly gone to the apostles and said, "I'm a believer in Jesus now, but I don't understand this Christianity thing. I want to preach it, so you'd better give me a crash course. Otherwise I could make some horrible blunders!" Could that be true? Did Paul learn what he knew of Christianity from Peter or from other apostles and Christians?

Then Hunt adds what he calls undeniable internal proof:

On the contrary, it was three years after his conversion that Paul finally came to Jerusalem. And when he attempted "to join himself to the disciples...then were all afraid of him, and believed not that he was a disciple." (Acts 9:26) Paul solemnly testifies:

> I certify you, brethren, that the gospel which was preached of me is not after man. For I neither received it of man, neither was I taught it, but by the revelation of Jesus Christ...I conferred not with flesh and blood; neither went I up to Jerusalem to them which were apostles before me, but I went into Arabia....
>
> Afterwards I came into the regions of Syria and Cilicia, and was unknown by face unto the churches of Judaea which were in Christ; but they had heard only that he which persecuted us in times past now preacheth the faith which once he destroyed. And they glorified God in me (Galatians 1:11–24).

That he is telling the truth is clear from the fact that Paul was the revealer of truths unknown to the other apostles. It was Paul to whom Christ made known by revelation (Ephesians 3:3–10) "the mystery which was kept secret since the world began" (Romans 16:25) and gave to him the privilege of preaching it (1 Corinthians 15:51; Ephesians 5:32; Colossians 1:25–27). He became the leading apostle and authority on Christianity, and the other apostles had to admit that he knew more than they and that he had indeed learned it directly from the risen Christ.

Paul wrote most of the epistles, more than all of the original apostles combined. It was he who stood up against the false doctrine being taught by the Judaizers who came from Jerusalem, where the apostles still resided. Paul confronted the apostles and church leaders in Jerusalem with this heresy (Acts 15) and changed the thinking of the church.[2]

One reason why there never has been a real attempt to discredit Paul's conversion (until seventeenth-century skeptics tried, without much success) is that the logic supporting its historicity is so strong. How else can it be explained that a man of his obvious brilliance could suddenly switch from being the chief opponent of Christianity to becoming its chief exponent? The conversion of Saul of Tarsus into a world-renowned Christian missionary is a fact of history.

THE CONVERSION OF LORD LYTTELTON

One of the most amazing conversion stories of the past has been well documented several times. Two skeptical eighteenth century English lawyers, Gilbert West and Lord Lyttelton (1709–1773), set out to disprove Christianity, only to be convinced that it was true. Typical of many honest skeptics, what they *thought* was lack of evidence was really lack of exposure to the evidence. When rightly exposed to that evidence they became Christians. In the new book *The Road from Damascus* author Bruce Corley tells it this way:

The Enlightenment took matters on a different course. A rising tide of skepticism in the eighteenth century threatened to sweep away the supernatural in Paul's conversion, along with other cherished truths, and called forth a variety of apologetic approaches. Those who doubted the miraculous sought other ways to explain what happened to Paul. One of these doubter's inquiries seems to have had an unexpected result. Early in the century at the end of an academic term, two Oxford scholars, George Lyttelton and Gilbert West, set a task for themselves during a long vacation to undermine two salient truths of Christianity. Each intended to demonstrate, respectively, that the conversion of Paul (Lyttelton) and the resurrection of Jesus (West) were falsehoods that did not happen as reported in the New Testament. When they met again in the autumn, they shared an astounding reversal. For Lyttelton had become convinced of Paul's conversion and West of Jesus' resurrection. Both published their finds as apologetic tracts for the faithful.

Lyttelton's eighty-page pamphlet, *Observations on the Conversions and Apostleship of St. Paul* (London: R. Dodsley, 1747) was widely circulated and is still reprinted today. His argument proceeded on the assumption that the facts surrounding Paul's conversion, by necessity, could be explained in only one of four ways: (1) Paul was an impostor who reported what he knew to be false, or (2) he was an enthusiast who was driven by an overheated imagination and thereby deceived, or (3) he was deceived by the fraud of others, whether human or demonic powers, or (4) what he declared about the cause and consequences of his conversion was true and, therefore, the Christian religion is a divine revelation.[3]

Recently while in Washington, D.C., I visited the rare books section of the Library of Congress. Sure enough, Lord Lyttelton's book was there, some 230 years after it was written. I was able to secure a copy and am happy to report that his sound reasons for accepting Proposition Four are just as relevant today as when written. Paul could have no rational motive to undertake such an imposture, nor could he have carried it on by the means we know he employed.

But let's suppose for a moment that he was an impostor. Why would he attempt such a thing? Lord Lyttleton suggested the following:

- To advance himself in temporal things for his own credit or power. Power over whom? Over a flock of sheep driven to slaughter?
- To advance his passions (power lust) under the authority of it and by means it afforded. Did he pretend any superiority over the other apostles?
- Was there the hope of increasing his wealth? His conversion meant the loss of all he had, as well as the hopes of acquiring more.
- Those he joined were homeless people held back from improving their fortune.
- Even the churches he established were richer than those in Jude. He refused even remuneration for his necessities (2 Thessalonians 3:8). He said the same thing at Ephesus (Acts 20:33).
- Could a disciple of Gamaliel think he could gain any credit or reputation by becoming a teacher in a college of fishermen?
- Could his preaching bring him any honor? "To the Jews it was a stumbling block and the Greeks foolishness." Contempt was the response for preaching this unpalatable message to the world. To Corinthians—"we are made as the filth of this world, the offscouring of all things unto this day."

What were the circumstances in which Paul declared his conversion to faith in Christ?

- Jesus, in spite of His purity and innocence, was crucified as an impostor for declaring Himself to be the Messiah. This intimidated others from following Him and accepting His doctrine, yet Jesus' followers recovered their spirits and actually taught His doctrines. They, too, were performing miracles and declaring Jesus had risen from the grave.

- The chief priests and rulers were not converted and had begun a severe persecution of Christians, of which Paul was a part, being himself a Pharisee taught at the feet of Gamaliel (Acts 7:9, 22–23).
- He was not content with persecuting these people in Jerusalem, but headed for Damascus to bring those followers of Christ in the synagogues to Jerusalem where they were imprisoned (Acts 7).
- The Damascus Road experience is where he became a disciple of Jesus Christ.

These circumstances bring us to the following conclusion:

- The evidence shows he had no thought of becoming rich by becoming a Christian.
- The glory of ambition was not his motive for becoming a follower of Christ.
- THEREFORE, we must believe that his conversion was supernatural and the account given to be true.[4]

PAUL'S CONVERSION HISTORY IS BELIEVABLE

It is customary among scholars to accept all ancient written records of events as recorded unless there is sufficient reason to doubt them. For example, if the people and places mentioned match with what is known and if there are no contradictions of substance, the records are accepted as credible. Two famous archeologists, William Albright and Sir William Ramsay, have examined the evidence regarding the ancient manuscripts of the Bible and have found them accurate. In Ramsay's case, this judgment produced a life-changing experience. Josh McDowell in his classic book, *Evidence That Demands a Verdict,* quoted the following:

Sir William Mitchell Ramsay, in 1881, was a young man of sterling integrity, unimpeachable character, culture, and high education. He had a sincere desire to know the truth. He had been educated in an atmosphere of doubt, which

early brought him to the conviction that the Bible was
fraudulent.

He had spent years deliberately preparing himself for
the announced task of heading an exploration expedition
into Asia Minor and Palestine, the home of the Bible,
where he would "dig up the evidence" that the Book was
the product of ambitious monks, and not the book from
heaven it claimed to be. He regarded the weakest spot in
the whole New Testament to be the story of Paul's travels.
These had never been thoroughly investigated by one on
the spot. So he announced his plan to take the book of
Acts as a guide, and by trying to make the same journeys
Paul made over the same routes that Paul followed, thus
prove that the apostle could never have made them as
described.

Equipped as no other man had been, he went to the
home of the Bible. Here he spent fifteen years literally "dig-
ging in for the evidence." Then in 1898 he published a
large volume on "St. Paul the Traveler and the Roman
Citizen."

The book caused a furor of dismay among the skeptics
of the world. Its attitude was utterly unexpected, because it
was contrary to the announced intention of the author
years before. The chagrin and confusion increased as for
twenty years more book after book from the same author
came from the press, each filled with additional evidence
of the exact, minute truthfulness of the whole New
Testament as tested by the spade on the spot. The evidence
was so overwhelming that many infidels announced their
repudiation of their former unbelief and accepted
Christianity. And these books have stood the test of time,
not one having been refuted, nor have I found even any
attempt to refute them.[5]

What is significant about this is that there are some fifty-six cities
and other geographical locations mentioned in the Book of Acts. Yet

this archeologist, and others who also have investigated, have found the ruins of these cities in exactly the places Luke described. You can be sure you would have heard if even one discrepancy had been found. The fact that none were identified indicates how carefully honest and accurate Dr. Luke was in the narration of the events he described. Is it reasonable to think that a historian so obviously fastidious to details would treat the repeated testimony of Paul less accurately? I think not! The details he narrated always served the main purpose of the book, to document the stories of individuals, churches, and even whole cities who bowed before the cross of Christ to receive the power to live for God.

PAUL, THE MODEL OF SALVATION

It should be obvious why some consider the remarkable conversion of Saul of Tarsus second only to the resurrection of Christ Himself as convincing evidence of the truth of Christianity. Now it is time to look at the model of salvation his transformation really was. Not only is it significant because Paul saw the risen Christ, but also because he recognized Him and bowed his knees to Him. In his own words to the elders of Jerusalem,

> And I fell to the ground and heard a voice saying to me, "Saul, Saul, why are you persecuting Me?" So I answered, "Who are You, Lord?" And He said to me, "I am Jesus of Nazareth, whom you are persecuting." Now those who were with me indeed saw the light and were afraid, but they did not hear the voice of Him who spoke to me. So I said, "What shall I do, Lord?" And the Lord said to me, "Arise and go into Damascus, and there you will be told all things which are appointed for you to do." (Acts 22:7–10)

We need not be confused by Saul's use of the word *Lord* to address Jesus, as some are who suggest it means merely *sir.* That may be true in Spanish, but it was not used that way in Greek as found in the Book of Acts. In each case, it is a New Testament term for God. Paul prostrated himself before this *Lord,* meaning

God, and said, "What shall I do, Lord?" Saul knew that kneeling before Jesus Christ meant surrendering his life, his sin, his strong will, and his future to this Savior. He did it in a moment by turning control of his life over to the Lord. Later, when he understood more of what transpired on that road to Damascus, he was to challenge others to "yield yourself to God" or "present your body a living sacrifice" to God.

Until that moment Saul was self-willed. Could he have been deeply under conviction of sin by the Spirit of the Lord as he heard the testimony of the dying Stephen or watched other unnamed disciples tortured and killed? That is known only to God. What we do know is that Jesus, who considers that "as much as you have done it unto one of the least of these My brethren you have done it unto Me," could say "Why have you been persecuting *Me?*" Saul knew he was being personally addressed and this was the crisis moment of his life, for he was faced with an eternal decision—to accept or reject Jesus Christ. By saying, "What will you have me to do, Lord?" he was repenting of the sin of self-will and surrendering his will to Christ. That is salvation!

The subsequent transformation of his life grew out of that experience of surrender to Jesus. Those of us who were young at the time of our salvation don't have much of a past life to be transformed from. But those who like Saul have directly opposed the will of God often experience dramatic transformations. Everyone who makes that choice will demonstrate sufficient change to prove to themselves and others that their conversions were real, whether that change occurs instantaneously or over many years of struggle. But the change will come as proof that God's Spirit dwells within them.

That is what the rest of this book is about—the tangible evidence in many believers of the life-changing experience they had at the cross. Even though each story is amazing, every one is true and verifiable. They all demonstrate the same thing: once sinners bend their knees before the cross to receive Christ, they receive the power of the cross to live an entirely new and godly lifestyle. I call this the power of the cross; the Bible calls it the power of God or the message of the cross. They are identical. For that power, demonstrating a lifetime change, is the main way God proclaims today that He is very much alive and in control, even though man denies it.

There are no human lives too difficult for God to change. But every change begins with salvation, and that comes by kneeling before the cross and saying, "Yes! Jesus Christ, I will have You rule over me. I give You myself, my sin, and my life. Do with it whatever You see fit."

Someone might say, "I don't like the sound of that. I want a better life, not a harder one. Just look at the life of Paul! Sure, he changed—but what did it get him? He was persecuted, tortured, imprisoned, rejected, and finally beheaded after thirty years of a harsh life."

But that is only part of the story! Jim Elliot, the martyred missionary, once wisely said, "He is no fool who gives up what he cannot keep to gain that which he cannot lose." Scripture teaches that all faithful believers will be rewarded for their labors, and that means Paul will receive every conceivable reward, crown, and blessing in the next life—and enjoy them for eternity! No, Paul was no fool—and neither will any of us be who "give up what we cannot keep to gain what we cannot lose."

Saul of Tarsus, who became Paul the Apostle, is one evidence that surrendering to Christ is the right choice. Paul went from persecuting Christians to preaching the gospel he formerly despised. His conversion story proves God is alive and well and working on planet earth in the lives of real people. Saul may have been a difficult case, but even he was no match for the power of the cross!

CHAPTER EIGHT

FROM
HAIGHT-ASHBURY
AND VIETNAM
TO THE CROSS

F or almost two thousand years God has revealed Himself in the transformed lives of millions of people like Saul, men and women who destroy themselves with hatred or murder, lust, obsession, etc. They have been changed by kneeling at the cross. It happened to Cornelius in Acts 10, to the Ethiopian eunuch in Acts 8, to Justin Martyr in the second century, and later to Polycarp, Augustine, St. Francis of Assisi, Martin Luther, D. L. Moody, Billy Sunday, Charles Colson, and millions of others.

Today, more than ever, with the rampant problems society faces from drugs, crime, promiscuity, depression, etc.—problems for which the world has little or no remedy—the power of the cross is still as effective as it was in Paul's day.

REBEL WITH A CAUSE

Gwinn Smith was a typical American high-school student in the late sixties. She enjoyed a good home life, living in a nominally religious household which attended a Latter Day Saints church in a San Francisco suburb. She was a bright student and a natural leader. In her junior and senior years she became an outspoken member of the radical anti-Vietnam War movement. She organized several high-school activities and was attracting quite a following, until school authorities cracked down and gave her a choice: "Stop your activism or leave school."

Her father began accompanying her to school in the hope that she would remain in school so she could graduate with her class. But she rebelled against all authority, even her parents. With time on her hands and rebellion in her heart, she was easy prey for the radical element of the antiwar movement at nearby Stanford University. In fact, Gwinn changed her name to Johnni, considering it more in keeping with her new lifestyle. She began hanging out with friends who not only introduced her to radical political positions, but also to radical moral activities, including drugs like marijuana and "speed." It wasn't long until she became disenchanted with the antiwar scene and decided to hitchhike to New York, where she had heard the *real* action was.

That trip changed her life—and all for the worse. Drugs, cigarettes, rebellion, and sexual sin became a way of life. The next two years became a blur that even today is hard for her to remember. She entered relationships with one man after another and got an abortion four months into a pregnancy. The Planned Parenthood "counselor" never offered any other alternative to Johnni, nor did she warn her of the guilt feelings that would haunt her afterward. This gave Johnni an even greater desire for more drugs until she was stoned out of her mind for long periods. Today she recalls those times as horrible. On three occasions during that period she remembers looking into the barrel of a revolver, which even in her drug-riddled mind terrified her.

On the verge of an overdose, Johnni somehow placed a phone call to her younger sister who became so terrified she shared it with their father. Together they flew to New York and brought Johnni back home, where she was able to regroup. But the call of the Haight-Ashbury scene was too much, and eventually she overdosed on drugs and almost died.

But God had not given up on Johnni. One night while heavily under the influence of "crystal speed," she caught a ride with two men who promised to drive her to a friend's house. When she realized they were going the opposite direction and into the worst section of Oakland, she made a desperate lunge under gunpoint for the door and was somehow able to stumble into the street. The men sped off into the night.

Johnni was so terrified and still under the influence of drugs that she couldn't even put a coin into a pay telephone to call a friend. Two large men, returning from a late-night Bible study, saw her plight and came to her rescue. They took her to a hostel set up for "hippie types" and got her into a good environment. She finally realized she needed help, but she refused to go home.

She then became involved with the Hare Krishna sect that was prominent in the area at the time. Its members introduced her to burning incense and praying some kind of mantra to the picture of their god, but did try to help her get off drugs. One day she looked at the blue guy in their pictures and said to herself, "Is this all there is? I don't know him, and I don't think he knows me." In desperation she recalled something from her childhood training and prayed, "Oh, God of Abraham, if You are real, help me and I will serve You the rest of my life."

A short time later she was invited to attend her sister's marriage to a young man active in youth ministries. Johnni, who by this time had been trying to reduce her drug intake but still couldn't quit a two-pack-a-day cigarette habit, admitted, "I felt dirty inside," even though she had borrowed a dress and cleaned up to attend the wedding. "I couldn't believe those people," she said. "They all looked like a bunch of Boy Scouts to me—and I felt dirty, even though I was all dressed up." One concerned young woman reached out to Johnni in an effort to give her the gospel, but Johnni responded with the old bromide, "I've got some changes to make in my life; besides, I'm not ready yet."

Two weeks later her sister called to invite her to her new home for the weekend; her husband was out of town for a youth activity. Johnni made her sister promise that if she came she would not be asked to go to church on Sunday. Her sister reluctantly agreed but insisted on picking Johnni up so she wouldn't have to hitchhike. They had a good visit that weekend, and on Sunday morning a friend came by to go to church with her sister. As the two young women stood at the door, Johnni felt an urge to go with them but was too rebellious to ask. Suddenly her sister said, "Johnni, I know I promised not to pressure you to go to church, but if you would like to come, we'll wait until you get ready." That is all it took for her to hurriedly get ready and go to the service. It was a decision that would change her life.

The service itself was quite uneventful. The pastor was away and someone else delivered a sermon that touched Johnni deeply. During an altar call, the minister asked his audience to bow their heads. Johnni ignored him and looked around to see who was going to go forward. When the speaker asked those who needed help from God to raise their hands for prayer, she was as surprised as her sister to find her own hand in the air! As she raised her hand, she realized that the God of Abraham had sent His Son to die on the cross for her sins and that the only way she would ever feel clean again would be to repent of her sins and receive Him.

The next moment she found herself going forward, where she bent her knees before the cross and received the Savior. Johnni got up off her knees a different woman. The war suddenly was over—the rebel had become a servant of the living God, and He was her personal Savior.

The joy and peace that flooded Johnni's soul was exactly what she had been looking for all those lost years. Instantly she became a "new creature in Christ," and gradually her life began to change. The first thing to go was the two-pack-a-day cigarette habit. Then the drugs and running with the wrong crowd. She found a job and began to see her entire life cleaned up. Attending church and Bible reading became a personal quest and it wasn't long before she began to sing in the choir.

One day Johnni felt led to change her name. She read in the Bible where after Abram committed his life to God, his name was changed to Abraham. Since Johnni represented the rebellious part of her life that she wanted to forget, she decided to take her middle name, Lenora, which meant light—a better description of her new life in Christ.

Lenora's new church featured a preservice prayer time in

which members would often ask fellow members to pray for lost friends or loved ones. Lenora's new Christian friend, Jeannette, had shared her burden for her brother, Jim. About four years after Lenora's salvation, Jeanette said, "Lenora, would you pray for my brother, Jimmy? He really needs the Lord." Both women were in the service the day Jimmy came forward to receive Christ.

Today, after serving her Lord for more than twenty-seven years, Lenora models what a godly Christian woman should be. Were you to meet her, you would think she had always been a Christian. She is the mother of four children, one a student in a Christian university preparing to serve the Lord. Her fourth child was adopted after being abandoned by drug-addicted birth parents. Although she is a victim of her parents' drug use, she now has a loving mother who is sacrificially giving her an incredible chance at a normal life.

From a rebellious Johnni bent on self-destruction to a godly Lenora, a submissive servant of Christ and a loving, faithful wife of more than twenty years and a wonderful, caring mother of four, this woman is one more living illustration of a soul transformed at the cross of Jesus.

THE TRANSFORMATION OF AN ANGRY MAN

According to all the rules of warfare, Marine Staff Sergeant Jim Woodall should be dead. He spent nearly two years in Vietnam, where he found himself in the middle of dozens of battles and "fire fights" that killed many of his buddies. It was almost as though God protected him supernaturally because of what He knew Jim would do when he returned home.

Jim was raised in an angry household where he and his older brother saw their alcoholic and brutal father beat their mother until she had hardly a spot on her body that wasn't bruised. He also beat his young boys, but eventually they grew up to be almost as big as he. Then the beatings stopped—but not the intense anger. The boys channeled their hostility into violent sports like football, in which they excelled partly because of their immense size and also because of their raging anger. Body contact sports were fun to them; it worked off their frustrations.

Their father rejected both boys when they became more protective of their mother. When Jim graduated from high school, his father refused to attend the awards banquet where he received the outstanding player of the year trophy; his coach acted as surrogate father. Jim was recruited by seventeen colleges and universities to play football, including an invitation from Coach Dick Vermeil of Stanford University (now the head coach of the NFL's St. Louis Rams).

This was the Vietnam War era, however, when football players were not exempt from military duty. Jim was drafted. Believing he would play football for the marines, he signed up—but ended up in some of the fiercest combat duty of the war.

One time he and a buddy were on sniper duty. He thought he saw a distant branch move. Mentioning it to his marine partner, the man raised his head to get a better look…and took enemy fire in the head, saving Jim from certain death. On other occasions his anger overcame normal fear, and he and his buddies escaped death by his acts of heroism—acts prompted by sheer anger.

When he returned home a decorated hero, his anger continued, partly because of the abuse and hostile spirit that confronted servicemen upon their return from a wildly unpopular war. On one occasion Jim beat a war protester within an inch of his life after being accosted by him on the street. His anger was so intense he blacked out and doesn't remember knocking the man through a plate-glass window. (He once did the same thing to a marine private for sassing a corporal under his command.)

Anger, of course, was not Jim's only vice. He had an enormous appetite for the fairer sex. He learned to be sexually promiscuous in high school and continued that practice through his three years in the Corps and for several years into civilian life.

In his twenties Big Jim began to realize his life was pretty empty, so he decided to go to church. After visits to three churches in the city were he was tending bar, however, he decided that was not his answer. He moved back to California where he had been raised and became a respectable businessman, filling his house with one live-in girlfriend after another.

Yet one day he looked around and it seemed to him as if he were surrounded by witnessing Christians. First it was a mother and her daughter who attended a charismatic Catholic church. They met him in the restaurant where he had breakfast every morning and never failed to share Christ with him. They even got him to go to their service in the basement of a Catholic church to hear an evangelist. But the evangelist came too close to Jim's sinful lifestyle so he walked out.

Then his brother's wife got saved and one week later his brother was born again. The two men were very close, and Jim could not believe the transformation in his brother's life after he had bowed before the cross. Soon Jim was enticed to attend their church, where he too came to realize that Jesus Christ bore his sins on the cross and rose again in order to save his soul. That night Jim Woodall went forward, bent before the cross of Jesus, and was marvelously saved. He got up off his knees a different man.

I have known Jim intimately now for more than ten years. It is difficult to reconcile his testimony of what he was before Christ with the man he is today. I have met his brother, mother (who later received Christ), and others in his family; they all vouch for the accuracy of his story. In fact, the former Jim was much worse than I have presented him.

One day as we were traveling together I asked him, "What was the first sign to you that you were really saved?" He replied, "On the way home from church I suddenly realized I was going to have to get rid of the woman I was living with." With his salvation only minutes old, he made the decision to sleep on the couch that night. He was busy going to school, studying, and working, so his girlfriend didn't get too suspicious the first night; but by Wednesday night she burst into the living room and said, "Okay, Jim, what's wrong? Have you found someone else?"

When he told her "I've found God," she blew up, sure he was lying. A heated argument prompted her to call her mother and ask if she could spend the night with her. When she flew out the door, Jim got on his knees and prayed for her. In fact, in the three days after his salvation he developed a deep concern for her soul. Before he finished his prayer, he heard a knock on the door—her car wouldn't start! He gave her a ride to her mother's and somehow he extracted a promise from her that she would go to church with him the next Sunday. She kept her word and later was marvelously converted. The two were never intimate again, of course, but she grew spiritually, married another man, and is today the mother of two children, all of whom are active in their church.

For the first year after his salvation, Jim gave himself to spiritual growth and to learning how to serve the Lord. Dating didn't interest him; he had enough of that in his old life. As he grew, his natural leadership ability and musical talents began to surface and he was given an opportunity to lead in worship. His growing love for the Lord and His Word was apparent in the way he led music. During that time he scarcely noticed the attractive brunette friend of his sister who sang faithfully in the choir. One day the pastor, obviously led by the Spirit, suggested they would make a good couple. One date led to another and soon he and the transformed Lenora (alias Johnni) were married.

On a mission trip to Mexico, God used Jim (through an interpreter) to win hundreds of people to the Savior. During the communist takeover of Nicaragua, God placed a deep burden on Jim's heart for the Nicaraguan people and the persecuted Christians in that country who were fleeing for their lives to Costa Rica and other neighboring countries. Lenora later came to share his burden and together they responded to the call of God and became missionaries to the Nicaraguan refugees. After raising support, they attended language school in San Jose, Costa Rica. Even before they became fluent in Spanish, they began visiting the many U.N.-operated refugee camps set up for thousands of Nicaraguans. Each Sunday they would take a group with them to conduct services for the refugees, thousands of whom received Christ. During that time Jim developed a burden to build a church and school near the Nicaraguan border; today both ministries have been in operation for almost a decade.

It was during the early stages of his refugee ministry that God brought Jim into our lives. My wife heads the largest women's organization in the nation, Concerned Women for America. In addition to fighting for traditional family values, Beverly used her mailing list of six hundred thousand women to help the victims of the spread of communism, largely in Nicaragua. In a miraculous chain of events, God led Jim to attend the National Religious Broadcasters convention where "he hoped to meet Beverly LaHaye." He heard she was interested in helping these refugees and wanted to offer his assistance. At that point Bev already had planned to take a group of her ladies to Costa Rica for "a fact-finding trip." The Spanish-speaking missionary she had previously lined up, called one day before departure to tell her his sixteen-year-old daughter had been involved in a serious auto accident, making it impossible for him to go. Since none of the ladies spoke any Spanish, she was left without a translator. By God's grace Jim and Beverly were providentially brought together at that conference and he dropped everything to serve as her translator on that and many subsequent trips.

First he became the director of CWA's Nicaraguan project in Costa Rica. Together they brought food, clothing, and shelter to thousands of refugees, leading several thousand to Christ through the many humanitarian and evangelistic projects they conducted. Tens of thousands of refugees know that God has not forgotten them because of the Woodalls' commitment to the Great Commission. After the fall of communism in that beleaguered country, many refugees returned home to do their part in restoring a normal life to their homeland. Some became pastors, evangelists, and government officials, while thousands more returned to live ordinary Christian lives. These transformed lives help to account for the great moving of the Spirit in Nicaragua today.

Jim's five years of service in Nicaragua and Costa Rica made it clear this former marine veteran had much-needed administrative skills. Today he serves as the CEO of Concerned Women for America, based in Washington, D.C., where he represents the Christian community before some of the highest leaders in the nation's capital. Jim actively serves as worship leader in a large church in the area and speaks at conferences whenever possible. He rejoices in the knowledge that the souls he led to the Savior and the churches he has had a hand in starting, both in Costa Rica and in subsequent trips to Nicaragua, are an eternal work of the Spirit of God.

BOWING AT THE CROSS

Jim and Lenora, two former rebels who bent their knees and wills before the cross of Jesus Christ, are prime examples of the miraculous, transforming power of the Holy Spirit. The spiritual work they have done, particularly the founding of New Testament churches, will live on long after them.

That is what Christianity is all about—sinners bowing at the cross of Jesus to surrender their anger, rebellion, lust, or whatever other sin has held them captive, and then receiving His forgiveness and the new life only He can provide. After they get up off their knees, they go forward to live the transformed life and to pass on that experience to others. And Christians have been doing that now for almost two thousand years!

A BIG-LEAGUE
SKEPTIC FINDS FAITH
AT THE CROSS

Not all those who bend their knees before the cross are flagrant sinners obsessed by some practice or habit that will destroy their lives before their time. But all are sinners. Some sinners, like Frank Pastore, were professional ballplayers who disciplined their bodies to extract the most benefit from them. In his case, he was a faithful husband in the midst of overwhelming temptation and the proud father of two delightful children. His sin was pride, skepticism, atheism, and arrogance.

As a professional baseball pitcher for the Cincinnati Reds in the days of The Big Red Machine, he was a star for nine years. He is also gifted with a brilliant and quick mind, a great combination if a man wants to live independently of God and seem to be self-sufficient. Frank tells his story best and has given me permission to share it in this book.

"It was early summer, I was seventeen years old, and life just couldn't get any better. I was young and healthy with a bright future before me. I was senior-class president at Damien High School in La Verne, California. I had earned an academic scholarship to Stanford

University, was dating a popular trophy (i.e., cheerleader), and the Cincinnati Reds had just offered me the largest bonus in Reds history to pitch for them if I would just pass up my scholarship and sign on the dotted line.

"The decision was really simple. I truly had only one guiding question: 'Which of the two paths will bring me the greatest happiness?' Translated, that meant 'What's the quickest way to become rich and famous—major league baseball or law school?' At seventeen, that was no contest. I signed with Cincinnati on June 6, 1975, and a few days later began my professional career with the Billings Mustangs of the Pioneer League.

"Four minor-league seasons later, in Riverfront Stadium on opening day, 1979, before a sellout crowd of fifty-six thousand, I appeared in 'the Show' as the youngest player in the National League. I was only twenty-one, and I brought with me my beautiful young bride of seven months, a blazing fastball, and a burning desire for success. My boyhood idol, Tom Seaver, had started the game but got into trouble early; I was called on to relieve him and get the team out of the inning. When manager John MacNamara called for me out of the bullpen, I floated to the mound with a standing ovation ringing in my ears. After a few brief words, Mac handed me the ball, and with a wink from catcher Johnny Bench (J.B.), I proceeded to do what I had done my whole life. I threw fastballs as hard as I could, hitters swung and missed them, and I was told how wonderful I was for performing so well. I loved every second of it. I did well that day and I enjoyed doing the postgame interviews almost as much as I enjoyed the standing ovations. After all the minor-league ballparks, all the minor-league spreads, all the minor-league bus trips, and all the minor-league paychecks, I had finally made it—I had finally made it to the major leagues!

ONE PITCH FROM HUMILITY

"After the game, J.B. called me over to his locker. Back then, rookies were seen and not heard in the clubhouses, so when a veteran—especially a Hall of Fame veteran—spoke to you, you jumped. I'll never forget the advice he gave me on that storybook first day. 'Kid,' he said softly, 'there's two things you need to know about playing in the major leagues. First, it's harder to *stay* here than it is to *get* here. And second, never get too cocky or too arrogant, because you're always only one pitch away from humility.'

"Great words of wisdom from one who had done it all and seen it all! He was right, of course, but at the time his advice went in one ear and out the other. At twenty-one, I already knew the meaning of life—to be happy—and the best way to be happy was to be rich and famous, and the quickest way for me to become rich and famous was to pitch in the major leagues for a long time.

"Over the next five seasons I set out for more, and along the way I accumulated all the right trappings of a successful young professional. I bought all the right status symbols (a Porsche, Mercedes, house, condo, etc.); I earned the respect of my peers (I became the Reds Player Rep); I put a little money away just in case, started an off-season construction business, had two great kids, remained absolutely faithful to my wife, and avoided abusing drugs and alcohol. Basically, I played life by the rules. Most of the guys on the team considered me a 'goody-good' because I didn't drink, do cocaine, or cheat on my wife. By default I hung out with the Christians, because they didn't do those things either.

"For twenty-seven years I was a practical atheist, an evolutionist. I rejected Christianity because I had been convinced it was false. Very simply, if there is no God and no afterlife, then our existence is utterly meaningless. Since there is no meaning to life, all that is left is to create meaning in this life as you go. For me, it was in winning the 'survival of the fittest,' and in our culture that translates to 'He who dies with the most toys wins.' I thought I could create my own happiness, my own meaning, if I became rich and famous.

"Funny thing was, although I became somewhat rich and sort of famous, I wasn't any more content than I was on the day I signed with the Reds. Even living the American dream didn't bring fulfillment. Playing life by the rules didn't bring it either. The issue isn't what is outside, the issue is what is inside.

"Since the first grade I had been taught to doubt the existence of God: The universe had just popped into existence out of nothing, evolution was a 'scientific' fact, miracles can't happen, the Bible's been changed, etc. During my whole life I had accepted the government's humanistic propaganda that the teachings of Darwin, Marx, Freud, Hume, and Kant had all combined to make religion obsolete. As these thoughts raced through my mind, my heart was drawn to the quality of life I had observed in my Christian teammates. When I found myself wanting to yield to my emotions and pray, I had to remind myself that 'God' wasn't real. He was merely a crutch for intellectual weaklings, an excuse for mediocrity and failure, a placebo for psychologically imbalanced people—although also an effective and soothing pacifier for whining, injured professional athletes.

"Although I may have had all the external signs of success, internally there was something wrong. Something was missing. There was a hole in my life that *more* wasn't filling. I tried to fool myself that the next good game, the next sports car, the next winning season, or the next contract would do the job—but they never did. I slowly began to lose faith that baseball would ever make me happy and fulfilled. I remember looking around the clubhouse one day and coming to the realization that although most of these men had become rich and famous, only a few were truly happy. That was very disturbing. Since I was six years old, I had wanted to be just like them—but if they weren't happy with all of the money and all of the success they had, what made me think I was going to be any different? The only guys on the team that seemed to be 'together' were the guys I regularly made fun of behind their backs, those religious fanatics who brought the Bible into the locker room and on road trips, those born-again Jesus freaks who believed in the Easter Bunny, Santa Claus, and people rising from the dead.

"Back then, I would not have considered myself a religious person—I was a realist. I was a realist because I believed only in what was real and true—things like science, history, psychology, chemistry, and physics. I believed that some being called 'God' may have caused the Big Bang, but I knew that evolution was a fact, that morality was culturally relative, and that environment and chemicals could account for all human behavior. Those were the things I had been taught in school. I did not believe that Jesus Christ was God, that He had been born of a virgin, that He had risen from the dead, that the Bible was inspired, that there was a literal heaven and a literal hell, or that there had ever been prophecies or miracles. Simply put, I just didn't believe Christianity was true.

THE PITCH THAT BROUGHT HUMILITY

"Then on June 4, 1984, in Dodger Stadium, all of that changed. J.B.'s prophetic words were fulfilled. I was cruising to a 3–1 victory with two outs in the eighth inning, when I made the pitch that eternally changed my life. Dodger Steve Sax rocketed a 2–2 fastball off my right elbow and my whole world-view shattered in one painful instant. Immediately, I knew my arm would never be the same again, and my career, as I had known it, had come to a tragic end.

"The crack of the bat still echoed through the stadium as every eye focused on me as I clutched my elbow and grimaced in agony. The eerie silence was broken by a collective gasp as the crowd turned to watch the replay on Diamond Vision. As I glanced up to take a peek at it myself, everything seemed to be happening in slow motion—it was all like a bad dream—and I just wanted to wake up from the nightmare. 'Why, God? Why!?' I prayed desperately on my way to the training room, but I had to remind myself no one was listening.

"Deep in my heart, I knew my life would never be the same. I had always derived my sense of security and self-esteem from my athletic performance. Baseball had been my god and my source of identity. For twenty years my identity was in *being* a baseball player, not in *playing* baseball. I had confused *what* I did with *who* I was, like many others. I was no longer going to *be* a baseball player. I had lost my identity; I was a nobody. That frightening reality crashed down upon me in thunderous waves of terror.

"As unlikely as it may seem, it was in the midst of all this that I was introduced to the concept that God was *real*. As I walked into the training room, my small but faithful group of friends—the Christians—asked me whether I would mind if they prayed for me. 'Of course you can pray!' I said. 'You can do anything you want if you think it'll help.' *How cute,* I thought, *the religious fanatics want to pray for me. Isn't that just like uneducated people to turn to a mythical god in a crisis situation?*

"Not long after that, Tommy Hume, the Red's Chapel Leader, invited me to his house for a barbecue and, if I wanted to stay, a Bible study. Tommy had asked me to come to Bible studies many times over the years, and I always came up with some lame excuse not to go. However, this time I agreed. I tried to tell myself that I couldn't stand the fact that these guys were so 'together' while I was falling apart. On the surface, I acted as though it really bugged me that they were so naive. But deep down I wanted to know more about this Jesus they prayed to.

"I arrived at Tommy's house and said hello to the regular bunch of guys: Duane Walker, Tom Foley, Danny Bilardello, and was introduced to a guy named Wendel Deyo, whom I recognized from some of the chapels I had attended. (They didn't tell me he was the national director of Athletes in Action and a twenty-year veteran of working with overpaid, prima-donna, insecure, non-Christian athletes.) After the hamburger-and-hot-dog thing was over, we got down to business. Wendel gathered us to start the study. Now, I had never been to a Bible study. Heck, I didn't even own a Bible! But I knew all about the Bible—it's unhistorical, it contradicts itself, you can make it say anything you want to, and it's been changed many times over the past two thousand years. But most of all, I was convinced it was simply wrong; there had never been any miracles—we just hadn't figured a scientific way to explain some things yet. One day we'd know how something came from nothing, or how all those Egyptian soldiers drowned in only six inches of water but 3.5 million Jews made it through unharmed! As soon as the opening prayer ended with 'amen,' I came out shooting.

"I launched all of my hurt, anger, and confusion in a fierce salvo of blasphemous missiles aimed at religion and Christianity. I fired for half an hour, attacking everything about Christianity. The guys were blown away—they looked like that guy in the popular commercial who's reclining in a chair in front of a speaker, his hair blown back by the incredible volume. They didn't interrupt once throughout the whole tirade; I didn't give them the chance to.

"When I finally stopped, believing I had successfully enlightened the guys to the truth about reality, Wendel spoke up for the first time since the amen. 'Wow. I've never heard anyone articulate their views with such passion and reason as you've just done. Frank, I simply can't answer most of the questions you've raised; boy, I don't even *understand* most of the questions! The guys had told me you were smart, but they didn't tell me you were this smart!' With my good arm I was patting myself on the back.

"'But, Frank,' Wendel continued, waving to the rest of the guys, 'we don't want to believe in myths, stories, or anything that isn't true or real. We want to believe in what's true. Right guys?'

"'Right!' they all answered in chorus, almost on cue.

"'So, will you help us?' he asked, placing the bait before me.

"'Of course, guys. You're my friends. I don't want you guys building your lives on lies,' I said, smelling the bait.

"'Great. Here's how you can help us. I just happen to have brought some books,' he said reaching behind the couch to grab some small paperbacks. 'These books present and defend Christianity better than we can. Will you have a look at them, and as you read, maybe write in the margins where the authors are wrong and why, so that we can think clearly about all these things? Then, after the next road trip, we can all get together again, and then maybe we can become happy and fulfilled, just like you!'

"'Sure, I'll be glad to help. Really, guys, disproving Christianity won't be very hard. I'll start with Genesis and prove to you why the creation story is an unscientific myth,' I said, swallowing the hook, line, and sinker, and pole, and dock.

"Wendel handed me three books. Now mind you, I had never met an intelligent Christian before—I thought the term was an

oxymoron like jumbo-shrimp—because before whenever I had
asked a Christian a serious question, they would invariably
respond, 'I don't know, but Jesus loves you!' That doesn't help a
whole lot if you don't know who Jesus is! The titles of the three
books handed to me were: *Mere Christianity* by C. S. Lewis;
Scientific Creationism by Henry Morris; and *Evidence That Demands
a Verdict* by Josh McDowell.

"That night, I began reading *Mere Christianity*. I read all night.
The next day at the ballpark, I snuck off the bench during the
game and hid in the weightroom to continue reading. I started out
with the intent to help my friends get their thinking straight, and
of course found myself even further confused. Over the next three
weeks, I read and reread the books. I devoured them. I can
remember the guys coming over to me several times to ask how
things were going and telling them that I was still working on disproving the Bible, but that it was just taking a little longer than I
expected.

"Then it happened. I was in Pittsburgh reading *Evidence That
Demands a Verdict* in the clubhouse during the game, when the
lights came on. It was my very first 'Oh!' experience—'Oh!' is the
most popular word in heaven among new arrivals. The reality that
a personal God had spoken the universe into existence out of
nothing; that His Son, Jesus Christ, had died on the cross for my
sins and the sins of the world; that He had validated His testimony
by rising from the dead before hundreds of witnesses; and that
Jesus was the way, the truth, and the life, and that the only way to
heaven was through Him—hit me like the blazing sun would
smite the eyes of someone who had spent a week in a dark cave.

"'Jesus, you're alive!' I whispered.

"Simultaneously I had two powerful emotions. The first was
joy—my sins could be forgiven! The second was anger—I was
ticked off that I had been lied to my whole life. It was naturalistic
evolution, secular humanism, and the other atheistic ideologies that
were the myths, not Christianity! Not once was I ever told there
were good reasons to believe in God or Christianity. I was simply
told that evolution was a fact and to ask questions about it was to

be heretical and unscientific. Not once through elementary school, junior high, or high school did I hear that there were problems—huge, gaping problems—with evolution. I realized I had been deceived my whole academic life, and I was furious. I could have died and gone to hell because people wanted to repress intellectual freedom and force their agenda on me! Why couldn't they just have presented the arguments both for and against Christianity and let me decide for myself, based upon the evidence? The issue should have been Truth, not Ideology.

"I prayed, 'Lord, I know that I am a sinner and that Jesus came to save sinners, and that He came to save me. Forgive me of my sins. I'm asking You to come into my life and change me. Make me the person You want me to be. I now promise to follow You, to the best of my ability, every day for the rest of my life. Thank You, Jesus, for being my Savior, I now want to make You my Lord. Amen.'

"It was only about two months after making that pitch in Dodger Stadium that I gave my heart, my mind, and my life to Jesus Christ. Nine years earlier I had gone into pro ball to get rich and famous. Finally, I *was* rich—rich with the knowledge that my sins were forgiven and that I would spend eternity with Jesus Christ in glorious fellowship. And I *was* famous—I may not have been in Cooperstown, but I was in the Lamb's Book of Life. Despite the injury and all the uncertainty of my career, I knew the void in my heart I had been trying to fill my whole life had finally been filled. My wife, Gina, came to Christ a short time later, and when our daughter was born in October of 1984, we named her Christina to commemorate our commitment to Him and to honor her."

How Long Has It Lasted?

The true test of a conversion experience is how long it lasts. The primary reason the conversion of Saul of Tarsus is such a powerful witness to the power of Christianity is that Paul lived constantly for over thirty years as a Christian and died without ever recanting, even though he was beheaded for his faith. It may surprise you to know that in some countries of the world today, like China,

Christians are still martyred for their faith. In our country such deadly persecution is rare, so we are left with perseverance as the test of genuineness.

In the case of Frank Pastore, we are confronted with a consistent and dramatic change, like that of Paul. Frank's transformation from atheism to becoming a defender of the faith is as exciting a story as his original conversion. We shall let him tell this also, again in his own words.

"I retired from baseball in June 1987, and because I had signed a professional contract out of high school, I became a thirty-year-old college freshman at National University in Irvine, California, that fall. In two years I received a degree in business and my wife and I decided to spend some time in ministry before going on to law school. We raised support and joined the national office staff of Athletes in Action, the sports ministry of Campus Crusade for Christ. While on staff, I had the chance to speak often and found I enjoyed answering people's questions about Christianity more than just about anything else. Walter Martin, Josh McDowell, and Henry Morris were my heroes, and I read nearly everything I could get my hands on that those guys wrote. After almost two years on staff, we decided that I could best serve the evangelistic effort of the church as an apologist, so we changed our plans from law school to graduate school—the only question was, Where?

"We researched the best programs at the best schools and concluded that the top apologetics program in the country was being run by J. P. Moreland at Talbot School of Theology, Biola University, near Los Angeles. Although I had played for seven seasons in Cincinnati, we never lived there year 'round; Los Angeles was our home. So we started the program in June 1991, and I graduated with a Masters in Philosophy of Religion and Ethics in December 1994. I currently direct the Talbot Institute for Biblical Studies, a church-based training ministry to help churches establish their own lay institutes for Christian education."

I met Frank when he preached in our home church one Sunday in 1997, thirteen years after his conversion. Not only is he still serving the Lord, he is actively trying to teach young people to examine the overwhelming evidence that Christianity is true, Jesus Christ really is the Son of God who died for the sins of mankind, and that He saves to the uttermost all who bow before His cross and receive Him as Savior and Lord. Frank loves to confront skeptics and doubters and is driven with the desire to equip others to be ready always to give an answer to everyone who asks, a *reason* for the hope that is within you! There *are* convincing answers to the questions of today's skeptics. Frank is using his talents to convince many that God and His Word are absolutely reliable. One reason he is so persuasive is that he has been there and has turned from skepticism to faith.

CHAPTER TEN

THE CROSS
TRIUMPHS OVER
CRIME AND VIOLENCE

C rime and violence are among this nation's greatest problems. Between twenty-two thousand and twenty-three thousand die needlessly each year at the hands of criminals, and the criminals are getting younger each year. Recently when a teenager shot three people, his only explanation was, "I just felt like killing someone."

Senseless killings are uncommon, but they are definitely on the rise. Many murderers never get caught, but victims and their loved ones always suffer. The cost of crime in this country is estimated as high as $674 billion annually. The cost of grief, pain, death, and human misery is incalculable. Our overcrowded prisons, costing American taxpayers more than $40 billion a year to operate, are doing little or nothing to rehabilitate violent criminals, even though the inmates are incarcerated for ten, twenty, or even forty years.

History records many illustrations of criminals who, after receiving Jesus Christ as their Lord and Savior, ceased their obsession with crime. Those who have lived the rest of their years as transformed, law-abiding men and women are examples of the power of the cross. At no time in history, however, has it become so apparent as now that conversion to Christ is the most effective means of dealing with criminals, particularly violent offenders.

It is well known that America, the freest nation in the world, has the highest crime rate in the world. Criminals have a field day in a free society and about 20 percent of our citizens take advantage of their freedom to rape, rob, kill, or to harm others. The Graham Institute for Prison Ministries compiled the following frightening statistics:

- There are an estimated 6 million violent crimes committed in America each year, with only 1.8 million actually reported.
- During the past 30 years, violent crime has increased 560%.
- Of the 1.8 million violent crimes only 580,000 result in arrests each year.
- Of the 130,226 convictions, 107,302 result in felony convictions.
- From 1960 to 1992 the crime rate in America increased 370%.
- There are currently 758 violent crimes per 100,000 citizens.
- There are currently 23,760 homicides each year.
- There are currently 4,903 property crimes per 100,000 citizens.
- 80% of all crimes are committed by 20% of the criminals.
- One-fifth of all violent crime is committed by kids under 18 years of age.
- During the last 10 years violent crime has risen over 30% in America.
- In Washington, D.C., 70% of all black males will be arrested by age 36. Philadelphia and Baltimore have similar statistics.
- There are 2.7 million cocaine and heroin addicts in America.
- The chances of an adult prisoner not returning to crime when released is 25%.
- The chances of a juvenile (17 or under) offender *not* returning to crime when released is 15%.
- The chances of a Christian inmate *not* returning to crime who finds a church, is discipled and mentored when released from prison is 90–95%.

Two of the startling figures above relate to the recidivism rate. After turning our prison system (that once existed to protect the population) into reformatory programs for criminals, the secularists have elevated the number of victims by releasing criminals before their sentence is complete and before they are truly rehabilitated. In addition, we have the largest number of citizens in prison of any free nation in the world and at a higher cost, in excess of $20,000 per criminal per year. The tragedy is that this expensive system is not working; as mentioned, it is expected that 75 to 95 percent of the violent criminals released back into society will return to prison, usually within three years. All this occurs at an unimaginable cost to innocent victims who are robbed, brutalized, or in many cases killed. Intense hostility is generated in victims, their families and friends, when they learn a loved one was victimized by a convicted prisoner who should still be in jail.

CHRIST MAKES A DIFFERENCE

The recidivism rate for those who have received Christ, become active in a Bible study program, and upon their release become active in a local church, drops to an incredible 5 to 10 percent. That is such a startling contrast to the poor success level of the most expensive reformatory system in the world, it cries out for evaluation.

During the past four years I have learned more about crime, criminals, and life in prison than in any of the forty years I served pastoring local churches. I have been mentoring or discipling a friend of mine, Bill Kennedy, who I believe was wrongfully sentenced to twenty years in a federal prison. His case is currently on appeal and I am confident his hate-filled prosecutor will be proven to have used illegal means in court to obtain Bill's conviction, either to increase his own record of convictions or because he was determined to "get" Bill for publishing one of the most conservative magazines in the nation. In the meantime, through frequent phone calls from him in prison (I cannot call him; he can call me) and by several visits to see him in Lompoc Federal Correctional Institution, I have learned more about the effects of crime on individuals, families, victims, and society than I ever wanted to know. Probably the most tragic result is the huge number of inmates who, if released, will go right back to the streets and continue in crime. They seem to learn little or nothing from their prison experience, other than how to commit crimes more effectively.

THE EXCITING PRISON MINISTRIES

I was amazed to find in the Graham Center report that "there are 450 prison ministries in America, seven of which are having national impact." The others, like my own mother's, are led by dedicated Christians who live near a prison and decide to take the gospel into the nearby prison—if they can find prison authorities willing to let them. It is revealing today that, unlike ACLU advocates who are so opposed to the gospel of Christ being preached on federal property, many prison officials are so desperate for help that they are willing to allow the message of the cross to be presented to their inmates. Most will admit they are impressed with the results of those who have had a genuine conversion experience. They understand that some prisoners are con men who relish the opportunity to get out of their cells. But even some of these have been converted to Christ and demonstrate remarkable change in their lifestyles.

THE BILL GLASS PRISON MINISTRY

As an ardent fan of the National Football League all my adult life, I followed with interest the stellar career of Bill Glass, the three time pro-bowl defensive end of the Cleveland Browns. I remember reading an account by one NFL running back who admitted he always hated it when a play was called for him to run around Bill's end; he knew he was in for a bone-jarring tackle.

Since I did not live in Cleveland, I did not realize that all through his twelve-year career, Bill was a dedicated Christian and was using his off-season time to attend seminary. After graduation and even before he gave up football, he was holding evangelistic meetings and was becoming one of the nation's leading crusade evangelists. Eventually Billy Graham urged Bill to give up football and go into evangelism full time while he was still in good health. After praying about the matter, he did. Then one day he was invited to hold meetings in a local prison. After that experience Bill was never the same, nor were several of the prisoners who saw this gentle giant compassionately telling these lost and broken men that God loved them and gave His Son to die for them. He explained to them how they could be released from their bondage of guilt and become new creatures by bending their knees to Jesus Christ and receiving Him as their Lord and Savior. Many did. Bill Glass has never lost his burden for prison ministry. Today he runs one of the premier prison ministries in the United States.

Thousands of criminals are transformed by the power of the cross through the Bill Glass Prison Ministry every year. Thousands of volunteers have come forward to help Bill sponsor two-day, "Weekend of Champions Crusades" all over the country. His celebrity status has enabled him to recruit other Christian celebrities, such as Coach Tom Landry and Roger Staubach from the NFL, country music stars, and in one prison a group of top motorcyclists who drove up and down the prison corridors as an enticement to get inmates to attend the outdoor meetings. When invitations to receive Christ were given, from 3,300 to 3,700 men invited the Savior into their lives.

CHUCK COLSON AND PRISON FELLOWSHIP

In 1997 the media commemorated the twenty-fifth anniversary of the famous Watergate scandals that forced the resignation of the president of the United States, Richard M. Nixon. Most people remember the name Chuck Colson as one of Nixon's closest associates who spent nine months in a federal penitentiary for his part in the coverups. Many who have read his book, *Born Again*, know that just before his indictment, he bent his knees to Jesus Christ and had an experience that transformed his life. His experience did not keep him from serving his prison sentence, but it certainly fortified him for those long, grueling months of confinement. In his book he told the details of his conversion.

A personal friend whom Colson deeply admired had proclaimed

his faith in Christ quite clearly and presented the gospel to him privately. Chuck knew and admitted that he needed something to fill the aching void in his life, but while he was deeply moved at the compassionate presentation of his friend, he did not receive Christ that night. So his friend, Tom Phillips, gave him a copy of C. S. Lewis's book, *Mere Christianity,* a classic presentation of the gospel by one of the clearest thinkers of the twentieth century. In it Lewis tells his own story of being a skeptical philosophy professor at thirty, how he made his life-changing decision, and how it transformed his life.

The next week Chuck and his wife, Patty, spent a week at the beach vacationing, and he read that book and made the most wonderful discovery of his life. Let him tell in his own words how he bent his knees before the cross of Jesus and said an eternal "Yes!" to Him:

> I knew the time had come for me: I could not sidestep the central question Lewis (or God) had placed squarely before me. Was I to accept without reservations Jesus Christ as Lord of my life? It was like a gate before me. There was no way to walk around it. I would step through, or I would remain outside. A "maybe" or "I need more time" was kidding myself.
>
> And as something pressed that question home, less and less was I troubled by the curious phrase "accept Jesus Christ." It had sounded at first both pious and mystical, language of the zealot, maybe blackmagic stuff. But "to accept" means no more than "to believe." Did I believe what Jesus said? If I did, if I took it on faith or reason or both, then I accepted. Not mystical or weird at all, and with no in-between ground left. Either I would believe or I would not—and believe it all or none of it.
>
> The search that began that week on the coast of Maine, as I pondered it, was not quite as important as I had thought. It simply returned me to where I had been when I asked God to "take me" in that moment of surrender on

the little country road in front of the Phillipses' home. What I studied so intently all week opened a little wider the new world into which I had already taken my first halting, shaky steps. One week of study on the Maine coast would hardly qualify, even in the jet age, as much of an odyssey, but I felt as if I'd been on a journey of thousands of miles.

And so early that Friday morning, while I sat alone staring at the sea I love, words I had not been certain I could understand or say fell naturally from my lips: "Lord Jesus, I believe You. I accept You. Please come into my life. I commit it to You."

With these few words that morning, while the briny sea churned, came a sureness of mind that matched the depth of feeling in my heart. There came something more: strength and serenity, a wonderful new assurance about life, a fresh perception of myself and the world around me. In the process, I felt old fears, tensions, and animosities draining away. I was coming alive to things I'd never seen before; as if God was filling the barren void I'd known for so many months, filling it to its brim with a whole new kind of awareness.

I wrote Tom Phillips, telling him of the step I had taken, of my gratitude for his loving concern, and asked his prayers for the long and difficult journey I sensed lay ahead.[1]

In the weeks that followed Colson was tried, humiliated, and sent to prison. Yet during all that time he received a newfound peace and serenity from his conversion, a peace that defies human explanation. Prison is never enjoyable, even for a Christian, and particularly when you know you are guilty. Naturally, many people questioned Colson's conversion. In fact, an attorney friend of mine who dealt with the Nixon administration before it came crashing down couldn't believe it when I told him Chuck Colson had become a Christian. Even though he was a Christian himself, my friend said vehemently, "I'll believe it when I see it!" That remark, of course, was based on the old Chuck Colson. Now, twenty-five years later, my attorney friend believes—as does a whole skeptical world—that Chuck Colson was transformed at the cross and began to live a whole new lifestyle, even before he went to prison.

Colson tells the thrilling story of how God sustained him while in prison and used his experience there as a positive influence in his life. But for our purposes, it is the long-term lifestyle change that is important. Once Colson was a disgraced White House lawyer; today, over twenty-five years later, he is one of the most sought after and respected Christian leaders in the country. He is a best-selling Christian author who has paid his debt to society and has been forgiven of his sins by God, the church, and by most of society. He has moved from opposing Christian principles to adopting them for himself and advocating them for the prisoners and others to whom he ministers.

Prison Fellowship, the ministry he founded, is one of the seven prison ministries with international impact today. To read his mail is an emotional experience. The letters recount the lives of men transformed while behind bars—some on death row can never hope to see the outside world, but they bend their knees at the cross, have their sins forgiven, and enjoy a new peace before man and God, in time to courageously face their inevitable death. Others have been transformed from a life of hatred and violence to become calm and sane and in their right minds. Many of them never enjoyed the normal love of a parent, were rejected and beaten, and grew up little better than animals. The first thing people notice after a criminal is converted is his change in attitude, followed by a true life transformation. Instead of being problem prisoners, some become models of the Christian way of life. Those who are released from prison and return to their homes to be good fathers, husbands, and neighbors are the real illustrations of the transformation power of the cross.

One factor seldom considered by secular authorities is that most prison ministries are not staffed by professionals, ministers, or trained counselors, but utilize trained laymen and laywomen whose only qualification is a burden to minister to prisoners in the name of Jesus Christ. One day while visiting my prisoner friend, I saw a typical Prison Fellowship group of nine people led by a black lay preacher. They brought their own song leader, musicians, and witnesses. I was reminded of the words of our Lord, "The harvest is plenteous but the laborers are few." They ministered that day to more than two hundred men, many of whom were hardened lifers.

PRISON IS A REAL HARVEST FIELD

Skeptics deny the authenticity of jailhouse conversions, just as they do deathbed or battlefield conversions. But time has proven they can be very valid. Certainly there are con artists in prison who feign a religious experience as an attempt to secure an early parole or lowered sentence, but a look at the evidence shows that the only lasting change for most prisoners is a genuine conversion that gives a man a hunger for the Word of God and a willingness to surrender to His will.

Many criminals today are drug addicts first and criminals second. It does not lessen the effects of their crime, for if they have killed someone, they are just as guilty, and the victim is just as dead. But once in prison where it is harder to get drugs, they sober up and realize, their drugs have caused an awful waste of lives. When their lives are in ruins it is easier to look to God for help than when they were living the "good life" (as they pleased) on the outside. But that does not lessen the genuineness of the conversion experience! While many on the outside are too busy for God and refuse to take the time to consider Him, prisoners have plenty of time! Time to think. Once sober and willing to face their sinful behaviors, many are consumed with guilt. That is when they are open to God. Such conversions, like Paul's, can be very real. The only way we know is by the recidivism rate—that is, by how many *do not* return to prison.

AN ILLUSTRATION FROM THE WASHINGTON POST

It isn't often the *Washington Post* has anything good to say about people of faith. An exception was found in a *Post* article on the recidivism rate headlined, "Redemption vs. Recidivism." Columnist

Pamela Constable paid begrudging acknowledgment to the fact
that men converted to Christ have a far better record of staying out
of trouble and not returning to prison than those who reject Him.
One of her illustrations was thirty-five-year-old José Lopez, who
converted to Christ in prison and had not been in trouble for five
years after his release. She described him as "a ninth-grade dropout
from Texas who says he used every drug invented and landed in
jail more times than he can count." She also said he had become "a
bona fide good Samaritan" and wrote that:

> In 1991, Lopez wound up at Fairfax, and by chance he
> briefly shared a cell with a pastor who had been arrested on
> a traffic violation. He decided to become baptized, prayed
> his way through a one-year prison term and went straight to
> live with a minister after being released in early 1992.
>
> Today, Lopez is a man on a mission. He owns a remod-
> eling business in Alexandria called Good News Home
> Improvement, is married to a fellow parishioner and owns
> a cozy house filled with snapshots of a church project in
> Colombia.
>
> "God has kept his hand on me, but you have to put on
> that armor every morning," he says. "Of 288 people I was
> paroled with, only two of us are still out. Sometimes I run
> into people I knew in jail, they're on the street, into alco-
> hol, they say they can't get out of that life. I try to give
> them a little work when I can, but I get chills thinking I
> could still be out there."[2]

A similar press report in the *Washington Times,* a paper more
favorable to people of faith, cited a study done in New York state.

> Prisoners who serve time reading the Bible are less likely to
> commit crimes after release than those who don't, accord-
> ing to a new study.
>
> Two groups of inmates—201 criminals who attended
> Bible study and 201 who did not—were monitored after

release, and only 14 percent of the ex-cons with the Christian instruction were arrested again.

Members of the group without Bible study showed a 41 percent arrest rate after release from the four different New York prisons, according to the research by Lamar University criminologist Byron Johnson.

"Programs targeting core values can be effective in reducing recidivism," or repeat offenses, said Dr. David Larson of the National Institute of Healthcare Research, which sponsored the research. "Current prison programs have not proven to be effective, as current rearrest rates, from 50 to 75 percent, continue to climb."[3]

This survey did not distinguish between Christian groups that used a distinctive discipleship program and those that did not and makes no attempt to single out those who had a genuine conversion experience. Even then, however, the recidivism rate for the 201 who studied the Bible in prison was over three times better than those who did not.

LOMPOC FEDERAL PRISON

I have met two chaplains during the four years of my friend Bill's imprisonment, both of whom have been very helpful to me. One day I told them I was writing this book and asked if they had any track record I could refer to in charting the recidivism rate at their facility. They amazed me! In the eleven years they have been ministering there, they have seen over two hundred men come to Christ, submit to discipleship, and be released. Believe it or not, they reported that "so far, *not one has returned to prison!*" That is an incredible record and offers clear and convincing evidence that there is power in the cross to transform lives, even those of hardened and often violent criminals.

GOOD NEWS JAIL AND PRISON MINISTRY

Every time I leave Lompoc prison I think, *If I were imprisoned here and was finally released to freedom, I would never do anything to cause me to return.* Yet upwards of 95 percent of hardened criminals do return to jail within five years of their release. On the other hand, the *Good News Jail and Prison Ministry* (GNJPM) reports that "92 –94 percent who have a support system [discipleship and involvement with a Bible-teaching church when released] do not return."[4] The ministry's figures are based on tracking men for at least five years after their release.

The president of this ministry once was imprisoned for shooting a police officer in a bar one night while under the influence of alcohol. After his conversion, he dedicated his life to helping other prisoners find the Savior and has spent over thirty-eight years since his release doing just that.

ANOTHER NEW CONVERT

My prisoner friend, Bill, spent the first year of his confinement committing his life to Christ and growing in the Word through Bible study. Gradually he began to share his faith and lead other men to Christ and disciple them. One man who saw something special in Bill's life was convicted of wrongdoing in his role as campaign manager for a state legislative candidate. After his big wave of bitterness began to subside, he sought Bill out, mostly on the jogging track where prisoners have a degree of freedom. Eventually he received Christ and has been transformed. His appetite for Bible study often extends to three hours a day. On one occasion when they were walking the track together, he said, "Bill, the best thing that has ever happened in my life was that I was sent to Lompoc, for here I met you and you introduced me to Jesus Christ." It is doubtful that when he is released he will ever return to prison. Why? Because Jesus Christ is still in the life-transformation business.

CHAPTER ELEVEN

ALCOHOLICS CHANGED AT THE CROSS

I t is almost impossible to exaggerate the alcohol problems of the United States. I don't have to prove we are reaching near epidemic proportions today; everyone is aware of it. All of us know of individuals who started out with alcohol and then graduated to drugs, slowly killing themselves along the way. I'm no exception; a friend of mine has abandoned his beautiful wife of twenty-three years and his three teenage sons, first because he lost the battle of the bottle and now because he is losing the battle of the needle. Alcohol abuse so changes the personality and habits of the abuser that he or she becomes a different person.

This American epidemic is so out of control, nothing the best minds can come up with can halt it. Recent surveys give us a glimpse at what the future holds. They indicate that marijuana use among ninth and tenth graders is rising at a frightening rate, which means alcohol use will increase catastrophically in ten years or less. Millions of young couples will start out their married lives with one or both partners facing a drug or drinking problem. And the divorce rate among such couples will be astronomical.

The only thing really working today to reverse the alcohol problem is leading people to Jesus Christ, who alone provides the power to change those who are addicted.

LAST FLIGHT FOR ILLICIT DRUGS

Kendra is a former flight attendant whose life was almost destroyed by alcohol. Here is her story, in her own words:

The Southwest Airlines jet was heading down the runway taking off when I reached out and released the emergency escape latch on the door of the plane. I was in an alcohol-induced blackout that day, working as a flight attendant. This major FAA infraction resulted in my being fired from my job and brought my world crashing down around me.

For twenty-six years alcohol had been my best friend—my only place to feel safe. But after that day, alcohol just wasn't doing enough in my life, so I went on a cocaine spree.

In nine months I lost my new car, my savings, everything I had, and ended up in a psychiatric ward at a hospital in Illinois. All I remember is that it was a horrible state of mind I found myself in.

My uncle, a pastor, came to visit me in the hospital and told me about Teen Challenge [ministry to drug and alcohol addicts and their families, both adults and youth]. He insisted that I go. The day I was released from the hospital, he drove me all the way to Teen Challenge, even though we did not have an appointment. I had been drinking all the way on this 300-mile trip and was quite drunk by the time we arrived.

But after an hour of crying and screaming, I calmed down, and they admitted me into the program. All I had was a duffel bag with a pair of jeans and one dress. The next morning I was so sick I couldn't get out of bed. I was shaking so much I couldn't even feed myself. My room-mate, who had also been an alcoholic for many years, helped feed me.

The next two weeks I went through terrible periods of sweats and nausea. But I experienced such a beautiful outpouring of love from the women. They prayed for me daily until the Holy Spirit was able to awaken me to the point that I would want life. I did not come from a Christian background; I knew there was a God, but I didn't know why He had to have a Son. Psalm 118:5 was one Scripture that became special to me, "In my anguish I cried unto the Lord, and He answered me by setting me free."

It was not easy for me because there were tremendous walls of fear in my life. I felt very, very unsafe all my life. Since the age of thirteen, I had found safety in alcohol. My mother was addicted to prescription drugs, and my dad was an alcoholic. I was sexually abused by a relative. I left home at an early age, full of bitterness and hatred and alone.

Alcohol continued to be my friend, my place of safety, all through high school and college, through career jobs in marketing and public relations, and then as an airline attendant.

Five times I entered secular drug treatment programs. We simply looked at the symptoms. The treatment was never penetrating enough to introduce the healing that was needed in my life. Within a few months I was back on alcohol after completing each of these programs.

Even though my life was in ruins when I entered Teen Challenge, a fierce struggle raged within me. I was resistant to change, not wanting to die to my old way of living. Many times in those first five months I would get frustrated and say, "I'm leaving!"

God helped me to see that I needed to make a commitment to Him. I don't know how He does it, but the Lord heals. I was able to move forward without the aid of alcohol or a tranquilizer. I began to feel safe in Him, and I was able to let go of the hurt from my past.

About this same time my family came to visit me. This was the first time we had all been together in years. My mother had been saved about eight years earlier. My brother had been the next one to become a Christian. Right there in the Teen Challenge prayer room, my father, weeping and with a broken heart, accepted Jesus into his life.

What a joyous time as my mother and father, who had been divorced for years, were able to ask forgiveness and share with one another!

After I graduated from the Teen Challenge Ministry Institute, I went to work for a marketing firm in Laguna Beach and worked there until God brought me to work on staff at the Teen Challenge women's home in Ventura, California. I became engaged and was married on New Year's Eve, 1997. This is another extension of God's healing in my life. Because of never bonding with my family, I was never able to establish intimacy, even with myself, let alone with others.

I thought I would never be free enough to spend the rest of my life loving someone else. So it's just a beautiful miracle of the restoration of God's love in my own heart. It just feels good to be free!

JOSH MCDOWELL AND THE POWER OF THE CROSS

Josh McDowell is famous today as a Christian apologist, having written the bestsellers, *Evidence That Demands a Verdict* and *More Than a Carpenter*. At one time he was the most popular college-campus speaker at Christian outreach events. To date he has addressed audiences at more than five hundred colleges. You may know him from his True Love Waits program that has helped multiplied thousands of teens maintain their sexual virtue until marriage. Or you may be familiar with his radio program or his ministry in Russia—and the list goes on.

But Josh was not always a Christian, nor even a very nice person. He was a born skeptic who loved baiting his professors, if they were Christians, or siding with atheist professors against any Christian students who were bold enough to speak up in class. He was also a very angry young man. Both of those problems were dramatically changed immediately after he bent his knee to the crucified Savior and turned his life over to Him. There are several similarities between Josh's transformation and those of the angry Saul of Tarsus who became Paul, the defender of the faith, some nineteen hundred years before.

Josh grew up in an alcoholic family with a bitter hatred toward his father, whose uncontrolled alcoholism was a constant source of humiliation. Even though he was a straight A student who went on to become an honors graduate in both college and graduate school, Josh was filled with enormous bitterness. Most people are unaware that intense anger can have the same effect on a person as narcotics and alcohol, inflaming the emotions while bypassing the mind. That is why many people do while angry what they would never do when they are calm, just like a druggie or an alcoholic. But let's let Josh tell his own story.

> I hated one man more than anyone else in the world. My father. I hated his guts. To me he was the town alcoholic. If you're from a small town and one of your parents is an alcoholic, you know what I'm talking about. Everybody knows. My friends would come to high school and make jokes about my father being downtown. They didn't think it bothered me. I was like other people, laughing on the outside, but let me tell you, I was crying on the inside. I'd go out in the barn and see my mother beaten so badly she couldn't get up, lying in the manure behind the cows. When we had friends over, I would take my father out, tie him up in the barn, and park the car up around the silo. We would tell our friends he'd had to go somewhere. I don't think anyone could have hated anyone more than I hated my father.
>
> After I made that decision for Christ—maybe five months later—a love from God through Jesus Christ entered my life and was so strong it took that hatred and turned it upside down. I was able to look my father squarely in the eyes and say, "Dad, I love you." And I really meant it. After some of the things I'd done, that shook him up.

When I transferred to a private university, I was in a
serious car accident. My neck in traction, I was taken home.
I'll never forget my father coming into my room. He asked
me, "Son, how can you love a father like me?" I said, "Dad,
six months ago I despised you." Then I shared with him my
conclusions about Jesus Christ: "Dad, I let Christ come into
my life. I can't explain it completely, but as a result of that
relationship I've found the capacity to love and accept not
only you but other people just the way they are."

Forty-five minutes later one of the greatest thrills of my
life occurred. Somebody in my own family, someone who
knew me so well I couldn't pull the wool over his eyes,
said to me, "Son, if God can do in my life what I've seen
him do in yours, then I want to give him the opportunity."
Right there my father prayed with me and trusted Christ.

Usually the changes take place over several days,
weeks, or months, even a year. My life was changed in
about six months to a year-and-a-half. The life of my father
was changed right before my eyes. It was as if somebody
reached down and turned on a light bulb. I've never seen
such a rapid change before or since. My father touched
whiskey only once after that. He got it as far as his lips and
that was it. I've come to one conclusion. A relationship
with Jesus Christ changes lives.[1]

A FUNERAL TO REMEMBER

Mr. McDowell lived only fourteen months after he received Christ,
but during those months he maintained victory over his lifetime
habit and began witnessing to all who knew of the kind of alcohol-
soaked life he had lived. Even though he was still convalescing
after his near fatal auto accident, Josh spoke at his father's funeral
and gave some interesting details of the power of the cross in his
life. This is what he said:

"Dad's life has been brand new these past 14 months," Josh
said to family and friends gathered before the casket. "Dad

has spent the past 14 months witnessing in prisons, giving his testimony, and sharing his faith. He also took time to renew a father-son relationship and even in the space of just a little over a year, spent quality time with me and established for me the kind of father role that I will want to give to my son some day."

There was no way to undo past damage to his body, however. Josh's dad finally collapsed and died because of the earlier destruction of his liver.

"But one thing was always on Dad's mind," Josh told the mourners. "He wrote me a letter before he died telling how he witnessed to different people in town—how he wanted them to have the deep peace and power that he found." Josh took the letter from his pocket and read it to those listening. One by one, as they heard their names mentioned, they looked down or shuffled nervously.

"'I talked to Owen at the hardware store today,' Dad wrote me, 'and Owen said Jesus was fine for me, and maybe one day he'd consider coming to Christ—but not just now. Son, I sure hope he doesn't wait as long as I did to give his heart to Jesus. Pray with me for Owen, and Sam McClennan…'"[2]

Josh did not read the letter to embarrass his listeners, but to show them the love his father had for their eternal well-being.

You can laugh at Christianity, you can mock and ridicule it. But it works. It changes lives. If you trust Christ, start watching your attitudes and actions, because Jesus Christ is in the business of changing lives.

But Christianity is not something you shove down somebody's throat or force on someone. You've got your life to live and I've got mine. All I can do is tell you what I've learned. After that, it's your decision.

Perhaps the prayer I prayed will help you: "Lord Jesus, I need you. Thank you for dying on the cross for me.

Forgive me and cleanse me. Right this moment I trust you as Savior and Lord. Make me the type of person you created me to be. In Christ's name. Amen."[3]

AN ALCOHOLIC NFL STAR IS TRANSFORMED

Sean Gilbert was "the meanest, toughest, and baddest guy in a Ram uniform" for four years before being traded to the Washington Redskins, according to the *Times* sportswriter, T. J. Simers.[4] Drunk most of the time off the playing field, it often took two men to block his six-foot-five-inch frame during a game. He registered ten sacks in '93 and sixty-one tackles, all the while consuming inconceivable amounts of alcohol on the way home from games. Simers called him the best player on the Rams team and said, "The best player for the Rams, while downing a pair of 40-ounce beers after practice each day, getting tanked before he got on the plane for an away game, and smashed on the way home, was making plays, sacking the opposition's quarterback and acting every bit like a hard-hitting football player."

He would get sick from all the alcohol consumed. "I was having fifteen shots, five or six mixed drinks, seven or eight beers.... I'd see other guys in the locker room, and there was something different about them. I couldn't understand how they could leave here each day and not stop to get a beer." Gilbert had the fame, the fortune, and a party every night—but he had become so unhappy, so angry that he frightened Nicole, who had known him since their sweetheart days together in high school. "I had the houses, the cars, the money," Gilbert says. "But none of it brought happiness. I would still argue with my girlfriend, still be upset, still be lonely..."

He lived with Nicole, his high-school sweetheart and the mother of his two children, but was on the verge of losing everything. An angry fit after the Pro-Bowl game found him home from a binge following the game. "I was scared," Nicole says. "Why was he ruining his life like this? He was on a road to destruction, drinking, smoking, and going out every day to strip bars; he was way out there doing terrible things I can't even imagine he was doing. After the games, sometimes we would go out with other people and everything would be fine, and then we would go home and he would go out with the guys again to do whatever. Night after night there was no way of knowing when he would come home, and when he did, he would fall asleep in a stupor."

Finally one night after a particularly angry tirade following a binge, she decided to leave. "I was leaving and taking the kids with me back home to Pittsburgh, and I was not ever coming back," Nicole says. "I was just fed up. I was not going to subject my kids to such treatment—to be yelled at for no reason. No child in any household should be put through that."

God used that experience as a wake-up call for Sean Gilbert. That night, in desperation he called David Rocker, a journeyman player, who had a real ministry in the spiritual lives of other players. David was surprised to receive a call from "the most intimidating player on the Rams roster." But he jumped into his truck and drove to his home where he explained the gospel to him. Before long Sean Gilbert humbled himself before the cross and committed his life to Christ.

"That night he became reborn," Rocker reported. Just like that—overnight. It was the last night Sean Gilbert took a drink. No more parties. No more strip joints. No more substance abuse. "One day he's the old Sean and the next he's different, the difference being God just showed up," Nicole says.

The next day Gilbert called a meeting of the players and gave his first testimony. They looked at each other in disbelief. "Could this be a joke?" If so, we need more jokes like it, for Sean has been transformed. Now he plays with equal intensity and drive, but he has no need for alcohol and drugs after the game. Today he is serving a different Master. In coming to the Redskins he joined a team that has a history of many Christian athletes. When Joe Gibbs was the coach and the team won two Superbowls, there were as many as fifteen Christians on the squad, including all-pro cornerback Darell Green, "the fastest man in football." Many teams are finding that Christian athletes take better care of their bodies and on average do not limit the length of their career through alcohol and drug addiction.

Who knows what difference one man can make on a football

team? But after the new Christian Sean Gilbert joined the Redskins, the team won five of its first six games, and during that entire season it never lost by more than seven points. Three of its losses came through missed field goals.

But what's more important than a good season is that Sean Gilbert is a different man! Nicole, now Nicole Gilbert, and her children have a different husband and father. The cross has not lost its power!

THE TOWN DRUNK SOBERS UP

One of the most admired pastors in America is Dr. Adrian Rogers, considered by many to be the best preacher in the country. When he became the pastor of Bellevue Baptist Church in Memphis, Tennessee, the congregation was in serious decline. Today the church holds two Sunday morning services in its new 7,500-seat auditorium on a 165-acre campus. His sermons are carried daily on radio and TV throughout the nation. He tells the following incredible story of a once-incorrigible drunk:

> When I was a pastor in Fort Pierce, Florida, Mr. Al Cross was the town drunk. He had been through many alcoholic rehabilitation programs, some for weeks on end. As Al later said, "I went in a dumb drunk and came away an educated alcoholic, but the problem was still there."
>
> Somehow Al was able to maintain his job at the telephone company, but on Friday night when he got his paycheck, he would go to the bar, put his money on the counter, and drink until he fell off the stool. Friends would carry him out and roll him underneath one of the fruit packing houses in that part of the town and he would spend the night on the cold dirt. He had a godly praying mother whose heart was broken over his drunkenness.
>
> One day Al Cross came to see me. In plain and straightforward language he said, "I am a hopeless, helpless drunkard. I have tried everything, but the one thing I need is God. Can you help me?"

I explained to Al the wonderful redemption that is in the Lord Jesus Christ and the power of His blood. Al slipped down on his knees with me, prayed and asked Jesus Christ to come into his heart. That was Sunday afternoon. That night he came forward to make his profession of his new faith in Christ and was baptized.

The next day was a workday at the church. We were clearing property for a parking lot. When I arrived about 8:30, I found that Al Cross had been there from about sunup. His shirt sleeves were rolled up, perspiration was on his brow, and he was clearing trees from the property that would become the parking lot. From that moment on his energy seemed to be tireless, his spirit unflagging, his praise unceasing.

Al Cross did not have a formal education but became an avid student of the Word of God. He could preach better than the majority of preachers that I know. He had a winsomeness and a love that was incredible. I dare say that thousands came to Christ through the impact of this man's life.

Ultimately he became a deacon in that church where I pastored and became one of my dearest friends. Subsequently, he became a staff member at an alcoholic rehabilitation camp where he served until his death. He took great delight in leading other alcoholics to Christ and teaching them how to walk in victory. He called them "jewels from the devil's junkpile."

On one occasion I witnessed to a man in that same city who was reputed to be the meanest man in town. When I asked him if he wanted to be saved, he said, "If I thought God could do for me what He did for Al Cross, indeed I would." That man also gave his heart to Christ.

If ever I saw a radical, dramatic, and an eternal change in a man, it was the change I saw in Al Cross that resulted in getting on his knees and receiving the Lord Jesus Christ.[5]

AN ALCOHOLIC PSYCHOLOGIST FINDS NEW LIFE

Luis Palau is one of the most popular evangelists in the world, attracting thousands to his crusades, particularly when speaking in his native Spanish language. He also produces a special radio report heard every day throughout America. He tells the following incredible story.

> I had just stepped in the door of my hotel room when the phone rang. It was the desk clerk. "Mr. Palau, someone in the lobby is anxious to talk with you. Will you come down and see him?"
>
> It was 1:45 A.M. My day had been filled with back-to-back evangelistic crusade meetings, and I had just left the studio where our live, call-in television program, *Luis Palau Responde,* had been broadcast throughout El Salvador.
>
> My first thought was, *I've been up since 7:00 yesterday morning, and now some drunk wants to talk!*
>
> I went down to the lobby to find a rather distinguished-looking gentleman waiting. He was visibly shaking. "I watched your program three hours ago," he said, "and it hit home to my problem. I began to weep and my teenage daughter said, 'Dad, why don't you go and talk to him? He might be able to help you with your drinking problem.'"
>
> Not only did he have a drinking problem, he also confessed he was persistently unfaithful to his wife...even though he was a well-known psychologist who counseled others. "I can't control myself. I'm living like a dog!" He pounded his fist on the coffee table, then pleaded: "Is there any hope of change for a hypocrite like me?"
>
> I presented Christ in His Almighty Power to the less-than-sober, but earnest psychologist. Finally he said, "I want to receive Christ right now." He got on his knees in the middle of the lobby, where I led him in prayer.
>
> A week later, during the final live television broadcast, the very last phone call went like this: "Mr. Palau, do you

remember the man you talked to at 2:00 in the morning in the hotel? That was me."

I asked, "Have you experienced any change this past week?"

"A complete change! And now my wife is here to talk to you."

"Have you seen a change in your husband this past week?"

Indeed she had, and she wanted to receive Christ too! On the air, the miracle of regeneration took place—before an estimated audience of 450,000.[6]

That is the power of the cross. These stories illustrate its unlimited ability to transform and reshape and renew even the most desperate human lives. There is no power on earth like it. And it is still changing lives today!

CHAPTER TWELVE

THE POWER
OF THE
CROSS OVER DRUGS

nother of today's most serious national problems is rampant drug abuse, and to the secular world there is no remedy in sight. Drug use is strangling younger and younger age groups, and with the proliferation of drugs grows the ever-increasing robbery, prostitution, and crime necessary to support the habit. Recently an expensive set of personalized golf clubs that had been given to me were stolen. When the investigating police officer interviewed me, he said, "They were probably stolen by a drug addict who will be lucky if he sells them for $30, but that will get him a couple more fixes, and that's all he's interested in right now." No wonder so many new subdivisions are advertised as "gated communities." It's the only way the secular world has of coping with the escalating, drug-induced crime wave.

Neither Republicans nor Democrats are having much success in dealing with this growing epidemic. I have met leaders from both parties who cannot control their own addictions. We have our national drug programs, federal drug czars, and now a three-star general who commands a large task force. He has declared a war on drugs—but since that position was declared, the nation's use of drugs has risen considerably.

The near total impotence of the world at helping drug-obsessed individuals is a telling commentary on its secular philosophy.

Although billions of federal and state tax dollars are spent on drug rehab every year—plus an equal amount given by generous individuals to help drug victims—the cure rate is a pathetic 1–15 percent, and even some of those relapse. Easily the most effective means of helping what are considered to be "the hopeless cases" are those programs that utilize spiritual resources, beginning with bowing before the cross and experiencing the power salvation provides. In most cases the results are just the opposite of secular attempts to help drug addicts. Such rates run as high as 75–90 percent or more who get off drugs and never return to that lifestyle.

THE TEEN CHALLENGE PHENOMENON

Dave Wilkerson was a street preacher with a burdened heart for the broken people he saw everywhere on the streets of New York City. Many were devastated because of the sin of drug addiction. It soon became obvious that addicts brought to the foot of the cross were empowered to go out and walk a whole new way of life, drug-free. If you have read his best-selling story, *The Cross and the Switchblade,* you know about the remarkable transformation of young people who were introduced to Jesus Christ. Wilkerson founded the ministry of Teen Challenge in New York in 1958 and has watched his ministry grow until it has ministered to multiplied thousands of drug and alcoholic addicts and their families. It is probably the most successful program of its kind in the nation, with Teen Challenge Centers in 130 cities of the nation and one in Puerto Rico. All offer help in Jesus' name to both male and female, adults and youth—whatever their addiction.

I never pass a young person raising money for Teen Challenge without giving him or her a donation, because the organization has such an incredibly high success rate and because it introduces at least 80 percent of its participants to Jesus Christ. Teen Challenge also refuses to take money from federal or state governments, thus avoiding restrictions on its programs. Consequently Teen Challenge and other Christian ministries must be totally supported by interested Christians and other individuals.

GOVERNMENT VALIDATES SUCCESS

Smarting at the success of Christian-based rehab programs, and in the face of their own expensive but ineffective programs, two government-sponsored studies were launched that confirm the Teen Challenge claims of "a 70 percent cure rate for the drug addicts graduating from their program." In 1993, The National Institute on Drug Abuse (NIDA), part of the U.S. Department of Health, Education, and Welfare, funded the first year of a study to evaluate the long-term results of Teen Challenge programs. The medical doctor in charge of the survey had herself headed a New York City Hospital Methadone Clinic, so she was familiar with the subject. The main purpose of the study was to demonstrate that introduction of a religious component into the treatment of drug addicts is the one aspect which produces the largest success rate.

Keep in mind as you evaluate these statistics that about 20 percent or more of the Teen Challenge graduates refused to accept Christ, for one reason or another. Also remember that the government's own cure rate for its rehabilitation programs was running at 1–15 percent. The results of this survey clearly indicate the success of the Teen Challenge program in the following areas:

- The Teen Challenge definition of "drug-free" means abstaining from all use of narcotics, marijuana, alcohol, and cigarettes. 67% of the graduates are drug-free as indicated by urinalysis. (86% stated they were drug-free on the questionnaire.)
- 72% of the graduates continued their education upon completion of Teen Challenge. These graduates either acquired their G.E.D. or pursued a college level education.
- 75% of the graduates indicated they were currently employed. 73% of the graduates were self-supporting and earned their own salary. Of those who were currently employed, 58% had been at their present job for over one year.
- 87.5% of the graduates did not require additional care in drug treatment programs after leaving Teen Challenge. Over

90% considered themselves addicted to drugs before entering Teen Challenge.
- 67% of the graduates were regularly attending church. 57%
of the graduates were involved in church work.[1]

Although the government has verified the success rate of the
Teen Challenge programs, it still refuses to subsidize them. It evidently would rather continue impotent programs without God
than admit that the real effectiveness of Teen Challenge and similar
programs derive from the power of the cross. All Teen Challenge
centers and other Christian drug-rehab agencies freely admit that
conversion to Jesus Christ is at the very core of their programs.
The federal government's refusal to assist the successful Christian-
based programs can be nothing short of bias.

University of Tennessee Survey

The real success of a drug program cannot be measured immediately. Such programs often last six to fourteen months because drugs
have such a devastating effect on people. Once outside the drug-free
environment of the center, the individual is confronted with an awesome amount of temptation in the form of old friends and acquain-
tances who still live out the drug lifestyle. Such recovering addicts
need to become active in a local church, obtain education (many are
young and drugs took them out of the educational process), and
work. Each of these needs is important, for wholesome associations
are critical. The Scripture teaches, "Evil company corrupts good
habits" (1 Corinthians 15:33).

One of the more effective centers, located in Chattanooga,
Tennessee, commissioned Dr. Roger Thompson, head of the
Criminal Justice Department, to investigate the success of the program. Were dramatic lifestyle changes both apparent and long-
lasting?

Interest was expressed by the Teen Challenge of
Chattanooga, Inc. leadership and Board of Directors to
conduct a survey of alumni so as to determine their suc-

cess in recovering from alcohol and drugs. The survey was conducted beginning in the summer of '92 and concluding in the fall of '94. Among the many issues examined in the survey, the major ones included the individuals' status in the following areas: drug-free lifestyle, employment, legal, educational and church attendance.

Research herein focused on those successfully completing the induction program of Teen Challenge of Chattanooga, Inc. These men spend 4–6 months in the Chattanooga program and then transfer to a Teen Challenge training center in Cape Girardeau, MO; or Rehrersburg, PA; for an additional 8–10 months of training. Alumni from a 13-year time period (1979–1991) were included, totaling 213 individuals. A random sample of 50 alumni was selected for this research project with a 50% response. This adequate response allowed us to analyze the success of the Teen Challenge program in the following areas:

- It is noteworthy that 72% of the respondents had drug treatment prior to entering Teen Challenge of Chattanooga, Inc. Survey indicated that there have been no additional drug treatment program(s) in the lives of 88% of the respondents since Teen Challenge. In terms of program recommendation, Teen Challenge was named by 88% of the respondents as the treatment program most beneficial.
- 60% of the respondents continued their education upon completion of Teen Challenge. The areas include getting their G.E.D., or pursuing college level education.
- 72% of the respondents indicated their current status as employed. Further analysis of the 28% not employed yields 8% are students and 20% are unemployed. 50% of those who are employed have been at the same job for over one year. 60% of the respondents stated that exercising truthfulness and honesty about the past has helped rather than hurt employment prospects.

- 60% of the respondents were either under the jurisdiction of the court and subject to community supervision or had charges pending when entering Teen Challenge. As of their current legal status 76% are free of legal interference.
- One of the major areas that was researched to determine the success rate of Teen Challenge was the drug free states of the respondents. The survey indicated from the respondents that 67% are abstaining from illegal drugs and alcohol.
- 76% of the respondents attend church regularly. 60% have become members of a local church.
- Over 60% of the respondents indicated that their relationship with family was categorized as being good in comparison to fair or poor or no change.
- 92% of the respondents claim that Teen Challenge has had a great impact upon their life.
- The main focus of Teen Challenge of Chattanooga, Inc. is that of being a spiritual growth center where biblical principles are taught. 80% of the respondents credited developing a personal relationship with Jesus Christ as a major influence in helping them to stay off drugs.

As a result of this survey, indicators of success include: stabilized lifestyle due to their personal commitment to Jesus Christ, employment with some level of stability, financial independence, an absence of trouble with the police, an ability to enjoy freedom with condition or supervision and little need for additional drug treatment once completing the Teen Challenge program.[2]

Statistics can be cold, but these numbers tell of real people, most of whom were hopeless cases and probably would be dead today had they not been introduced to Jesus Christ and been transformed by the power of the cross. I asked Teen Challenge to send me some examples of how real people were changed at the cross, and they sent me so many I couldn't begin to use them all. The following few are typical of the changed lives.

Even Doctors Become Drug Addicts

Wayne Keylon, president of Teen Challenge of St. Louis, sent me many soul-wrenching stories of individuals hopelessly gripped by drugs until the day they bowed before the cross and surrendered to Jesus Christ. The following one is typical of the effectiveness of the Teen Challenge ministry.

> Joshua is a personal friend of mine, a hard-working medical doctor, energetic with a beaming smile. He was raised in the church, married to a beautiful wife for fourteen years, and they were expecting their first child when tragedy struck which brought his world crashing down. The excitement of being there for the birth of their first child turned to incredible pain—the child died at birth.
>
> The doctor tells it like this: "As I stood there holding my beautiful but lifeless baby, I can't explain how painful that experience was; it devastated everything in my life. At that point I lost interest in medicine, I lost interest in life. Our marriage went on, my medical practice continued, but the joy was gone. For years I had used drugs occasionally for 'recreational' purposes. After the death of our child, I turned to heroin on a daily basis. In two short years I lost my wife and was stripped of my license to practice medicine, with no hope of that being reinstated for at least ten years. The next two years I was a full time heroin addict, supporting my daily habit of $200–1000 through selling drugs. After five years of daily heroin use, I was desperately trapped. A great battle raged inside me, and I was losing.
>
> "One Thursday night I took so much heroin that I should have died. Early the next morning I went to the drugstore to buy more needles. As I turned to leave, a drunk sitting on the floor right next to the cash register grabbed my arm and said, 'This is going to be the last time you get high; otherwise you have no hope.' I walked out shaking, feeling scared and naked. How did he know I was

using drugs? Later that day, I decided to go to the Teen Challenge center.

"It was there, in a small chapel that I bowed before the Cross of Jesus, opened my heart and said, 'Jesus, please help me!' Those simple words began to break the darkness that had controlled my life. Suddenly I began to see a light inside me. At that very moment in my mind I saw a picture of Jesus carrying a cross on His back. I determined right then I would not betray that Man carrying that cross for me.

"They gave me a bed that Friday night, and I slept all night. The next morning I got up and for the first time in five years I did not start the day with heroin. Instead I ate breakfast and began reading the Bible. All day Saturday and Sunday I read the Bible and never had any symptoms of withdrawing from heroin. With my medical background I knew what to expect—at least three days of aches, fever, sweats, nausea, sleeplessness, depression, and an over-whelming craving for more drugs."

On Monday morning when Joshua went to the chapel service, he told the staff and students, "I want to publicly admit that I have become a Christian."

They all gathered around Joshua to pray for him. "Words are not adequate to describe the beauty of the feel-ings I experienced that morning as we prayed. It was more than pleasure, greater than any 'high' from drug use."

The weeks and months that followed were filled with intense study in God's Word and the discipleship classes at Teen Challenge. Upon graduation, Joshua completed an internship at a church in California where a graduate of Teen Challenge is the pastor. Here also began the difficult adjustment of returning to society with honesty, no longer living a double life as he had for so many years.

Four years after graduating from Teen Challenge, Joshua began attending a theological seminary, preparing for a leadership position in the ministry.

THE TRANSFORMATION OF JOHN DOUGLAS

John Douglas is another young man helped by Teen Challenge to turn his back on drugs and instead embrace the Savior. Here's how he tells his own story:

> At age 17 I had zero hope and zero future. My mind was destroyed by hallucinogenic drugs. Getting high was the only thing I had to look forward to in life. My parents had spent thousands of dollars seeking help for me, but with no results. After visiting Teen/Life Challenge (Nashville) in Madison, Tennessee, my mom brought home the book, *The Jesus Factor,* by David Manuel. After reading the book I wrote a note on the last page, "I need God's love more than drugs, yet I'm confused. I feel used. I want off the merry-go-round of drugs."
>
> The next day, Jimmy Lee, who at the time was Teen/Life Challenge's director, came to visit me at my home. I gave him the note I had written. I was literally in a drug-induced psychosis (on an LSD trip) that night when I saw the Teen Challenge choir from Rehrersburg, Pennsylvania, perform at Belmont Church in Nashville, Tennessee. Even in that condition I wanted the same kind of peace and joy I saw on their faces.
>
> I agreed to enter Teen Challenge of Chattanooga. As Lee drove me to Chattanooga, I talked about being invisible and threatened to jump out of the car. The LSD I had taken that previous week caught up with me, and I had lost contact with reality.
>
> For the first ten days at Teen Challenge, I thought I was either a flying saucer or invisible and people were trying to kill me. I was disruptive to the program. During one church service, I stood next to the pastor because I thought I was Jesus Christ and people were there to see me. That preacher put his arm around me and continued preaching.
>
> Not seeing any improvement, the staff planned to send me to a hospital with a psychiatric ward. One morning I

was so disruptive in class they sent me to the director's office. Wayne Keylon prayed for me with tears rolling down his cheeks.

Later that morning one of the staff, tired of listening to my incoherent babbling, told me to sit down, shut up, and start reading the Bible. He opened it to the Gospel of John. In the next 30 to 45 minutes I read the first few chapters of John, and in that time God literally restored my mind. I understood I was desperately lost. I went to the prayer room and turned my life over to the Lord.

Not every person coming to Teen Challenge experiences such a dramatic healing, but for me it was a real turning point. I completed the Teen Challenge of Chattanooga program and transferred to Mid-American Teen Challenge Training Center in Cape Girardeau, Missouri. Upon graduation, I moved to Rockford, Illinois. My involvement with a church street ministry was vital and kept me from falling back into drugs.

Eventually I married, returned to Nashville, and began working for Teen/Life Challenge. I have counseled hundreds of men involved in drugs and helped them find Christ. Personal evangelism has been a high priority in my life since becoming a Christian.

In 1987 I left Teen Challenge to start a roofing business. My business cards, check, and yard signs have a logo that says, "What the world needs is Jesus." I try to live in a way that entices others to follow Christ. Today I have a wonderful wife and two remarkable boys. If Christ had not impacted my life, I would most likely be dead or locked up in some institution or penitentiary with my brain fried out. I try not to take that for granted.

VICTORY OVER A TWENTY-YEAR ADDICTION PROBLEM

Dr. Larry Lewis, then president of the Home Mission Board of the Southern Baptist Convention, saw a miracle of God's transforming power in the life of a twenty-year addict. He wrote,

Shattered fragments of her mother's porcelain animal collection littered the floor; the bookshelf, which only moments earlier had held the delicate treasures, lay in their midst. Another argument had begun. In her rage, she ran at him. The blow to her face made her wince. Though it was 3:00 in the morning, she ran—out the door, down the street, searching for help.

Sirens told her that help was on its way. To the police, it would be another routine incident of domestic abuse. But for Kathy Phillips, it was the end of the routine. For two years, she had suffered at the hands of an abusive boyfriend. But for 20 years, she had suffered from the abuse of her own hands—hands that held the liquor bottle to her lips, hands that exchanged money for cocaine, hands that lined the cocaine for snorting. Tonight she would end both kinds of abuse.

Kathy's decline into drug abuse was not predictable. Growing up, she had it all. Parents who loved her, a church, friends, popularity. But after graduating from high school in Arlington, Oregon, she wanted to do things "her way."

"I couldn't get a handle on who I was," says Kathy. "I lived for the moment, and only the moment motivated me. I had no goals, no direction, no vision. Then I found drugs. And it became the drugs that motivated me."

She started using cocaine and drinking alcohol. Wherever she went, she quickly learned where to find drugs. She was unable to escape their hold on her. After working in a nursing home, she enrolled in nursing school. While there, she lived with a drug dealer but remained drug-free except on weekends. But the day she graduated from nursing school, she snorted cocaine, and for the next 15 years didn't stop. She remembers: "The more I did, the worse it got. The people I hung out with were rougher, the activities I got involved in more questionable. I wrote bad checks. I considered prostitution. Everything in my life revolved around drugs."

She finally moved back in with her parents. They didn't know about the drug addiction. When they found out, they were hurt and disappointed, but their love for her did not end. They tried helping her, yet, even with their support, the drug abuse continued. Then her father died. A few months later, her mother died. The two people who had such high hopes for her life were suddenly gone. Believing no one would ever love or care for her again, she started smoking cocaine, a method more potent than snorting.

"I became paranoid. I wanted to isolate myself from everything. I came home in the evening and bolted the door behind me. And, with blankets on my window blocking out the light, I got lost in a cocaine high." Her live-in boyfriend, also a drug addict, abused her frequently. Though sometimes threatening to leave, she knew she wouldn't. Good or bad, he was someone there for her. But then, one evening, he went too far. The crash of the bookshelf and the scattered pieces of precious porcelain symbolized what had become of her life. She knew she could no longer continue living the life of abuse. Broken, she reached for help.

She went to a psychologist to learn why she had a drug problem. Not finding an immediate answer, she went to self-help groups that told her, "Fake it till you make it." She had faked it for years, but she knew she wasn't going to make it. She turned to Alcoholics Anonymous (AA), going to as many as six meetings a day.

At the time, Kathy was living with a man who was also involved in AA. He was staying clean, and they encouraged each other. Sometimes he read his Bible at night, and she was intrigued by that. He visited a church one evening, and came home with information about a treatment program called S.A.F.E. (Setting Addicts Free Eternally). He asked Kathy if she wanted to attend a meeting. Kathy thought, "I can't believe I'm going to try something else.

What difference will it make?" But she went, and what she found made all the difference in her life.

Jamae Smith, wife of S.A.F.E. director Troy Smith, was speaking to the group that night. At the meeting, Kathy heard words of hope. Words of encouragement. She heard about a Father who loved her more than anyone. He had a plan and purpose for her life.

"Oh, how I needed to hear that! After the meeting, I literally grabbed Jamae and pleaded for help. I told her I didn't know what to do. Jamae explained that Jesus was the answer I was looking for; then she led me to the Lord. At that moment, my heart was full of life. I knew it was going to be a different life—a better one than I had had before."

The journey had begun—a journey of recovery. Kathy began to deal with her emotional instability. She dealt with the death of her parents for the first time. "God gave me hope, and in His Word, I read promises that I claimed every day. I learned to deal with anger, and I had plenty of anger after 20 years of drug abuse. I learned what it's like to be stable. I learned that, by having a personal relationship with Jesus Christ, everything falls into place. Now, I am accountable and responsible to Him."

The bondage of drugs had been removed. Kathy is no longer an addict or even a recovering addict. Kathy proclaims, "I am free." She continues to have disappointments. Sometimes she even craves the high of drugs. But now Kathy knows the One who can help her overcome her self-destructive desires.

Kathy knows what it takes to remain free—God's perfect strength working in her life. She says, "Now, I know what to do when I'm hurting—I saturate my mind with God's Word and rethink my thought process. I know how to get out of the pit of despair. God showed me, and now I want to show others His hope and strength. I want to give them a second chance, just like God gave me."

S.A.F.E. continues to be part of Kathy's life. She now works in the ministry, running a small coffee shop that helps provide income for ministry needs. And she helps others break the bonds of addiction.

Troy Smith remembers meeting Kathy for the first time: "She was so sad, crying all the time. The difference between now and then is remarkable—a true testimony of God's work in her life."

Kathy Phillips credits the power of the cross for her release from drugs. "I'm different, and it was God—and God alone—who made the difference."

I find it intriguing that the ministries reaching out to addicts today are not limited to certain denominations, but seem to grow up out of local needs and people who can lead in meeting those needs. Some provide national training, but all have one thing in common: they first lead the addict to a saving knowledge of Jesus Christ. None of them is in the business of helping addicts without first introducing them to the One who can give them the power to overcome their addiction. This begins at the foot of the cross which, depending on the addiction, begins the long, tough process of transformation. In most cases, the people working in these ministries are themselves former addicts. The Bible tells us we can "comfort others with the same comfort we ourselves were comforted of God." Very simply, a recovered addict is a good role model for an addict. A visit to almost any such ministry will find more success stories like the ones described in this book.

JAY STRACK—THE TRANSFORMED "DRUGGIE"

My friend Jay Strack was like many addicted to drugs today. His journey into serious addiction began before his senior year in high school. It started in his home, broken by alcohol. When Jay was only eight his father, a severe alcoholic, left the family for good. Jay remembers grabbing his father around the knees on the front lawn of their Florida home and crying, "Daddy, please don't leave us." But he did leave, placing an emotional scar on that little boy's life that only Jesus Christ was able to heal years later. His mother married another alcoholic a year later, and before long they, too, split up, deepening the scars on young Jay's heart. He told his story in the book, *Shake Off the Dust.*

The carefree innocence of childhood ended for me that day. A light turned off in my soul; things would never be the same. In the years that followed, my life went from bad to worse. Mother constantly reached out for happiness but never found it. Men came and went from our lives regularly, but I ignored them all, determined not to get hurt again. In the meantime, my real father sank further and further into alcoholism, unable to hold a steady job. He, too, was searching for answers but came up empty-handed.

One of my stepfathers had a teenage son by another marriage. When the two moved in, the teenager molested me and threatened to kill me if I ever told anyone. Bitter and confused, I withdrew even further into myself, afraid to tell anyone for fear I would be rejected again. I can see now that my distrust of everyone grew from my feeling that everyone had hurt me in one way or another. Through all of my troubles, I developed an intense hatred for alcohol. It had ruined my life; it had taken my father, sent away my brother, and demoralized my mother. "If there is one thing I'll never do," I vowed, "it is take a drink."

My big break came in junior high when I made the football team. Now I can make it, I thought. I'm finally one of the cool kids. After a game one night the captain of the team brought out a case of beer and began to pass it around. I was shocked. "Don't you realize what this stuff can do to you?" I asked.

"Yeah, isn't it great!" someone replied.

"But you guys don't realize what this stuff has done to my dad and to our family!"

"Come on, kid. You're not afraid, are you?" the team captain challenged.

"Chicken!" somebody shouted. "Maybe you ought to go home." But that was the last place I wanted to be.

Suddenly, I found myself doing what I had vowed I would never do—drinking alcohol. It tasted awful, but everyone acted like they were having such a great time that I went along with them.

I began to drink in excess regularly, and the very actions and attitudes I had despised in others became evident in my own life. I wanted to drink away my problems. I went to endless parties where almost everyone got drunk and where some nights I got very sick. But I kept insisting I was having a great time.

For me, as for so many others, alcohol was a "gateway" drug that led to other drug addictions. I was unaware of the cycle that alcohol would lead me into. But it wasn't long before I began to smoke marijuana, which led to my taking pills and then hallucinogens. Finally, I shot speed. I began to sink further and further into drug abuse.

Eventually I was arrested four times for drug possession with the intent to distribute and driving under the influence, and I was sent to the Lee County Detention Center in Ft. Myers.

One night "under the influence," I lost control of my car while hallucinating from drugs and hit a whole row of taxicabs, causing thousands of dollars' worth of damage. Panicked, I jumped out of the car and ran away. The police pursued and apprehended me for hit-and-run, possession, and being under the influence of drugs. To make things worse, I punched the arresting officer. By the time the judge was through with me, I had lost my license and been sentenced to three months in the detention center.

In the detention center I was alone with myself and my thoughts. The friends I had lived for forgot all about me. There were no girls, no parties, no rock 'n roll, and not even a television.

Every time I was busted for drugs, I would vow I'd

quit. I would endure the withdrawals at the detention center—perspiration engulfing my body, endless diarrhea. Through shakes and nausea, I would wonder, *Why can't I give it up?* And I would quit. I quit a hundred times. But I went right back.

The doctors at the detention center told me I was getting to be a lost cause. They said I had to want help, but nobody seemed to understand. I did want help, but I didn't know where to get it.

For me, drugs provided an escape from my problems and failures. Drugs gave me a false sense of power and control. But when the high ended, I crashed back down to reality in brutal despair. I smoked my first joint on a dare. I didn't want to be different or excluded from the rest of the group, so I gave in to their pressure. Soon I was smoking it regularly. The harsh smoke began to taste sweeter. I liked what it did to me. It gave me a quicker and more pleasant high than alcohol ever had.

I soon learned that once you cross the line to marijuana, it becomes easier to say yes to any kind of drugs. I began taking anything people offered me. I liked amphetamines ("speed") the best because they created an instant rush and left me high for hours.

The day I was finally released from the Lee County Detention Center, I was ready to make a new start, but I felt too weak to do it. I had seen enough of the detention center to know I didn't want to go back to it ever again. But I didn't know how to quit.

When school started up in the fall, it didn't take long for me to fall right back into the routine of getting high every day. Kids were passing around drugs like first graders trading candy at lunch. Drugs were everywhere. Guys were selling dope in the bathrooms, the hallways, the cafeteria, and sometimes even in class!

During this time, Charlie, a guy at school, invited me to a Bible study. Charlie stood out from the rest of the gang. He was clean-cut and usually smiling, and everyone knew he didn't use drugs. He consistently invited me to Bible study and daily told me about a God of love who wanted to be my heavenly Father. He told me over and over, "I care. I'm praying for you." That night I believed him, and the next night I found myself turning my car on to Central Avenue and driving to a small green stucco house where the Bible study was held.

Charlie had said to "come as you are," so I showed up in cutoff jeans and sandals. As soon as the door opened, I felt a flood of warmth and love. No one stared at my hair or my clothes. Instead, I was greeted by hugs and acceptance. An older woman, who I learned later was Rick's mother, smiled and said, "Welcome, son."

The small room was crowded. I recognized several kids from school, which made me immediately put up a front. "I'm just here to get Charlie off my back," I joked. But they seemed genuinely glad to see me, so after a little while I relaxed. Someone handed me a Bible, and sitting cross-legged on the floor, I listened as kids all around me talked about how real Jesus was in their lives. They were excited about knowing Him personally and getting strength from the Bible. I was curious but skeptical. Then it was Rick's turn to speak. He opened his Bible and read from 2 Timothy, chapter 3. I didn't know much about the Bible—in fact, I had never read one in my life—but I found myself listening intently. According to what I was hearing, I was a sinner, but Rick added that God loved us just the way we were—with all our bitterness, anger, sin, and rebellion.

I wore a surfer cross, which was popular then, and had seen crosses everywhere; but for the first time, I understood what the Cross was all about. The same One whose name I'd taken in vain loved me enough to die for me on that Cross. The most life-changing aspect of what I heard was that Jesus had risen again and that He is alive today.

As Rick brought the evening's message to a close, he stressed that every individual must make a personal choice to accept Christ as Savior. He told us that a simple prayer of belief, asking for forgiveness, was all that would be necessary to receive a new life and a new heart. This was God's promise to us. "Call upon the Lord," he said, "and He will answer you."[3]

That night Jay bent his knee and his will before the cross of Jesus and was saved. Even more, he was transformed by the power of the Spirit of God. Sure, he was tempted—a lifetime of drug abuse leaves the door of temptation wide open. Yet he tells about the time he went to Fort Myers Beach and sat on the sand.

As I struggled with the aftershock of depression, I began to write all of my sins in the sand. The list got longer and longer. But as the tide kept coming in, the waves began to wash away the list. As I sat there watching, I realized that God's grace had washed away my sins. I watched until the water covered the list and it was completely gone.

That is what God has done for me, I thought. *He has washed away my sins. I don't need to let the past get me down anymore. It's gone forever.* When I stood up to leave, the sun was setting in splendid hues of red and gold against the clouds on the horizon of the Gulf. The warm air felt fresh and clean, and so did I.[4]

The first big victory in Jay's newfound life came one week after he was saved.

A guy gave me one-hundred-dollars' worth of good speed. "Just take it," he said, shoving it into my hands. "But I don't want it," I tried to say, as he hurried off. As I stood there holding the package I wondered what I was supposed to do. I can't just throw this away. But God seemed to speak directly to me. "Oh yes you can! Get rid of that stuff," Jay, He seemed to say. I hesitated only a moment before I walked to the boys' room and flushed it all down the toilet. You cannot imagine the joy and relief I felt! I had said no to drugs for the very first time and I felt great about it! I was free and the past no longer had a hold on me![5]

That was many victories back. Jay became a powerful witness on campus the rest of his senior year. A pastor helped him enroll in a Christian college where he did well and later went on to seminary. When I met Jay in the early eighties he was pastor of a booming church which he had started in his hometown of Fort Myers, Florida. He invited me to come for a Family Life Seminar and we have been friends ever since.

It was obvious that Jay has the gift of evangelism. Soon other churches began inviting him to come for meetings, and today he holds citywide evangelistic crusades all over the country. Jay also lectures on high-school campuses, where because of his past he gets rapt attention from the students, particularly where drugs are rampant. School principals welcome him in, not because he is an evangelist but because "he has been there," where many students are or are headed. Hundreds of young people come to the meetings as a result of his high-school lectures and thousands are receiving the salvation message he offers.

One indication of the respect this transformed alcoholic has earned from his peers is that he has served as president of the Southern Baptist Evangelists' Association and, for the past decade, has been a member of the Executive Committee of the Southern Baptist Convention. He is married to a dedicated Christian wife and has two children who are being raised in a Christian home. For half a lifetime he has demonstrated the power of the cross to transform an otherwise hopelessly lost life. Jay often says, "Had I not accepted Jesus and given Him my life, in all probability I would now be dead of an overdose." And he is not alone. Millions of dedicated Christians share a testimony like his.

DRUGS NO MATCH FOR THE SAVIOR

A whole book could be written citing thousands of such illustrations—hopeless people bound for an early death caused by drugs. Some had tried everything before they were introduced to the Christ who died for them and rose again from the dead to forgive their sins. It was He who empowered their lives with sufficient resolve to overcome their lifetime addiction. Many of these new converts become contagious witnesses of the grace of God, introducing their drug-riddled friends to the Savior.

This message is so common today—in centers, churches, and homes—that it cries out to all who are willing to hear: "God is alive today and proves it by transforming the lives of those hopeless victims of drugs who bow before the Cross and receive the Savior."

CHAPTER THIRTEEN

THE CROSS
OVERCOMES
DEPRESSION

T wenty-three years ago I wrote a book titled, *How to Win over Depression,* which became an enduring bestseller. Today more than one million copies are in print, and at the publisher's request I recently revised and updated it. I had to change very little, which indicates to me that depression is still a serious problem. *Newsweek* magazine once wrote, "There is no doubt that depression, long the leading mental illness in the U.S., is now virtually epidemic—and suicide is its all too frequent outcome."[1]

In 1996 there were nine thousand more suicides in the United States than homicides. Think of it—more than 33,000 people took their own lives. Most of these were depressed individuals who had lost all hope that their life could ever be happy.

But this is not the whole story. For every depressed person who takes his own life, there are probably a hundred more who think about it or whose depression ruins their marriage, their career, or a personal relationship with friends or relatives. It is impossible to calculate the high cost of depression.

Medical science has made incredible progress on treating depression in the past twenty-three years and now provides incredible help for the 10–15 percent of depressed persons who have some genetic or chemical cause for their condition. This problem has been known to plague as many as four generations in a single family. Usually this tendency is seen in those family members who inherit a melancholy temperament. That is why some children in a family of depressed individuals will skip it, because they inherited a sanguine or phlegmatic temperament. Such individuals whose depression is temperamentally or biologically induced seem to respond well to medication administered by their doctor. Even so, certain side effects to the new drugs can be almost as harmful as the illness itself, as the following story illustrates:

> Several years ago, a woman informed me that she had found her husband's diet pills to be the perfect solution to her depression. She did not realize, however, that those diet pills were probably a form of amphetamine which was never intended for permanent use, but for short periods to help in food intake reduction. In addition to cutting down on one's appetite, they also stimulated the "pleasure center" of the brain just above the hypothalamus gland, producing a feeling of euphoria in direct proportion to the amount of amphetamine taken and the user's natural immunity level.
>
> The trouble with amphetamines is that they become addictive—even dangerously so. The body's natural immunity level responds to this drug, making it necessary to increase the dosage to continue the same effects. In addition, the exhilarating "high" that amphetamines produce is followed by a corresponding "low" which, not surprisingly, sends the individual into a worse depression than before he began to take the drug.
>
> The woman mentioned above, like scores of others, compounded her problems by taking her husband's pills. Not only did she feel worse after taking his "diet pills," but her husband was upset that his pills had disappeared. I have repeatedly observed that people on diet pills are usually irritable and the pills tend to aggravate a bad situation. Her first visit concerned an emotional problem. After taking the amphetamines she added a marital problem.[2]

One of the advantages of not being a medical doctor is that I cannot prescribe medications in trying to help the depressed. Instead, I must use my only available resource, the supernatural ministry of the Holy Spirit. The life-transforming experience of bowing at the cross and receiving Jesus Christ is the first step in helping a depressed person. Of the more than one thousand depressed people I counseled in my role as pastoral counselor, I was never able to help anyone who would not first receive Jesus Christ. My Bible-based technique has helped multiplied thousands of individuals, judging by the letters and messages I have received from readers. Even some counselors trained in psychotherapy have told me they were ineffective in helping the depressed until they read my book and adopted its principles. The key to success is the life-transformation that begins at the cross.

Depression is an emotion. And although depression can be chemically altered through medication, it can seldom be done without cost, mainly in unwanted side effects. When the depressed person is introduced to the saving power of God through Jesus Christ, however, then he has access to the supernatural power of God to change his life by altering his emotions.

THE TRANSFORMATION OF A DEPRESSED DOCTOR

It never ceases to amaze me how God sends me real-life illustrations to help my readers understand a particular subject. Recently two doctors and their wives dropped by my office. One of them, about forty years of age, was carrying a copy of the original printing of *How to Win over Depression*. Before asking me to autograph it, he told me this thrilling story and gave me permission to use it.

> After being a physician for several years, during which he married and had three children, he was gradually overcome with severe depression. Recognizing that he was becoming suicidal, in 1984 he agreed to be hospitalized. After being treated for three weeks, he became convinced that the people working on him "really didn't know what they were doing." At the end of three weeks he got a pass

to go home for a visit. Somehow that made him even more depressed. The next day he was strolling through a shopping mall and stopped at a bookstore. He told me, "The title of your book stood out from all the other books on the shelf—*How to Win over Depression.*" At that point in his life, he was not sure it was possible to be victorious over that dreaded disease. He had tried everything the medical profession had to offer and was no better off for his efforts.

In the book he discovered there was hope. He was particularly struck by my positive assertion: "I am confident that you or those you love do not have to be depressed." For the first time someone was offering him a way out. He read the whole book! As a non-Christian, he was also struck with the realization that my book offered help from a dimension he had never considered—the "spiritual side." He was used to trying the mental, emotional, and physical sides, but did not realize there was a spiritual dimension he had left unexplored. In the sixth chapter he was impressed with the need to surrender his life and will to Jesus Christ, or as he said, "put Christ on the throne of my life. I was driving my car when I distinctly invited Christ in and surrendered my life to him. Nothing happened immediately. When I got back to the hospital, I watched a football game, and as I turned off the TV I noticed I felt different in my spirit. It was almost as if a great cloud was lifted off me. I began reading the Bible regularly, and the owner of the Christian bookstore got so well acquainted with me that he kind of discipled me in a warm and caring way. It was not long until it dawned on me—I was not only growing as a young Christian, but I was experiencing permanent deliverance from my depression!" (Keep in mind, he told me this eleven years after his experience.)

By this time tears were running down his wife's face as she said, "I have been married to two different men—the depressed man he was before his conversion and the man he is today!"[3]

The second doctor testified that his friend really was a transformed man. He had been a Christian prior to his friend's experience at the cross and, although he had never had a problem with depression himself, he had seen his colleague demonstrate the power of God in overcoming this disease after Christ came into his life—so much so that he recommitted his own life to Christ!

Unfortunately, much of today's secular counseling is futile. I have known of individuals whose depression caused them to see a psychotherapist twice a week for over six months, then once a week for twelve to eighteen months—and still did not overcome their problem. On the other hand, I have seen individuals bow at the cross, have their sins forgiven, and immediately begin to live new lives in Christ, free of depression. If because of habit they face the rejections, insults, and injuries of life with self-pity, the depression returns. Not because Christ is not still in their lives, but because they have negated the power of Christ resident in them by violating the biblical command, "In everything give thanks; for this is the will of God in Christ Jesus for you" (1 Thessalonians 5:18). When a depressed person receives Christ and begins thanking and praising God by faith for the victory that is his in Christ, he begins to experience genuine victory in Christ. Conversion has a distinctly therapeutic effect on a new Christian's emotions.

THE DEPRESSED WARD OF THE STATE

In quiet desperation, an extremely depressed young woman began attending our church. She had been a ward of the state of California in the psychiatric wing of a nearby hospital for four years. Prior to that she had been in training as a nun, but after two years her depressions closed in upon her, and she dropped out and became so severely depressed she had to be committed to keep her from taking her own life.

I first encountered Ann shortly after she came forward at the close of one of our services to kneel before the cross of Jesus and be born again. The first thing she said was that she felt "freed from my guilt for the first time in years." Guilt, of course, is a major cause of many depressions. When individuals get to the place of

Lady MacBeth, the star of Shakespeare's play by that name, and acknowledge "My sin is ever before me"—or in her case, the famous words "Out, out damned spot!"—what they really need is to bow before the cross of the One who died for their sins and experience the forgiveness He made possible.

Ann scared me during our interview when she said she was on sixteen drugs all at the same time. She didn't tell all of her doctors what prescriptions she had already been given, so she was taking them all. I was so concerned I did a brash thing—I urged her to stop them all. I thought this would encourage her to return to the last doctor to whom she had been assigned.

One week later she came into my office looking like a new woman. She had abstained from all her drugs and kept reading and studying the New Testament according to a program I have developed for depressed people. I have new converts read the little book of Philippians every day for a month. There is something about that little book of joy, written by Paul while unjustly confined to a Roman prison cell, that has a transforming effect. Then I have them read 1 John every day for a month to give them the assurance of their salvation. Last I have them read the Gospel of John.

By the time Ann had been on this program for two months, she was so improved I transferred her to my associate pastor in charge of counseling. She continued doing extremely well and all her friends could see the dramatic change in her even in casual exchange. She smiled all the time because she was happy for the first time in years. Her naturally gracious nature began to surface, and she became concerned about others, rather than always dwelling on how badly she felt.

Then it happened. She got a letter from her psychiatrist, ordering her to come in for a checkup or she would lose the government check she counted on each month. Instead of seeking outside advice, she naively went to his office. Evidently she had such a radiance about her, he began the interview by saying, "Ann, what has happened to you that you look so different?" She innocently replied, "Doctor, I have had the most marvelous experience. I received Jesus

Christ as my Savior and He has changed my life."

Evidently her psychiatrist was quite an insecure man, for he did a very unprofessional thing. He jumped up from behind his desk, stood over her threateningly and said, "Young lady, religion is a false crutch that will collapse under you and you will be back in here one day worse off than you were before!" The truth was, she could hardly have been worse off and still be alive.

The man's threatening manner caused Ann to run from his office in tears. Fortunately, she called our office from the hospital corridor. I was out of town, but she reached my associate who immediately instructed her to catch a cab to his office. He helped patch her back together by reclaiming the promises of God and by explaining to her that her doctor was typical of those who depended upon the wisdom of this age. The man neither believed in nor used the supernatural power of God to heal or help his clients. Ann left the pastor's office that day shaky, but with new hope. She was already in a support group for singles, and it was a big help to her. Within a few weeks she got her first job, began to take some classes in college, and was active in church.

Several years later I left the church in San Diego and began a traveling ministry. I was asked to speak at a Bible conference at Hume Lake Christian Camp, high in the Sequoia Mountains of California. One afternoon I bumped into Ann as she walked the grounds with three girlfriends, one of whom had been my secretary for a time. We embraced all around, and I was anxious to see how Ann was doing. She looked so radiant and at peace that I was not surprised to find she was doing extremely well, still walking with God and serving Him. She said she had never been back to see her doctor; she just didn't need him. I was amazed when she explained what she was doing professionally, for she was serving as the head of a technical department at a local San Diego hospital which uses Magnetic Resonance Imaging machines as well as other sophisticated and expensive electronic equipment—a very heavy responsibility for a former psychiatric ward of the state! Not, however, too heavy for one who was converted at the foot of the cross and is now indwelt by the power of the Holy Spirit of God.

One of the incredible things about the transformation of Ann and others like her is that they stand the test of time. She didn't receive "a quick religious fix," as some like to say in an attempt to brush off such miracles. Her life has stood the test of time. It has been at least six years since our encounter at Hume Lake, and ten years since her conversion and release from depression. She is still serving her Lord and maintaining a responsible work load at the hospital.

The cross has the power to do what pills, capsules, other drugs, and even therapy cannot do—deliver a person from a powerful addiction to depression.

THE TESTIMONY OF DORIS WADE

One of my close pastor friends is Dr. Richard Lee of the dynamic Rehoboth Baptist Church of Atlanta, Georgia. He is the author of several good books and conducts an effective TV ministry. I have preached for him several times and can vouch for the spiritual strength of his congregation. In a day when many churches have a weak Sunday night service or have given up on it altogether, his is one of the strongest in the nation. Like other pastor friends, he sent me the story of one of his counselees who met Jesus Christ at the cross and came away a transformed soul. I will let him tell it in his own words.

> Doris Wade grew up in a Christian home with a happy childhood. "I just loved it," she told me. "But suddenly at age thirteen, my wonderful world turned into hell itself! I withdrew into my room. I began to pull away from people. In fact, I was scared to death of people. I didn't realize it at the time, but I began to hang my head and stay away from people. I even stopped going out after church with our youth group on Sunday nights."
>
> Throughout high school, Doris remained a recluse, isolated from other teenagers and even from her parents. After high school, she attended Mercer University in Macon, Georgia, but still could not make the adjustment to dealing with people, especially her peers. As she struggled to find

herself, Doris moved back home and finished school at Georgia State University in Atlanta. Shortly afterwards, she met Cliff Wade. They fell in love and later married. In the meantime, however, Doris's father, whom she loved dearly, became ill and eventually died. Before he passed away, he urged her to get help for her depression, which seemed to be getting continually worse.

Like many believers, Doris was not sure whether she should seek pastoral counseling or psychiatric evaluation. Initially, she chose counseling from the pastor at her home church. "He was a great help and I felt such hope inside," Doris told me. "But friends kept insisting that I see a psychiatrist." So, Doris agreed to see a secular psychiatrist.

"When I first went to see the psychiatrist, I was immediately labeled 'manic depressive,' 'psychotic' and 'suicidal,'" Doris recalled. "What followed was like a black hole of hopelessness. I went through twelve years of therapy. Twice I tried to commit suicide. I got to the place where I just didn't want to live any more. Even at church I was a total blank. I couldn't even hear the music. I went through the motions of being a wife and a mother, but I was just like a 'zombie.' I felt desperate all the time. I was scared to death. Everything was like one gigantic nightmare. I was paralyzed with fear and I had no feelings.

"I had to do something, so after twelve long years, I tried a Christian psychiatrist. He had a sign on his door that said: 'This is the first day of the rest of your life.' But I used to think to myself, *This is no life! This is a nightmare!*

The Christian psychiatrist prescribed several medications and anti-depressant drugs for Doris. "Instead of getting better, I got worse," Doris explained. "I begged him to decrease the medication, but he insisted on increasing it. That's when I got the worst I had ever been! I couldn't sleep at night. Cliff sat up with me and just held me all night long while I cried and cried.

"The crying episodes were almost endless. I couldn't

control myself. Then, one day I was looking out the window, I cried out to the Lord for help, telling Him I couldn't go on another day. It was so vivid that I wrote down what He said to me, and I still have it to this day. It was on Mother's Day. God seemed to say, 'Doris, don't you know that I care for you? I know you are fearful and I'm going to heal you. But you are going to have to do what I tell you to do. Keep praying and trust My Son, Jesus Christ.'

"That was the turning point. It was like I had come to the end of myself and threw myself on God. And He caught me just in time."

In the meantime, Doris heard about a Christian counselor named Dr. Taylor, who taught a Bible study for company employees. She and Cliff decided to attend in October, 1987. "I remembered that my previous counselor had told me that I needed to tell myself the truth. The first time I went to Dr. Taylor's office I noticed a book on his desk entitled, *Telling Yourself the Truth,* by William Backus.

"I asked him about the book and he told me the Lord told him to buy it because somebody would need it. That night he knew the book was for me. I asked him if there was any hope that I would permanently recover."

"Of course there is," he assured her. "There is always hope in Jesus." He was the first person in a long time to give her any real assurance of hope.

"My doctors kept telling me there was no sure cure," she explained. "What really jolted me was when my Christian psychiatrist told me he couldn't promise that I would ever get better. But Dr. Taylor gave me hope that night, and I latched onto it with everything in me."

"Thou wilt keep him in perfect peace whose mind is stayed on thee" (Isaiah 26:3) became her favorite verse. Doris gave up the drugs she had been on for over thirty years and replaced them with Scripture memorization and prayer.

"It was a miracle," Doris affirms. "Suddenly, the darkness in my soul gave way to light. The first thing I began to notice was the music in church. It was like a great weight lifted off me and I felt good again for the first time in years. I sat in church and started to cry, but this time it was with tears of joy and relief. I could finally hear the music again and I knew I was free!"

DON'T FORGET THE SPIRITUAL SIDE

Dr. Lee's story about Doris confirms what I have discovered in my own counseling of depressed people. There is a spiritual side of human nature that is rarely touched by secular counselors, doctors, and psychiatrists. They may use medication and designer drugs or shock therapy, but they have no message for the crucial spiritual side of human nature. Blaise Pascal, the famous French philosopher and mathematician, was right when he said, "There is a God-shaped vacuum in the heart of every man that can be satisfied by none other save Jesus Christ." When that vacuum is occupied by the Holy Spirit, God provides a whole new spiritual dimension of life for the depressed individual. For the first time, he has the capacity to see the sun rise or hear the birds sing and the children laugh. I have seen it happen so many times in what otherwise can only be diagnosed as "the hopelessly depressed," that I anticipate it when a depressed person receives Christ.

And why shouldn't we? The three emotions supplied by the Holy Spirit when He comes into the new believer are "love, joy and peace"—the very things needed by the depressed. I am reminded of the little refrain that can be the song of all those without Christ, particularly the depressed: "He is all I need, He is all I need, Jesus is all I need!"

The few stories I have told here represent only the tip of the iceberg of those I could pull out of my mailbag. All of them illustrate the power of the cross to transform the depressed. Almost any Christian counselor who introduces the depressed to the saving grace of God has seen enough of life transformation to join me in proclaiming that God's power to overcome depression is one more evidence of the stunning power of the cross.

CHAPTER FOURTEEN

THE ONLY REMEDY
FOR HOMOSEXUALITY

I have been a practicing psychiatrist in the Los Angeles basin
for thiry-three years, and I have never seen a homosexual
turned around," said an angry psychiatrist who had agreed to
debate me on an LA talk-radio program. Then he made the mis-
take of asking me, "Have you ever seen one give up that lifestyle?"

Naturally I could say yes and added, "Through the years,
although that has not been my major area of counseling, I have
seen at least thirty homosexuals come to the cross of Jesus and
gain the necessary power to leave that lifestyle to live a normal
life."

He went ballistic, calling me "a liar" on live radio. And yet
what I said is absolutely true. During the twenty-five years I pastored in San Diego, my staff and I had seen over thirty men caught
in that misery-producing lifestyle come to Christ and "go and sin
no more." It wasn't always easy for them to gain victory, for homosexuality may be the most powerful negative obsession there is,
but I have seen too many come to Christ, get into a discipleship
program based on the Word of God, and commit themselves to
living as He would have them live, to question the genuine power
of the cross.

Transforming homosexuals is nothing new to Christianity. It

has been going on now for almost two thousand years. Let's face it, we had that problem clear back in the days of Lot when God destroyed the cities of Sodom and Gomorrah. Today, because of the death, burial, and resurrection of Jesus, there is a way to transform sinners of all kinds—it's called conversion.

The apostle Paul was the first to mention this problem as it confronted the early church. When faced with the gospel, many of these folks fell before the cross and tapped into God's power to enable them to come out of that lifestyle. Consider the apostle's words to the church of Corinth, a city located in the center of Greek humanism and homosexuality:

> Do you not know that the unrighteous will not inherit the kingdom of God? Do not be deceived. Neither fornicators, nor idolaters, nor adulterers, nor homosexuals, nor sodomites, nor thieves, nor covetous, nor drunkards, nor revilers, nor extortioners will inherit the kingdom of God.
>
> And *such were some of you.* But you were washed, but you were sanctified, but you were justified in the name of the Lord Jesus and by the Spirit of our God. (1 Corinthians 6:9–11, italics mine)

It may be hard for some Christians to accept that in the great church at Corinth where Paul spent eighteen months teaching the Word, many of the believers and leaders were former homosexuals. The true church of Christ has always opposed homosexuality and offered conversion as a way out of that lifestyle. It remains so today. In fact, Christians, churches, and Christian ministries that specialize in reaching out to hurting homosexuals are helping thousands come to the cross and then to escape that lifestyle. Many of those who have organized or provide leadership to such "exit" ministries are themselves former homosexuals. They have found victory over that lifestyle and are interested in helping others do the same.

On the other hand, the track record of the psychological and psychiatric profession has been so spectacularly unsuccessful in this area they have officially removed it from the mental-sickness category and today call it "normal," rather than face their inability to help change homosexual behavior. Yet untrained Christians who were former homosexuals *are* helping people by the hundreds to come out of that lifestyle! Many of those helped even marry and father children.

During my open-mike debate, one former homosexual who bowed his knee to the cross of Christ came immediately to mind. Long after his conversion, I saw his progress and spiritual maturity and eventually married him to one of our choice young women. Today he is a deacon in our church, an earnest soul winner, and the father of three children. I wished that day that I could have introduced him to the angry psychiatrist, but he would never have believed that my friend had spent thirteen years in the homosexual world before he met the Savior.

Three callers did come on line to tell the psychiatrist they had been homosexuals prior to being converted but had found in the power of the cross adequate resources to come out of that lifestyle. One man acknowledged he was now a pastor in the Los Angeles area and offered to give his phone number to help any who wanted to forsake that life. The psychiatrist was visibly shaken and I doubt he ever again agreed to discuss that subject on open-mike radio.

After I preached that night in a local church a man and his wife, members of the church, came up and said, "We heard your interview this afternoon on the radio and would like you to shake hands with number thirty-one who came to Christ and was delivered from that lifestyle."

A few weeks later I preached morning and evening in a great church in Sacramento. I used this story in my message, and after the evening service I noticed a couple in their late thirties waiting for me at the base of the stairs leading to the platform. He was holding a six-month-old sleeping infant, while a two-year-old held her hand. The wife said, "We want you to meet number thirty-two," so I shook hands with him, and they told me their story. He had been involved in the homosexual lifestyle since he was fifteen. Not until he was twenty-eight, thirteen years later, did he learn that God condemned that type of sexual expression and that the power of the gospel offered both a way of forgiveness and a way of escape. He received Christ as his Lord and Savior shortly thereafter. For four years he grew in the Lord through studying His Word, then fell in love with a single woman in the church. I met him at thirty-eight, a husband, father, and joyful Christian—ten years removed from the homosexual scene.

Very frankly, no one is helping homosexuals like that today! No religion, no therapy, no system of works—except the power of the cross.

Several times I have shared this story as I speak across the country. On most occasions I hear from former homosexuals who testify, "I am number thirty-five" or "thirty-nine" or one more than I had last mentioned. To date I am up to forty-eight men who have shaken my hand and identified themselves as delivered homosexuals. In every case it is the power of the cross that made the transformation possible.

One young man in Vermont identified himself as a former homosexual who read my book, *The Unhappy Gays,* and bowed before the cross to receive Christ. Now he is a youth evangelist. He says he has given ten thousand of those books to needy victims of that lifestyle.

THERE IS HOPE FOR HOMOSEXUALS

The power of Christ to transform homosexuals is living proof that conversion is a valid evidence of both God's existence and the reality of the Holy Spirit's power to transform even the hardest of harmful obsessions. One thrilling illustration is that of Anthony.

If there is such a thing as a typical homosexual, Anthony Falzarano fit the mold. He was raised in a New Jersey home where his father worked hard to support his seven children, but was psychologically absent. When Anthony was nine, a family member who had been molested by a local area merchant molested him. He was subsequently molested by a schoolteacher and by at least three other individuals. When he was sixteen years old he fell into the trap of a thirty-year-old attorney who would lure more impressionable teens into his home to have sex with them.

One year later, Anthony was introduced to the gay bars and, because of his youth and good looks, he became popular in the New York gay scene. He soon met the famous New York attorney, Roy Cohen. Roy Cohen was the attorney who represented Senator McCarthy during the Communist trials of the late 1950s. He also represented the Schubert and Nertherlander families, including the infamous Studio 54 discotheque. Anthony was involved with Roy for approximately two years. He introduced Tony to New York's high echelon gay scene that included some of the most famous political and influential leaders of the 1970s. It was a life of opulence and immorality. As Anthony looks back on this time in his life, he now realizes that the Lord Jesus Christ was calling him, and at the same time the devil was enticing and blinding him with the temporal pleasures of this world.

Anthony was nineteen years old at that time and had no idea of Mr. Cohn's notorious reputation. The Roy Cohn that he knew was always very kind and paternal to him. And, even though Anthony was offered the life of mansions, Greenwich, CT and Palm Beach, he felt very empty inside. Finally he decided to end his realtionship because he felt that his intentions with Roy were not honorable. Anthony really wanted a relationship with someone his own age, and this, he hoped, would fill the emptiness of his life. He was upfront with Roy and one night told him that he had to end their relationship because he was not in love with him. The very next morning, Roy Cohen's former boyfriend called Anthony and barked at him, "Are you crazy!…ending a relationship with Roy Cohn? I used him for years, and he gave me a Bently and a restaurant in Coral Gables, Florida!" Anthony felt sick to his stomach.

Although he knew he had opened Pandora's Box in entering the gay lifestyle, he knew he had a remnant of morals left, and he began to see the gay subculture for what it really was. However, he was so steeped in the lifestyle that he didn't think there would be a way out, due to his promiscuity. Anthony became, in his own words, "a sex addict." He estimates that he had sex with over four-hundred different sexual partners, always hoping that "Mr. Right" would be one of them.

Although raised Catholic, Anthony's knowledge of Scripture was not strong. His involvement in the gay subculture pushed him further and further away from the gospel, but he had Christ's message spoken to him directly in an extraordinary way. After having a clandestine rendezvous with someone he met through a personal ad, his "new friend" apologized for what he had just done. He admitted he was a backslidden Christian and said, "God doesn't want me to be gay!" And then he turned to Anthony, and said, "God doesn't want *you* to be gay, either." What the devil used for evil that night, God used for His glory. Anthony was open to hearing the truth about homsexuality. His friend Tyler then took out a Bible and began reading the Scriptures that pertain to homosexuality. That was the first time Anthony realized what God really said about being gay and that there was freedom from homosexuality through Jesus Christ. The verses he recalls from that experience are found in 1 Corinthians 6:9–11:

> Do you not know that the unrighteous will not inherit the kingdom of God? Do not be deceived. Neither fornicators, nor idolaters, nor adulterers, nor homosexuals, nor sodomites, nor thieves, nor covetous, nor drunkards, nor revilers, nor extortioners will inherit the kingdom of God. And such were some of you. But you were washed, but you were sanctified, but you were justified in the name of the Lord Jesus and by the Spirit of our God.

Shortly thereafter, Anthony left the gay lifestyle, got help from Exodus International, which is the largest ex-gay network in the world, and has now been out of the lifestyle for fourteen solid years. He is clean from sexual addiciton, pornography, masturbation and lust. Only the Blood of Jesus could have washed Anthony's red cloak as white as snow. He has now been married for fourteen years, and he and his wife, Dianne, have two wonderful children, Mary Victoria and Carter David. He currently directs a Christ-centered, Washington, DC, Exodus chapter called Transformation Christian Ministries, and is national director of P-FOX (parents & Friends of

Ex-Gays) a Christ-centered outreach to parents, siblings, and friends who have friends stuck in the gay lifestyle.

It may be hard for some Christians to accept that in the church at Corinth where Paul spent eighteen months teaching the Word, many of the believers and leaders were former homosexuals. The true church of Christ has always opposed homosexuality and offered conversion as a way out of any lifestyle. It remains so today. In fact, Christians, churches, and Christian ministries that specialize in reaching out to hurting homosexuals are helping thousands.

One of Anthony's burdens is that the church do a better job of reaching out to recovering gays. As a churchman myself, I am sure we could do more to help the many hurting people of this crazy, mixed-up world. The church must take a biblical stand against homosexuality, but we also need to offer more personal help to those who are trying to come out of that lifestyle. They need to be personally discipled in the Word by a godly man willing to make whatever time investment it takes to save another from that miserable life of sin. Some gays think the church is against them, when they ought to see it really is their friend and offers the only real help available today, the cross of Jesus. We need to be understanding of the deeply entrenched gays who struggle to come out of that addictive lifestyle.

Like overcoming any addiction, God deals with us as individuals. I have met alcoholics who met Christ at the cross and immediately lost all interest in alcohol, while others fought the craving every day of their lives. So it is with homosexuality. Some drop it at the foot of the cross and are rarely tempted again. Others struggle every day of their lives and sometimes fall. At such times the individual needs loving understanding and help. One thing the church ought to be famous for is forgiveness. All of us have been forgiven, not just once, but as our Lord told Peter, "seventy times seven." I have learned that it is possible to love the sinner while hating his sin. The challenge is to convince him that if he falls, you still love him. It is difficult for the church to take an inflexible stand against the practice, but still show love for and a willingness to forgive the sinner. But it is worth the try, for in so doing we can help a desperate soul live a new life in Christ.

Near the end of our conversation, Anthony told me he was planning to attend a conference the following weekend for ex-gays at Asbury College, where more than six hundred former homosexuals were expected to celebrate their victory in Christ. All have one thing in common: There was a time when they bent their knees before the cross of Jesus and said, "Yes, Jesus Christ, I will have You to rule over me." Today, the Holy Spirit enables them to take on a whole new way of life, just like Anthony who has been delivered from that lifestyle for over fourteen years. During those years he has helped many gays overcome their addiction, some who have married and raised families. But for all, even the man dying of AIDS resulting from his former promiscuity, there is the confidence that his sin can be forgiven and there is a better life to come. Like all sinners who come to the cross, there is hope for a better life—if not in this world, at least in the next.

FROM HOMOSEXUALITY TO SPIRITUAL THERAPIST

Joe Dallas is a husband of eleven years, a father of three, and professionally a Christian therapist who helps hundreds of sexually obsessed people each year, most of whom are homosexuals. Joe has not always been a Christian, or a heterosexual for that matter. There was a time when he was obsessed with promiscuous sex, heavy into pornography, and a practicing homosexual. He was seduced by a man when he was eight and as a teen embraced the idea of "gay sexual freedom" in the early seventies.

At sixteen Joe became a Christian and because of his musical talent (he plays the piano well), he became heavily involved in Christian ministry. During that time he took a "puritanical attitude toward sex" and gave it no place in his lifestyle. That attitude can only last so long, for God made us sexual creatures with a natural desire for sexual expression. He gave us marriage as His one legitimate means of expressing that desire.

At twenty-two Joe drifted back into homosexuality, and like many who travel that route, he became defiant and rebellious toward God. It is easy for any sexual sinner to blame society, the church, God or his cultivated homosexual desires for his sin. This opens up any individual to the wiles of the devil; such was the case with Joe. For six years he became sexually promiscuous, living with the manager of a gay bar while having an adulterous affair with the wife of a former friend. She became pregnant and aborted what would have been his first child. During that time he was miserable, twisted by wanting to live that lifestyle yet convicted by the Spirit of God that his activities were unscriptural and morally debased.

Joe's rebellion turned into deception the day he attended a "gay church." For the first time, he was formally taught to disregard the verses in the Bible that condemned homosexuality. Instead, he was taught that a monogamous gay relationship was all right. Adultery, drugs, alcoholism, pornography, and promiscuity were wrong, but the homosexual and lesbian lifestyles were all right. As he looked around at the audience, he was impressed that they sang the same evangelical tunes he was familiar with, observed communion, yet openly paired off with partners of the same sex. He did have a problem with the way they overlooked any Scripture that didn't agree with their theology, even to suggesting that there were only two commandments, "Love God and love one another." [Note how easily such thoughts do away with, "thou shalt not commit adultery" and the seven other commandments. But who can see that when desperately trying to justify a behavior that Scripture so plainly and roundly condemns?]

For six years Joe tried to live the "gay Christian" life, but never enjoyed peace with God. Somewhere in his background he had been taught that it was imperative that all teaching should be tested by Scripture. If the Bible condemned the behavior—as Romans 1 certainly does condemn homosexuality—it was wrong. Gradually the voice of God from within was preparing him for that special night in 1984 when he turned on Christian TV and heard Chuck Girard share his personal testimony. Although Chuck's sin had not been homosexuality, Joe was captivated by how Chuck had come to the cross and acknowledged his sin. Joe was impressed with how Chuck did not try to excuse his behavior or blame someone else for it, but admitted to both God and man that he was a sinner

in need of forgiveness. He received that forgiveness and became a
new person.

The thought burned in Joe's heart, "If I've been wrong in my
acceptance of the homosexual lifestyle, the Bible will show me."
He got out an old Bible and looked up all the verses on homosexuality and he recalls, "It was as if scales literally fell off my eyes and I
saw what God said about it. I then saw a trail of devastation in that
lifestyle. It plunged me into a deep depression that lasted about a
month." Finally, Joe visited a strong Bible-teaching church in his
area where he once again saw that God specializes in forgiving sinners, no matter how deep their sin. What His Son did on Calvary's
cross was to cover the sins of all who would call upon Him.

This time when an adult Joe was willing to face his sin and
surrender all to Him who died on that cross, his life changed. Not
only did he gain forgiveness and the inner power of God, but the
men of his church surrounded him with love—a pure love not for
anything he could do for them, but a love just because he was one
of them, a man who had sinned and brought that sin to the cross
of Christ. Their genuine Christian love had a profound effect on
his spiritual growth during the next years of his life.

One year later Joe met Renee. On their second date he told her
all about his past, because as he said, "I could see this is a woman I
could fall in love with." They decided to go slow in building a
Christian relationship—which they did, one and a half years of
dating before becoming engaged, and another year and a half
before they were married. Today they enjoy a beautiful love relationship and three children.

During that time Joe took special training to become a
Christian therapist so he could help troubled individuals escape
from the sexual permissiveness of our day. He founded Genesis
Counseling, a ministry that has helped hundreds of people come
out of all kinds of addictions: to pornography, drugs and marijuana,
alcoholism, compulsive smoking, and homosexuality. In fact, Joe
has seen "over three hundred homosexuals come out of that
lifestyle." His ministry has been written up favorably (because he
has helped so many people) by the *Los Angeles Times* and several

other periodicals, both secular and Christian.

It should be noted that Joe's "treatment" begins with introducing addicts to the cross, which alone has the power to save and transform anyone who will bend their knee to the Christ of that cross.

Joe's peers have shown their approval of his ministry by electing him president, for three years, of Exodus International. All eighty chapters throughout this country and in several foreign countries specialize in helping homosexuals come out of that lifestyle—and like Joe, they begin their therapy at the foot of the cross. Joe has written three books, *Desires in Conflict, Unforgiven Sins*, and his most recent, *A Strong Delusion*. Like so many men and women who bow at the cross of Jesus, Joe Dallas got up to give his life in his Savior's service and has spent it helping others experience that power to break their addiction.

A HOMOSEXUAL AND THE POWER OF THE CROSS

Pastor Jack Hayford is not only the much-loved pastor of the booming Church on the Way in Los Angeles, he is also appreciated as a TV and radio preacher known for his in-depth teaching ministry. Recently, he presided as emcee over the Promise Keepers "Stand in the Gap" prayer gathering in Washington, D.C., which was attended by well over a million men and was reported as the happiest rally of any kind in the nation's capital. In addition, he has written more than five hundred hymns and songs. He is particularly known worldwide as the author of "Majesty," one of the most popular hymns enjoyed by churches of all denominations. "Dr. Jack," as he is known affectionately by his congregation, tells the following incredible story of a transformed homosexual who proved by his changed life the reality of his conversion experience.

I'll call him Charles—and I was first introduced to him when he wrote me a letter of testimony. He wasn't in any way trying to impress me, but he simply wanted to tell me about an important growth point in his life. Along with the letter, he included a check; he was excited to explain that it was the first time in his life he had ever tithed, and he was especially happy about this early step of discipleship.

However, it was because of another thing he mentioned in his letter that I contacted him. I asked him to stop by and see me between Sunday morning services, noting that we would have only about ten minutes to talk. It was clear that Charles was a young disciple who needed affirmation and encouragement, and his letter had made a valuable point that I felt deserved reinforcement.

He had explained how, about eighteen months previously, he had come to Jesus Christ as his Savior and Lord. Although he had been very deeply involved in a homosexual lifestyle, he had sensed this was wrong but was still no less caught in the grip of his weakness. His conviction that he needed to change was not the result of anyone's pounding into him a religious agenda, a mandate to submission, or his having received a forceful persuasion that homosexuality was a distortion of his created identity. But the Holy Spirit had simply brought Charles to understand that he was confused about his true person, and that he needed God.

Shortly after he received the Lord, Charles began seeking to establish his life in Christ and to search for a church to attend. In his letter to me, he explained the struggles he had faced in doing so. First, there was his own challenge to continue in his walk with the Lord. The only friends he had at that time were the ones from his homosexual lifestyle. Not only had he realized he needed to move out of that environment, but as soon as they knew of his commitment to Christ, they had completely rejected him anyway.

At the same time, as he looked for a church in hope of finding a haven of strength as a new disciple of Jesus and a home for fellowship with new friends and a family of faith, he encountered an incredible series of additional painful and vicious rejections. Although he earnestly sought a place of continuing worship, everywhere he visited he was dismayed as, over and over, he heard unkind and often hateful remarks about homosexuals—even though he had not told anyone he had come out of that background. Having met Charles, I could see by his appearance and demeanor that no one would have suspected his past orientation, so his observations were clearly not born of situations where he might have been a precipitating factor in prompting the negativism and lovelessness which so grieved him. His grief was not due to any misguided sense of duty to defend the lifestyle he had forsaken, but of his sense of the said violation such attitude revealed of the gentle love of God that had found and forgiven him, and saved his soul.

As he continued his story, he said, "Pastor Hayford, I simply couldn't find a place to be, but it was during that time of searching that I found The Church on the Way. It was here that I did find a place where the love of God and the holiness of God were preached side by side. It was the answer to my deepest hopes, that there could be a place where there was as great a love for lost people as for the Lord Jesus Christ—and I began to grow." It was then that he referred to the tithe check he had mailed, which he indicated was, for him and in light of his own economic as well as moral past, a sign of that growth and of his will to walk in the way of the Lord in every respect.

To my view, Charles stands as a classic "today" evidence of the power of the cross to change the human personality. But it isn't only because of the story so far, by reason of the fact a man was delivered from a disoriented view of his true sexual identity, to becoming a tithe-paying member of the church. Beyond that evidence of the cross at work, in Charles' case I have been most deeply moved with a "follow-through" episode in his life in Christ.

About six months ago, the man who was formerly Charles' "lover" suddenly was overcome by the advance of the HIV virus in his system, and moved into the vicious, climactic phase of AIDS working its ravages on the human body. For some reason, former friends had little interest or time for the man now, and Charles—though out of touch for some time—heard about his situation. Knowing that his former friend had no help or support and needed someone to care, he realized he could not be indifferent and be a true follower of the Lord Jesus. So Charles, being a healthcare professional, went to see the now-dying man who had formerly been his partner in sin.

When his friend opened the door, the man was completely disarmed—at first, appearing irritated, then more patiently but brusquely asking Charles why he had come. Charles simply replied that he had come to take care of him. And that's what he did. For the ensuing weeks, day after day following his demanding schedule at work, Charles made professional visits to his friend; washing the body of the near-helpless man, treating his abscessed sores, cooking meals, then helping feed him, and also providing simple care for the condition of the man's apartment. Of course, he always maintained his own standard of holiness in Jesus Christ, while giving himself to show God's love— even at the risk of exposing himself to an infectious environment.

During these weeks of voluntary care for a dying homosexual, Charles did not once speak a word to the man about Jesus. His friend already knew fully well where Charles stood, and Charles believed all he was to do was care for him and let his love through Christ speak to the man.

One of my most unforgettably moving conversations of recent date was the day Charles came to my office and said, "Pastor Jack, I am so overwhelmed—I need to tell you something." He proceeded to describe how, just the week before, and after over three months of the above mentioned care having been given, his friend looked up at him one day as Charles—with purity of motive and method—washed the foulness from his body. He said: "Charles, I have watched the way you have cared for me with the love of God during this time. Now I know what you have is real. Even though I mocked and rejected you when you received Him, I know that I need Jesus just like you know Him. Will you pray with me and show me how to come to know Jesus Christ too—today?"

With tears, Charles related to me how he led the man to Christ; amazed at the degree of God's grace shown to him, to not only be saved from a past of confusion but to be a redemptive instrument in recovering another with whom he had lived out that confusion. "Pastor, I didn't have any idea the Lord would let me be an instrument of seeing him saved. I felt so unworthy because of my past sin, but I knew I had to at least show the love of Jesus."

It was only a month later his friend was buried. But it is in that ruined life, now forever saved, that it seems to me the most glorious, yet humble expression of Charles' testimony, new life and practical witness reveals the power of the gospel. In this account lies a primary feature of the power of Calvary that is sometimes overlooked. You see, when Charles set out to help his friend, facing the risk of rejection and the risk of infection, he moved onto Calvary ground. He moved beyond being a follower of Jesus who cares about the things of Christ, a person who was willing to lay down his life for Christ. He came to minister—to simply serve, in Jesus' name. No platitudes, no posturing, no preachments. He simply gave himself in the interest of another, with no knowledge of the miracle God would work through him.

Thus we are reminded again: The power of the cross multiplies itself in kind. It lies not so much in greatness or might of human action, for it is characterized in weakness as man sees it (1 Corinthians 1:21–25). But in the laying down of our lives to serve and care for others, in the same way the power of the Holy Spirit replicated the loving life of Christ through Charles, we see a picture of the life-changing, cross-power of God to be received in all our lives.

There is a glory in the cross of Calvary, waiting to be released every day through you and me as we allow ourselves—beyond obstacles, in spite of rejection—to be instruments of the love of God as it is revealed in the abiding, transforming, life-giving power of the cross.

CHAPTER FIFTEEN

EVEN GUILT FALLS
BEFORE THE CROSS

J ohn Bunyan, in his classic allegory *Pilgrim's Progress,* written in 1681 and still one of the best loved books of all time, portrayed his hero climbing a long and arduous hill with a great pack on his back. Many were the temptations and digressions that con-fronted him, but Pilgrim continued his climb. The further he went in the heat of the day, the bigger and heavier his pack became.

At the top of the hill he saw hope—a beautiful cross with a tomb nearby:

> Now I saw in my dream, that the highway up which Christian (or Pilgrim) was to go, was fenced on either side with a wall, and that wall is called Salvation. Up this way therefore, did burdened Christian run, but not without great difficulty, because of the load on his back.
>
> He ran thus till he came at a place somewhat ascending; and upon that place stood a Cross, and a little below, in the bottom, a Sepulcher. So I saw in my dream, that just as Christian came up to the Cross, his burden loosed from off his shoulders, and fell from off his back, and began to tumble, and so continued to do, till it came into the mouth of the sepulcher, where it fell in, and I saw it no more.

Then was Christian glad and lightsome, and said with a merry heart, *He hath given me rest by his sorrow, and life by his death.* Then he stood still awhile to look and wonder, for it was very surprising to him, that the sight of the Cross should thus ease him of his burden. He looked therefore, and looked again, even till the springs that were in his head sent the waters down his cheeks. Now as he stood looking and weeping, behold three Shining Ones came to him, and saluted him with, "Peace be to thee"; so the first said to him, "Thy sins be forgiven;" the second stripped him of his rags and clothed him with change of raiment; the third also set a mark in his forehead, and gave him a roll with a seal upon it, which he bid him look on as he ran, and that he should give it in at the celestial gate. So they went their way…. Then Christian (Pilgrim) gave three leaps for joy, and went on singing:

> Thus far did I come laden with my sin;
> Nor could aught ease the grief that I was in,
> Till I came hither: What a place is this!
> Must here be the beginning of my bliss?
> Must here must the burden fall from off my back?
> Must here the strings that bound it to me crack?
> Blest Cross! Blest Sepulcher! Blest rather be
> The Man that there was put to shame for me![1]

This short passage, dealing with one of the most important issues of life—sinful man bowing before the cross and losing the burden and guilt of his sins—helps us understand why this marvelous, three-century-old allegory is still a popular book. It is based on truth, the truth of Scripture. When pilgrims find their way to the cross—usually heavily burdened with the guilt of their sins before God—they are instantly forgiven and cleansed of all unrighteousness.

The elation that Pilgrim felt as soon as he became a Christian is not unusual. I felt the same thing, and many people I have prayed with have responded with "I feel so much better!" Some ill-advised souls have responded to such a feeling by saying, "I know now that I am a Christian because I feel so much better," but that "feeling" is no guarantee we are saved. Salvation is guaranteed by the Scriptures, not by any feeling, however grand.

But we all know what such a person means; he suddenly has a new "peace with God," described in Romans 5:1. "Therefore, having been justified by faith, we have peace with God through our Lord Jesus Christ." The word *justified* has been simplified by breaking it down to the sound-alike, "just-as-if-I'd never sinned." By faith in the sacrifice of Christ on the cross and His resurrection from the dead, we have "peace with God." That is what fills us with joy—or in Pilgrim's case, the feeling of elation. Usually, the greater the extent of our sin, the more guilt we experience, and consequently the greater our elation after we have been forgiven at the cross.

As you may remember the story, this salvation experience didn't solve all of Pilgrim's problems. But by becoming a Christian at Calvary, he started on the road to victory and a new life. So it is for everyone. First, sins must be forgiven by the grace of God; then we enjoy peace with God because the guilt of our sins has been cleansed by His blood; then the power of the cross to begin living a transformed life is made available to us through His indwelling Holy Spirit. It all begins at the foot of the cross when the "pilgrim" on the journey of life cries out "Yes! Jesus Christ, I will have You become my Savior and Lord!"

GUILT, THE OLDEST RESULT OF SIN

The first sin in the human race was committed by Adam and Eve when they rebelled against God and ate of the forbidden tree. That evening when God came to the couple in the Garden, they were afraid and hid themselves from His presence. They had previously enjoyed uninhibited fellowship with God, but immediately after their sin they became afraid of God. When God asked where Adam was, he admitted "I was afraid" (Genesis 3:10). Sin always separates man from God because it makes him afraid of God. Unless he seeks forgiveness at the cross like Bunyan's Pilgrim, man usually becomes rebellious and angry at God, much like Cain in Genesis 4 after being confronted with his murder. Rebellion leads to even greater sin, followed by more fear and guilt. In fact, in several places in the Bible, "sin" and "guilt" are used interchangeably because they are so closely related.

Adam's fear is a universal follow-up to man's sin. It results from our conscience built into us at birth, one of the sure signs we are human beings. Some people, like Cain, turn to a lifetime of rebellion due to the guilt of their sin. God has only one means of forgiving sin, the shedding of sin, for as the Scripture says, "Without the shedding of blood there is no forgiveness" (Hebrews 9:22, NIV).

The Bible provides a short course in forgiveness, using many illustrations. In the Garden it was the blood of a lamb which God Himself shed to cover the nakedness of Adam and Eve. Cain and Abel were commanded to offer a lamb sacrifice; Abel did, while Cain refused. Instead, he brought the best of his produce, a sacrifice which God refused. From then on through the Old Testament, sin was covered only by the shedding of the blood of a spotless lamb, in anticipation of the cross when God sent His only begotten Son. From then on, guilty sinners by the millions have had their sins forgiven by looking back in faith to that cross and saying in their heart, "Yes, Jesus Christ, it was for me You died."

For two thousand years there has been no further need for a blood sacrifice, because "Jesus paid it all" on the cross. He died "for the sins of the whole world." As the writer of Hebrews so beautifully put it:

> But Christ came as High Priest of the good things to come, with the greater and more perfect tabernacle not made with hands, that is, not of this creation. Not with the blood of goats and calves, but with His own blood He entered the Most Holy Place once for all, having obtained eternal redemption. For if the blood of bulls and goats and the ashes of a heifer, sprinkling the unclean, sanctifies for the purifying of the flesh, how much more shall the blood of Christ, who through the eternal Spirit offered Himself

without spot to God, purge your conscience from dead works to serve the living God? And for this reason He is the Mediator of the new covenant, by means of death, for the redemption of the transgressions under the first covenant, that those who are called may receive the promise of the eternal inheritance. (9:11–15)

The salvation that results when "Pilgrims of life" come to the cross is first shown when the burden of their guilt is lifted. That is what produces the "feeling of peace with God." At last the war is over; we can again enjoy fellowship with God because of the sacrifice of His Son Jesus!

AFTER THE CHOICE—GUILT

Concerned Women for America produced a powerful video of sixteen women giving their personal testimony after having an abortion. They ranged over all ages—one looked too young even to get pregnant, another could have been the girl's grandmother. Each told her own story, some with gruesome details about the pain and suffering she endured. One compared the vacuum-like sucking sound of the abortion "to a jet on takeoff." All reported the aftermath of guilt they suffered because they "had destroyed my baby." Or as one said, "I would never think of taking another person's life, but by having an abortion I have killed my own baby! This act haunts me every day of my life." One woman reported that her abortion had taken place thirty years before, yet it still troubled her.

I couldn't help surmise, since there was no ring on her finger and no mention of other children, that this latter guilt-ridden woman never escaped the consequences of her act; and now, at a time in life when she needed a life companion, she could not trust herself to build such a relationship. What a price to pay for guilt! But frankly, such a story is not unusual.

THE TYRANNY OF GUILT

As a counselor for many years, I have dealt with scores of people, both men and women, who have suffered the tyranny of guilt.

Nothing seems to create more guilt than taking another person's life, including aborting one's own child. I saw this several years ago when my wife introduced her first video on abortion at a CWA convention for about twelve hundred women in the nation's capital. We were not prepared for the reaction. Thirty-seven women rushed weeping from the room during the video. I happened to be in the back of the auditorium and as a pastor/counselor for so many years, I tried to comfort some of these women. It was overwhelming! The video had stirred up guilt-producing memories that were too much for these women to handle.

Several of these women needed to be introduced to the Savior and kneel at His cross by faith and seek His forgiveness and salvation. Others, who had already done that, needed to be reminded that God remembers our sin against us no more and that "as far as the east is from the west, so far has He removed our transgressions from us" (Psalm 103:12). I have found that some forgiven people have a difficult time accepting God's forgiveness, not a surprising discovery when it's clear they have trouble forgiving themselves.

"MAN'S WISDOM" HAS NO ANSWER

My first contact with electroshock therapy was an unhappy experience for everyone involved. I was only twenty-three and the pastor of a small country church. I was still in college and hadn't taken any counseling training yet. Like most people at that time, I assumed that psychiatrists, who are medical doctors, knew what they were doing when they put electrodes on a young woman's head and gave her such an electric shock it sent her into convulsions. The young woman's parents were deeply concerned at the near comatose condition in which this treatment left their daughter, yet they had to watch her go through a series of thirty such treatments. When she returned home, she was a zombie for months. Even after she recuperated, she exhibited telltale signs of her ordeal that may have lasted her entire life.

At eighteen years of age this young, unmarried woman had an abortion rather than face an unwanted pregnancy without a husband. The guilt was more than she could bear, and her behavior became so bizarre her family doctor thought she was losing her mind. Instead of sending her to the church or her pastor (after all, what do *they* know?), he sent her to a psychiatrist. He recognized her "guilt neurosis" and prescribed shock therapy. Somehow he was able to find out generally where that part of her memory bank was located and obliterated it with inhumane doses of electricity. (Today they have discovered that ECT, as it is called, is not as effective as they originally thought; it is now used only as a last resort. They also have found it is just as effective to use much weaker doses of electricity, so the convulsions, which are still severe, are not nearly as bad as they were four decades ago.) What he in fact accomplished was to blot out her memory of everything that happened in the last few years of her life—her promiscuity, her pregnancy, and her abortion included. She could remember them no more.

Unfortunately, the family did not ask for spiritual therapy, and I was so young I didn't push myself into the scene, though she had already been committed to the sanitorium before I heard about it. But I still believe if that young woman (whose parents came to faith in Christ late in her teen years) had been confronted lovingly with the cross of Jesus, where her sin could be faced and confessed, she may have been able to escape the tragic results of too much electroshock therapy in the hands of a secularist. For the two years I was this family's pastor, the girl was never herself, according to her parents. Years later I heard that her memory returned, albeit with "gaps."

The same thing happened to a young woman in my second church where the daughter of an active Christian family was spirited off to a sanitorium due to "depression." She also received thirty shock treatments that changed her personality and blotted out part of her memory. I now realize that this very sensitive, perfectionistic young woman (of a predominantly melancholy temperament) couldn't handle the guilt accompanying an affair she had at the age of nineteen. Like so many such cases, once the boy used her, he dropped her, and she was plunged into a depression that her parents thought required treatment by a psychiatrist.

Experiences like these probably are what God used in challenging me to major in pastoral counseling in graduate school, and helped point me to a lifetime of counseling people both personally and through several of my books.

In cases of depression caused by guilt, a better remedy than shock treatment is to bring a person by faith to the foot of the cross to seek the forgiveness of sin. There is no sin known to man that God will not forgive if we will confess it to Him and accept the shed blood of Christ as our means of cleansing.

A CASE IN POINT

Karen was an active member of our growing congregation whose first counseling encounter really frightened me. "Ten years ago I had thirty shock treatments which lasted five years," she said. "Then I had thirty more. Lately I find myself descending into that same syndrome." Through hot tears she said, "I don't want to go in for more shock therapy."

As I looked at this attractive woman in her midforties, I noted immediately her melancholy, perfectionistic temperament. She had been raised in a minister's home and had been a dedicated Christian most of her life. She married an unsaved man whom she was instrumental in later leading to Christ, and he became quite an outstanding witness in our city. Like many Christian husbands who get too involved, he grew apart from his wife. Somehow I felt inclined to ask her, "Is there some sin in your life you have never shared with anyone?" Suddenly she burst into tears. Finally she acknowledged having an affair with a man on two occasions some twelve years before. As she walked down memory lane, it was obvious that her sin totally controlled her thoughts. Within two years of her affair she was so depressed she had to seek therapy. The shock treatments worked for five years, then she had to have another set—and now their effects were wearing off.

I will never forget Karen's response to my question, "Have you ever confessed that sin to God?" She replied, "At least a thousand times!" My first response was, "Karen, that is 999 times too many." And biblically it was. Yet any conscientious person will admit that sins which really trouble us seem easier for God to forgive than for us to do so.

Just to make sure Karen understood, I explained the gospel message and invited her to kneel with me and pray one last time, acknowledging to God in my presence what she had prayed so many times before. In some cases, it is better for the person to confess in the presence of a counselor, although it is not essential. In her case, I thought it was. Then I gave her two assignments. First, she was to do a Bible study on forgiveness. I showed her how to look up all the verses on forgiveness in a concordance and write them on a yellow pad. Then I asked her to reduce this list to a single page, teaching her personally what God Himself said about forgiveness. This is good therapy for any Christian! Then I assigned her the task of thanking God every day for His forgiveness and instructed her to refuse to ask for forgiveness again, because she already had received it. When she asked "What should I do each time I remember my sin?" I said, "Thank God on the basis of 1 John 1:9 for His forgiveness."

During her second interview Karen told me that for the first week, she had to open her Bible to 1 John 1:9, put her finger on the text, and pray, "Thank you, dear Lord, that on the basis of this verse you have already forgiven me of my sin." As deeply ingrained as her guilt was, I could understand that. Gradually, she could by faith simply thank God for His grace and forgiveness. The more she thanked Him for that past forgiveness, the more her guilt faded and her depression lifted.

I am happy to say that I pastored Karen and her husband for at least ten more years. I saw their son go into the ministry and their daughter marry a fine Christian young man. She never again saw a psychiatrist and never again had to undergo shock therapy. The power of the cross did it again! The power of forgiveness that she finally appropriated gave her twenty years of victory over guilt. Why? Because she finally accepted the fact that her sins were cleansed by His blood and that "He washed them white as snow." Today she is in heaven, enjoying the reality that was hers on earth for twenty years.

CARMEN'S STORY

As I looked at Carmen, the strikingly attractive vice president of communications for Concerned Women for America, I could hardly believe her story. Raised in a nonchurched family in a small Arkansas town, nevertheless her parents dropped her off faithfully every week at Sunday school. Though she dreamed of her parents accompanying her to church and of sitting down as a family and reading the large family Bible her mother had purchased from a door-to-door salesman, her dreams never materialized.

Following the steps that many of her peers had taken, Carmen walked the aisle of her church to acknowledge that she believed in Christ and was baptized. During her teen years she became active in choir and other church-related youth activities. Though she learned what "good girls" should and shouldn't do, and though in fact she remained a virgin throughout high school, she was never discipled in the Word of God. She knew the simple gospel message, but Christ had never been honored as Lord of her life.

Even today Carmen remembers making the deliberate choice to abandon her virtue and to engage in sex with a boy she was dating after her high-school graduation. After only one sexual encounter, she became pregnant. Because she had worked so hard for the college scholarship she had received, Carmen moved ahead with college plans as though nothing had changed in her life. It wasn't until the seventh month of her pregnancy, during a rare trip home from school, that she had a tearful confrontation with her parents regarding her condition. As was the general practice in the early 1970s, Carmen and the father of the baby were encouraged to "do the right thing" in a bad situation and they were married, even though they did not love each other.

Their marriage is a textbook case of near impossibility. They were both angry because they had to drop out of college; he had to take a menial job to support his wife and child and seldom joined her in church. Three years later, a second son was born. Feeling trapped and prompted by selfish motives, Carmen left her husband, filed for divorce, and moved to Houston, Texas.

Lonely and insecure, she and her two boys moved in with a man of questionable character. Hoping to reconcile differences with her parents over her living situation, and still stung by the guilt of her divorce, Carmen married the man. He moved his three children from a previous marriage into their home, and she found herself a mom of five at age twenty-five. Four years later, the marriage ended when her husband left her for another woman.

As a two-time marital loser, Carmen felt worthless on a personal level, even though she was doing well in her career as a customer service manager in a major supermarket chain. Corporate executives saw her obvious talents and began promoting her up the corporate ladder. That is when she made another bad decision: "to make it big in the corporate world." Carmen took every course and every opportunity the company provided until she became Director of Public Affairs over a two-state area. Finally she had it all—the designer clothes, the big salary, the beautiful house and the flashy sports car—but she didn't have God, nor did she have a good feeling about herself. She says now that during those days, she turned the raising of her boys over to baby-sitters and child-care centers while she lived in the fast lane.

During this time she developed a bitterness toward men. Much of her life was miserable due to men, she thought, so she decided to use them as they had used her. Carmen was promiscuous during those years, joined the feminist movement, and had two abortions. When her eleven-year-old son, Jason, chose to go live with his father, God gave her a wake-up call.

She was depressed in her lifestyle, particularly in relation to her boys, and far away from God. That is when she received Jesus Christ as her Lord and Savior, a life-changing experience. In the midst of her despair, she reached back to what she had learned in Sunday school as a child, and all alone called out to God for a second chance. Somehow she knew that the Bible could help her. After finding one and not knowing where to turn, she simply opened it down the middle and began reading the fifty-first Psalm. God used the words of King David, as he cried out to God after his adultery and sin, to help lead Carmen to Himself:

Have mercy upon me, O God, according to Your lovingkindness; according to the multitude of Your tender
mercies, blot out my transgressions. Wash me thoroughly
from my iniquity, and cleanse me from my sin. For I
acknowledge my transgressions, and my sin is ever before
me. Against You, You only, have I sinned, and done this evil
in Your sight—that You may be found just when You speak,
and blameless when You judge. Behold, I was brought forth
in iniquity, and in sin my mother conceived me. Behold,
You desire truth in the inward parts, and in the hidden part
You will make me to know wisdom. Purge me with hyssop,
and I shall be clean; wash me, and I shall be whiter than
snow. Make me to hear joy and gladness, that the bones
which You have broken may rejoice. Hide Your face from
my sins, and blot out all my iniquities. Create in me a clean
heart, O God, and renew a steadfast spirit within me. Do
not cast me away from Your presence, and do not take Your
Holy Spirit from me. Restore to me the joy of Your salvation, and uphold me with Your generous Spirit. Then I will
teach transgressors Your ways, and sinners shall be converted to You. Deliver me from bloodguiltiness, O God, the
God of my salvation, and my tongue shall sing aloud of
Your righteousness. O Lord, open my lips, and my mouth
shall show forth Your praise. (51:1–15)

Carmen knew that Jesus died on the cross for her sins and the
sins of the whole world. That night she surrendered her past, her
present, her future, and her children to Him—and was forgiven,
just as He promised. Even before she got up off her knees, she
sensed the sweet peace of God and remembers the incredible
peace that flooded her soul. "I slept like a baby that night for the
first time in months," she shared. Not an uncommon experience
for sinners who experience sins forgiven!

Carmen has never been the same since that night! The very
next day she called the man she was dating and said, "I don't think
we should see each other again. I have found God, and I'm going

to get my life right!" And she never saw him again. For a long time she did not date, but devoted herself to her younger son and to growing in her new faith. She had a hunger for God and His Word and found a church home, but she had no one to disciple her personally, so growth was slow.

Finally she began to ask God to bring a man into her life with whom she could grow spiritually. During that time she was faithful in taking her son Joshua to his Little League baseball games. It was here that God chose for Carmen to meet Bob. As only God could plan it, Bob's daughter, Holly, from a marriage that had ended years before, was the only girl on Joshua's team!

At first, Bob and Carmen's only contact was at the games where they talked about their kids, their work, and their lives outside of baseball. It wasn't until after baseball season had ended that Bob invited Carmen to lunch and encouraged her to attend church with him. It seems he had been praying for a godly woman who could share his new commitment to Christ. When she told him where she and Josh attended church, he said, "That's where Holly and I go to church!" Different service times had kept them apart.

Their first lunch date actually scared them both. They found they had so much in common and enjoyed each other's company so much, Bob didn't ask her out again for six months. Carmen, being the perfect lady she now is, refused to call Bob. Then one evening when she was jogging, who should jog up to her but Bob? He said, between puffs, "I've been thinking of calling you to go to dinner." She accepted and they began a courtship that lasted until they were married, about a year later. Bob's daughter came to live with them and Carmen's older son, Jason, returned home to her.

Soon after their marriage they began attending the Oak Ridge Baptist Church in Houston, where Dr. Gordon Suddeth, an excellent Bible teacher, is the pastor. Their first Sunday there was "Sanctity of Human Life Sunday," and Carmen wept all through the service. For the first time, she saw her abortions as the great sin they really were. Fortunately, she also saw that God has made provision for any sin to be forgiven, even the taking of unborn life.

That day she gave not only her sin to God, but also her life to help those going through crisis pregnancies.

After praying for an opportunity to serve, she was asked to become director of a local crisis pregnancy center. The only problem was, they couldn't guarantee a salary. Bob had just started a new business, and they had been depending on Carmen's salary to make ends meet. They prayed together and decided she would leave her seventeen-year corporate job and its seeming security to step out on faith and serve the Lord.

During that time Carmen was invited to speak on many high-school campuses, where she challenged young girls to "say no to sex outside of marriage" and to "remain pure for the man you will marry someday." One feature of her talks described how to say no without offending, and still mean it. The response from the kids was so tremendous this became one of her favorite aspects of the ministry.

As Bob and Carmen grew spiritually, they agreed to make themselves available to God, no matter when or where he called them. Knowing Carmen's heart for women, Bob signed her up as a member of Concerned Women for America. When the first issue of *Family Voice Magazine* came from CWA, Carmen saw the only job advertisement that CWA has ever placed. The ministry was in search of a vice president of communications. Bob agreed that she should inquire about the position. After comparing the job description with her resumé, Bob said, "You have the exact qualifications they are looking for!"

The Lord truly "restores what the locusts have eaten," for today Carmen enjoys a rich and full marriage, close relationships with her children, and is doing what she wants to do most. She is serving Jesus Christ in her home, her church, and across America, standing for His truth and righteousness. And she loves it!

YOUNG PEOPLE SUFFER GUILT TOO

Pastor Gareld Murphy, my son-in-law, was on my staff when I pastored in San Diego. During that time he led hundreds of young people to Christ and helped hundreds of other high schoolers to find God's will for their lives. Many are in the gospel ministry today.

Recently he told me that he just married one of "his" girls, Susan (not her real name), to a dedicated youth pastor. The two of them have a bright future ahead as they begin a lifetime together serving the Lord.

That brought back memories of the night he invited thirty high-school students into his home for me to interview when I was writing my book, *Against the Tide: How to Raise Virtuous Kids in an Anything Goes World.* I wanted to hear real young people share where they were in the sexual jungle they lived in every day. We omitted interviews with young people from our Christian school so we could concentrate on the needs of public schoolers.

When we broached the subject of teenage sexual activity and virtue, Susan, who was seventeen at the time and had been a Christian only for a few months, surprised everyone by bursting into tears. When she finally regained control, she told us that she was not a virgin. "I was not raised in a Christian home. In fact, my mother had different men in our home all the time. When I was fifteen she was more concerned with my becoming pregnant than she was with my remaining a virgin. She told me it was OK to have sex, just make sure you always use a condom. As a result, I am no longer a virgin. But now that I am a Christian, I don't live that way anymore." Then, through more tears, she blurted out what really troubled her: "Now I realize I will not be a virgin on my wedding night."

Susan's obvious pain provided a wonderful teaching experience for the rest of the group. Any kids who might secretly be thinking about becoming sexually active were suddenly brought face to face with the reality that virtue is a priceless treasure. Once lost, it can never be reclaimed. Contrary to the thinking of this world, virtue *is* important.

Pastor "Murph," as the kids called him, pointed out to Susan and the other young people present that all those experiences were nailed to the cross of Jesus. They represented the life of Susan before Christ, but now she was a new creature in Him.

Consequently, by keeping herself pure from this point on, she could experience what we call "secondary virginity." That is, she could practice chastity from salvation until marriage.

During the time Susan attended the youth group, she grew by leaps and bounds and put dating on a back burner in her life. She graduated from high school and attended a four-year Christian college, where she met the man of her dreams, a young man totally committed to serving God the rest of his life. Susan, too, had gone to that school so she could learn how best to serve the Lord. (Personally, I have found the best foundation for a lasting and happy marriage is when the two young people have already made a commitment to serve God before they ever meet each other.)

Ultimately, the day she dreaded most finally came. She had to tell this wonderful ministerial student, who had been raised in a Christian home and had kept himself sexually pure all his life, about her pre-Christian life. By that time, however, he loved Susan, knew who she was in Christ, and knew she was the one God had selected to be his wife. If God could forgive Susan, and He certainly did, then he could, too, for she had acted in unbelief and in ignorance of God's moral standards. He loved and admired the woman he had come to know, and today she is his wife.

When they walked down the aisle to the altar where Pastor Murph married them, they committed themselves to God and each other "for as long as they both shall live." I treasure the thought of the guilt-ridden and weeping teenager who had been transformed at the cross, now becoming the wife of a minister, a young man mature enough to see she was a new creature in Christ Jesus. Together they will help hundreds of young people avoid that misery-producing lifestyle.

That picture of Susan and her young husband at the altar is a beautiful picture of the power of the cross! Guilt is strong, but not nearly as mighty as the cross of Christ. Jesus is Lord over all—and that includes guilt too.

CHAPTER SIXTEEN

A
MULTICULTURAL
PHENOMENON

The life transformation of those who bend their knees to the cross of Jesus is not a cultural or ethnic phenomenon, but a universal one. We see this principle already at work in the New Testament. Paul, for example, was a Jew steeped in Jewish teachings and traditions, while Dr. Luke was a Greek thoroughly trained in the medical science and philosophy of his day. Add the Romans and Galatians, Egyptians and other Europeans mentioned in the Bible, and you have many graphic illustrations of a variety of ethnic peoples transformed by the power of the cross. Among them were slaves, soldiers, merchants, and all manner of occupations, races, and backgrounds. All came away from the cross as transformed people.

And it's still happening today.

NEW GUINEA HEADHUNTERS

Dr. Henry Brandt, a dedicated Christian psychologist, has traveled the world teaching biblical principles to people on almost every continent of the world from almost every imaginable cultural background. Just after returning from a trip to New Guinea, he told me of the remarkable transformation of formerly naked headhunters deep in the jungles. For centuries it was unsafe for white men to be seen by these people. Even the government was so afraid of contacting them that it had no idea how populous they were. Yet twenty years before, two Wycliffe Bible translators had sought out the tribe to learn their language and translate the Bible into their own tongue. First they had to teach them to read their own language. When they could finally read the life of Jesus from the Gospels for themselves, thousands of the natives received the Savior.

By the time Dr. Brandt arrived to hold a conference for church leaders who had gathered from across the vast jungles, they were clothed, safe, and gracious—no longer a threat to the white man or even to their traditional enemies. In fact, they had welcomed Dr. Brandt warmly. Western culture was foreign to them and they knew nothing about cars, boats, electricity, etc., but they were genuine Christians and lived like it. This is a change totally inexplicable, apart from the power of the cross.

NIGHTMARE TRANSFORMED INTO BLESSING

I will never forget the announcement in 1956 that sent shock waves throughout the nation, even the world. Five young missionaries had been killed in Ecuador, their bodies found floating face down in the Curaray River in the eastern jungle of Ecuador. *Life* magazine featured pages of firsthand reports and photographs, while *Reader's Digest* later published another story. Many Christian periodicals carried news about this incident. But it is not just another event in church history; it is evidence of the power of the cross in lives wholly yielded to Him.

God's hand had uniquely prepared Nate Saint, the pilot of the little yellow plane that carried the men to their "Palm Beach" on the riverbank. Raised in a strong Christian home and eager to have God's will in his life, at the age of fourteen Nate had contracted osteomyelitis in his right leg. After months of recovery and regaining his ability to walk again, he continued to foster his interest in airplanes. At nineteen, when World War II needed good men, Nate enlisted in the army air corps. It was his great joy to be enrolled in the air cadet training program; he was on his way to becoming an army pilot! He was excited to see how $25,000 worth of pilot training was being provided for him.

Exams over and passed, he and other cadets went on a cross-country hike to test physical fitness. That night his dreams began crashing around him as he noted a redness about the scar on his right leg. On his twenty-first birthday, his flying career in the army was suddenly over. What happened to God's plan? But ever trusting his heavenly Father, he waited and prayed. It was with thanksgiving that he learned the army would allow him to take the exam for a mechanic's license.

It was at this juncture that my brother-in-law, Bill Lyons (who then served as a chaplain's assistant in the army air corps), met Nate Saint and saw the power of God's peace at work in this young man's life. (They both became missionaries after their army experiences.)

Later, when the Lord brought Nate in contact with a new program for pilots to assist missionaries in remote locations, he knew that was where the Lord wanted him. All the training he had received now fit into God's plan for him and his new wife, Marj. He was a pilot, a mechanic, and a missionary—one of the first MAF (Missionary Aviation Fellowship) circuit pilots, dedicated to helping missionaries reach tribes in remote areas.

In his book *Evidence That Demands a Verdict,* Josh McDowell, a careful researcher and excellent writer, quotes Rachel Saint as she recounts the rest of the story. Rachel was Nate's sister and had gone to Quito to learn the Auca language (Auca is actually a Quechuan word for "savage").

On January 8, 1956, the whole world was stunned by the word that a band of Auca Indians, the fiercest of Ecuador's aborigines, had fatally speared an American missionary pilot, Nate Saint, and his four co-workers, Jim Elliot, Roger Youderian, Ed McCully and Peter Fleming. After official investigation confirmed the tragedy, Ecuadorian troops and missionaries serving adjoining tribes formed an expedition upriver to bury the victims. They found the plane demolished, its fabric torn to shreds.

The pilot was my brother. He and his companions were engaged in what has since become known as "Operation Auca," a mission to carry the gospel of Jesus Christ to this unlettered, Stone Age tribe in the vastness of the Amazon.

Through one miracle after another, as told in *The Dayuma Story*, all five killers confessed Christ as Savior. I believe it is significant that the first to believe among the Auca men were the five living killers—Kimo, Minkayi, Gikita, Dyuwi and Nimonga. When the first baptismal service was held in Tiwaeno, a little more than two years after our entry into the tribe, four of the five were baptized. The fifth was in the second group of baptisms. In this case my brother Phil did the baptizing. Each of the wives also opened her heart to the Lord Jesus Christ and received baptism.[1]

What the world deemed a tragedy and a waste of human resources became the vehicle that opened the gate for the power of the cross to enter a tribe. Soon after the murder of the five men, Rachel and Betty Elliot (Jim's widow) and her little girl, Valerie, went to live among those tribespeople—they did not fear women—to further their language study and to translate the Scriptures for the people. Today, most of the tribe's members have bowed their knees before the Savior and accepted Him to be the Lord of their lives, giving evidence of God's power to the uttermost.

What but a confrontation with the living Jesus Christ could prompt such forgiveness and love, a response which defies all natural inclination? The missionaries' actions mirror those of the Savior Himself who prayed, "Lay not this sin to their charge, Father. Forgive them, for they know not what they do." Remember that within forty days of crucifying Him, thousands were repenting at the foot of His cross and crying out, "Have mercy on me, surely this was the Son of God!" No other power demonstrates such forgiveness!

THE GENERAL WHO BOWED BEFORE THE CROSS

General Mario Avilez was a Nicaraguan freedom fighter who helped to overthrow the oppressive Samosa government. He was a hero to his people, but like many of the freedom fighters, not a communist at heart. He was a womanizer and drinker and very popular with his troops, but his only gesture toward Christianity was that he married a beautiful young woman who prayed for him every day.

After the revolution was won in 1979, he was sent to Cuba to study communism and to become indoctrinated in the ways of the new pro-Castro regime. In 1981 he was given charge over the entire southern command. One day he stopped some police who were dragging a Nicaraguan farmer through the dusty streets of his town. He was told, "It is to teach him a lesson not to hold back part of his harvest from the government." It seemed the man had saved enough to feed his family and found that was contrary to the law. General Avilez ordered the police to let the man go and they did so—but before long it became his turn to be jailed.

The black shirts arrested Mario and kept him in a two-foot-by-six-foot metal box for several days. During that time a woman who sounded like his wife was supposedly beaten and raped in a cell next to his. (Later he discovered it was a Sandinista government tactic to keep patriots and hero leaders in line.)

Returning to his command, the general began planning to take his family to Costa Rica, where refuge was offered to political refugees. Once he established his family in the area around San José, the nation's capital, he went back to his homeland and volunteered to become a Contra freedom fighter under General Eden Pastora. Recognizing this experienced veteran as a patriot to Nicaragua, Pastora made him a general in his army and he led many battles against the communist-led Sandinista troops, soon becoming a hero to the Contra cause. During one of these battles he was seriously wounded and taken to Costa Rica, where his Christian wife tried to nurse him back to health. During that time he recognized that God loved him and had a wonderful plan for his life, that he had been spared for a purpose.

During his convalescence he bowed before the cross of Jesus and received Him as his Lord and Savior. He was instantly transformed. Not only was his personal life recreated, but he developed a hunger for the Word of God. He was not content merely to study the Bible; he went to Bible school so he could learn to share God's Word and his faith.

When I first met Mario, he was giving his testimony in a refugee camp, along with missionary and former Vietnam marine veteran, Jim Woodall. It was interesting to see how this highly respected former army general was so well received by the people. Even in jeans and a white shirt, the people stepped aside as he walked, showing respect for this warrior.

TWO OPPOSING GENERALS MEET

Jim Woodall told me about an incredible incident that took place in the mideighties when he was invited to an evangelism conference in Guatemala. He asked Mario to go with him, and together they arrived a bit before the conference started. Learning there was a preconference prayer meeting to be held in a hotel room where they were staying, they walked in and began mingling with some of the leaders. Suddenly Jim felt Mario stiffen and saw him staring intensely at a man across the room. Both men locked their eyes upon the other as if no one else was in the room. A holy hush settled on everyone as two warriors saw each other under totally new circumstances. The other man, General X (to spare his identity), had commanded the Sandinista Army which had engaged General Avilez's troops on many occasions. These men had often killed each other's soldiers and more than once had attempted to kill each other.

As they each stared into the other's eyes, they began to move slowly toward each other. No one had to tell Mario that General X also had bent his knees to Jesus Christ and had become a new creation in Christ. He just knew! When they reached the center of the room, they threw their arms around each other and began to weep and fell to their knees. Everyone in the room followed suit—

and the prayer meeting was on. Many of those present were total strangers, but they all sensed the Spirit of the Lord in that place. The cross's power to change people's hearts and attitudes had become extremely apparent.

Now that his country is free again, Mario Avilez has turned down many offers to serve from its president, Violetta Chamorro, preferring to dedicate his time to helping establish and build Christian churches and ministries in his country. He returned to his home and as a businessman has helped many Christians set up what he calls "micro businesses" in a nation where many are destitute and need his professional touch to help them get started.

And, of course, Mario has proven himself a faithful and loving husband to Lejia, the prayer warrior who led him to the cross that changed his life.

THE TRANSFORMATION OF A TOUR GUIDE

Jorge Taylor is the owner of one of the most successful tour agencies in Costa Rica. It was not always successful, nor was Jorge always a Christian. He was a typical Latin male, extremely handsome, likable, and a real ladies' man. Even though he married one of the most beautiful women in Costa Rica, like many men in his country, he had a mistress and others on the side, loved to drink and party, and was very popular. He had an excellent command of both English and Spanish so was popular among North Americans as a guide.

At a time when his marriage was in ruins, his wife, Alicia, met a missionary who led her to the cross. Discouraged by her husband's infidelity and partying, she decided to become a model wife with God's help. The missionary discipled her in the Word and convinced her that only God could change her husband, and He would use her Christian example to do so. Every night when Jorge came home, rather than replaying the scenes to which he had become accustomed, he found his clothes neat and clean, his home ideal, and a gracious, loving wife. One weekend when he happened to be home, Alicia asked him to go to church with her. It was there Jorge Taylor heard the true message from God, that He indeed had sent His Son to die on the cross for Jorge's sins, that He rose again, and that He wanted to save him.

That Sunday evening Jorge went forward and knelt before the cross, signifying that he was repenting of his past and turning his future over to the One who loved him so much. The transformation in his life has been extraordinary. With God's power, this handsome man has cleaned up his act, is faithful to his wife and children, is active in church and Bible study, and is a favorite with missionary groups needing to travel throughout the country. Big Jim, the missionary who discipled Jorge, introduced him to tithing and investing in the work of God. From the day Jorge started to tithe, he sensed the blessing of God on his business and the Lord has allowed him to invest generously in many Christian activities in his church and related ministries.

Currently Jorge is copastor (and still tour agency owner and director) of a booming church in San José, which he and his pastor founded. Many souls have found Christ there, and already the congregation has started a Christian school in the church during the week. Someday I would like to see this church—it didn't exist the last time I was in San José—and meet some of the people he has led to the Savior. Because of the power of the Spirit in his life and his ability to translate from one language to another, he is a favorite of the Christian speakers who visit Central America. When he translated for me one time, I kidded him about elaborating on my message for the good of the congregation.

THE MOST WATCHED MOVIE IN HISTORY

The showing of the movie, *Jesus,* is another indication that the message of the cross knows no cultural barriers. The film is a reenactment of the Gospel of Luke, so all that must be done to show it to various ethnic and language groups is to translate the soundtrack. In that way it can be shown in any country of the world.

Last year, Bill Bright, president of Campus Crusade for Christ International, received a gold copy of the four hundredth language version of the movie, a film that once was no more than a dream in his mind. To date, millions of people have bent before the cross of Jesus and experienced His power for themselves after viewing this movie. We should not be surprised by such a response. Jesus said, "And I, if I am lifted up from the earth, will draw all peoples to Myself" (John 12:32). John looked into the future to see a day when an innumerable host of people would respond to the gospel from every tongue and tribe and nation. That prophecy is starting to be fulfilled in our lifetime.

HOW GOD USES ONE LIFE

Bill Butler was a fighter pilot in World War II who made it home without a scratch. He was a fun-loving playboy who fell in love with a beautiful woman named Betty, who came from a fashionable San Diego family. They made a strikingly handsome couple. The two sons they had together became the joy of their lives. Only one thing was missing from their lives: God. They didn't reject Him, like many Americans; they just never knew Him. Consequently, they made no place for Him in their lives. Partying and the good life were the only gods they served.

When he was thirty-five, Bill went on a skiing trip to the Colorado River with several of his friends. They were having a great time, drinking and skiing, until just before dark, when one of his daredevil buddies did a circular whip at high speed, trying to splash water on their campsite. Evidently he didn't see the overhanging branch of a tree and hit his head so hard he died instantly.

It was decided that two of his friends would take the boat downriver and report the death to the authorities, while Bill would sit by his friend's body in case animals might attack. They were gone until daylight, so Bill sat all night by a fire next to the body of his dead friend, grieving and reflecting. *What if that had been me?* he wondered. He realized that night he was not prepared to meet God.

Shortly thereafter he met an old friend named Paul, who had just received Christ and had started to bring his family to our church. Paul was an interesting and very successful businessman in the city. Raised in a liberal church, he had never heard that he should accept Jesus Christ personally to be saved. He and his new wife had been searching for something in their lives when Paul brought home Fulton Orsler's popular book, *The Greatest Story Ever Told.* Over several Sunday evenings he read to his wife and daughter the story of the life and death of Christ. The Sunday night they finished the book, Paul turned on the television and heard Billy Graham preaching the first real gospel sermon he had ever heard. When Billy gave the invitation, Paul knelt on the carpet in front of his TV, invited his wife and daughter to do the same thing, which they did, and all three bowed before the cross of Jesus and invited Him into their lives to save and guide them.

Paul was never the same again! He became a contagious witness to their social set. He invited one man to have lunch with him in a bar so he could give him the gospel. The man he was witnessing to said, "If you are a Christian now, why are you here in this bar drinking beer?" The thought that testifying over a drink might not be appropriate had never occurred to Paul.

He also shared his new faith with Bill Butler, an old friend. The skiing accident had prepared Bill to humble himself before the Savior, and he too bowed his knees before the cross. No sooner had Bill come to faith than he wanted his wife and two sons to be saved. Paul invited them to church and I had the privilege of baptizing them and watching them grow spiritually by leaps and bounds. In the fall they started bringing their sons to our Christian school and to all the church services. They had a true hunger for the Word of God and became contagious witnesses of their faith.

Somewhere in his past Bill had been made aware of missionaries, who he thought had wasted their lives in some "God-forsaken jungle somewhere." Now he saw them as real heroes of the faith. He was especially captivated with the work of the Wycliffe Bible Translators from our church who had given their lives in some jungle to translate the Bible for the illiterate peoples who seemed so responsive to the Bible as soon as they learned to read.

The remarkable conversion of whole tribes moved Bill deeply. He visited some of them and saw former headhunters now converted, "sane and in their right minds," and realized this was something he wanted to have a part in. As he got acquainted with missionaries, he recognized they knew more about the Bible and helping people spiritually than they did about practical business practices. So he met with the leadership of Wycliffe and together they founded Wycliffe Associates. Today many missionaries are on the field doing translation work because Bill and his associates were able to help them get the support of others to serve in such remote places.

Later Bill founded Christian Resources Management, a ministry to raise money to help radio, TV, and other missionary endeavors. One of his clients during the seventies and eighties was Brother Andrew, who smuggled more Bibles into Russia and other communist countries than any other known individual. Bill and his associates helped raise the money to produce those Bibles.

Only God knows how many people have come to faith directly and indirectly because Bill Butler knelt at the cross and has served his Savior now for over thirty years. I am looking forward to that day when the full accounting will be revealed in heaven.

THE BORDERLESS GOSPEL OF CHRIST

And so the cross continues to transform lives, knowing no nationality, ethnic, nor cultural barriers. The gospel truly is "the power of God to salvation for everyone who believes, for the Jew first and also for the Greek [gentiles]" (Romans 1:16).

It is safe to say there are millions of Pauls and Bills who have had the same life-changing experiences. That is what makes Christianity grow. One person hears the message of the cross, bows before it to surrender their past, present, and future, and then goes forth to live the transformed life that once again proves there is a God who manifests Himself through the power of the cross.

CHAPTER SEVENTEEN

THE FOOLISHNESS
OF MAN'S WISDOM

I n between visits to her psychiatrist, a severely depressed woman in her early thirties came to me for counseling. I couldn't convince her that she should stop being angry at her parents for what she called "her overly strict childhood" and instead thank God for their gift of life, protection, and a comfortable lifestyle. Instead she decided to accept her psychiatrist's advice, which, according to her was, "your problem is you were raised by legalistic parents and are too rigid in your standards to be happy. You have an exaggerated standard of right and wrong. You should relax and have fun." She claimed her psychiatrist ridiculed her virginity and suggested she become intimate with men.

She returned to see me about a year later, more heavily depressed than before, five months pregnant…and still single. And for this advice she paid more than $100 a session!

That is when I began to understand Paul's meaning, "the wisdom of this world is foolishness with God" (1 Corinthians 3:19). Since then I have realized that it doesn't matter what field of humanistic wisdom, or wisdom of this age, that a person follows. If it starts without God, it will end up at worst harmful or at best just plain "foolish". The only exceptions are those who happen to stumble onto a principle of God which helps them. Otherwise, they will be forced to look back over a lifetime and say, "foolishness" or "futility."

It is supremely foolish to refuse to acknowledge that the power for life transformation—and for that matter, societal or cultural change—begins at the foot of the cross. Without the cross, there is little or no possibility of tapping the power it takes to overcome the obsessive compulsions or harmful habits of life.

CONFUSED ABOUT HUMAN NATURE

All observant people are aware that our culture is in trouble. With drive-by shootings, gang wars, ten-year-old murderers, twelve-year-old mothers, fifteen-year-old drug pushers, fourth generation welfare recipients who have no desire to work, and twenty-four-year-old unmarried grandmothers, it should be obvious to all that something is drastically wrong in our country. We have spent over six trillion dollars on welfare during the thirty years of the Great Society—the amount of our national debt—and there are more people on welfare now than when we started.

No one can accuse the originators of these problems of not having good intentions. Most of them are intelligent, well-educated people high up in government, the media, the entertainment industry, or in education. Yet most of what they do to improve our society backfires and creates bigger problems than what we had when we began. The big question is, *why?* The answer is, they are wrong about God, human nature, moral absolutes, and the role of government in national and individual life.

One of the first principles a student of logic learns is that "if you start out on a wrong premise, you will end up with a wrong conclusion." So whether you call it secular humanism, socialism (communism without a gun), or liberalism (socialism through the ballot box), it is all foolishness. And after fifty or more years of this kind of anti-Christian thinking, our cultural decline proves it.

Fifty years ago my widowed mother worked the night shift in a Detroit factory. She got off work at midnight and took two city buses to get home. Years later I asked her if she was afraid to be out on the streets so late. "No," she said, "it never occurred to me that a woman wasn't safe on the streets of Detroit after dark." But that was before judges, law professors, social workers, and parole-board members who were confused about human nature began to look on criminals as victims and refused to make them pay for their crimes.

Even some Supreme Court members have taken the legal handcuffs off the criminals and put them on the police. A violent criminal can often be arrested and out on the street again before the arresting officer can finish the paperwork. The criminal justice system is so twisted today by its antibiblical philosophy that a murderer can be out of prison in six to twelve years. That way, instead of killing just one person, he can kill four or five in his life-time. The result? Ordinary citizens, particularly women, are afraid to go out on the street after dark. *And that is wisdom?* It sounds more like *foolishness* to me. The safety of our culture has all but been destroyed by the decisions of some of the brightest and most-educated minds in our society. Their problem is, they reject God and His moral values and do not understand human nature.

The Founding Fathers of our country knew better. They were overwhelmingly Christian in their philosophy; consequently, they established our constitution and system of law on the premise that human nature was fallen, just as the Bible said. They believed in moral absolutes that people must obey, otherwise chaos would reign. They believed men and women were responsible to God for their behaviors and lifestyles.

Contrast that with the Los Angeles riots after the Rodney King beating, when the city was all but destroyed. For five days the *Los Angeles Times* carried articles justifying the out-of-control actions of the rioters by saying, "Feel their rage." Instead of holding them accountable for their behavior, people were excused for looting, robbing, beating, and even killing others. That is not the rule of law; it is the rule of the jungle. Yet it was sanctioned by some of the brightest minds of our society. They have bought the false notion of Rousseau, the French skeptic who thought human nature was perfectible and merely needed the right environment in which to blossom. They reject the biblical tenet that man has a fallen human nature and that the "heart is deceitful above all things, and desperately wicked" (Jeremiah 17:9).

The idea that "men are criminals because they are poor"—the foundation of our national criminal justice, welfare, and social system today—is a foolish concept based on the refusal to accept the fallen state of human nature. If the idea were true, there would be no white-collar crime today, for only poor people would break the law. But all of us know that to be untrue. Some of the wealthiest and most powerful people in society, including millionaires, have cheated, robbed, and murdered others. Besides, it is an insult to the majority of the poor and the majority of the rich who are *not* criminals to make such a statement.

Rich or poor, criminals break the law because they have a fallen nature and think they can get away with it. That is why mere reformation does not work. The only thing that does work is regeneration, or conversion, in which the power of the cross changes the nature of the individual. Conversion occurs when a man or woman says, "Yes, Jesus Christ, I am a sinner. I have sinned against heaven and in Your sight. Forgive me now and come into my life." Only then, like the prodigal son, are sinners ready to get out of their pigpen of drugs, alcohol, abuse, crime, and immorality to become new creatures in Christ. Only then do they have the power to overcome the obsessions of a lifetime.

4 PERCENT RECIDIVISM RATE—A CASE IN POINT

We have already seen that our national recidivism rate runs at 85–95 percent, despite the $40 billion a year we spend on our prison system (not counting an equal amount for prison construction). Contrast that with Humalta Prison in San Jose des Campos, Brazil.

Prison officials are not hampered there by the ACLU and other liberal American thinkers. Consequently, they can introduce their prisoners freely to Jesus Christ. Once converted, a prisoner is held accountable to attend Bible study and a course in Christian character development. He is required to learn a trade and make restitution to his victim and to earn a living to support himself when released.

Does it work? Over the last twenty-five years where it has been tried, only *4 percent* of Humalta's former inmates have reoffended! As Prison Fellowship says, "Everyone wins...victims are compensated and restored...offenders go on to a new life, communities are safer...and taxpayers get a reliable system that works."[1]

If it works so well, why don't we try it in this country? Because the leftist leaders of our nation reject the power of the cross, considering it foolishness. In reality, their own attempts to solve our nation's crime problems are foolishness—but they stubbornly cling to them, preferring godless chaos to godly peace and safety. Interestingly enough, Dan Rather recently did a television piece about the upcoming test case of Prison Fellowship that features prisoners who agree to attend a discipleship program prior to their release—all financed by voluntary contributions. Can you imagine the opposition of the ACLU and other humanists who oppose tax money being used to promote the very successful method of keeping men from returning to a life of crime?

SEX EDUCATION WITHOUT MORAL VALUES

It has long intrigued me that ordinary working people were not the ones behind the explicit sex education industry that has transformed education in our country ever since the sixties. Instead, it has been the Ph.D.s and Master-degreed educators, sociologists, psychologists, and medical professionals who have destroyed the moral standards of an entire generation. Almost no advocates of radical sex education (which teaches 45 million children and youth far more about sex than they need to know for their age level) are carpenters, plumbers, factory workers, or parents. Instead it is championed by the liberal elite who insist that children must know all about condoms and "safe sex" (possible only through fidelity in marriage) while refusing to teach abstinence. Whole communities have erupted in conflict over the obsession of secular humanists to impose their anti-moral values about sex on our nation's schoolchildren.

Launched in the sixties and seventies at a cost of billions of dollars—supposedly to curb sexual activity, teen pregnancy and venereal disease—the programs have instead increased every one of these problems. Today it is claimed that 51 percent of the girls and 67 percent of the boys in an average high school are sexually active. Sexually transmitted diseases are rampant and teenage unwed pregnancy has never been higher, and the human suffering connected with these abuses is incalculable.

The educational elite has created an obsession for sex at an age when our children and youth need an obsession on learning. Our once great school system is in shambles, not because of lack of money—education is the second largest industry in the nation (behind healthcare) and spends over two trillion dollars every decade. Yet our children are receiving an inferior education. Only 30 percent are good readers, and one-third can't read at all when they graduate. But they know more about sex than any group of young people in the history of mankind!

It is telling that academic performance has gone down in direct proportion to the increase in emphasis on sex education. Parents and taxpayers are being defrauded by highly educated "wisdom of man" thinkers and their foolish assumptions about our children. They believe in evolution and that children are merely animals who have the right to satisfy their urges and desires. Since they do not believe in God, they reject moral absolutes as irrelevant for this age.

The abstinence movement that has lowered the rate of sexual activity among unmarried teens in recent years has been sparked by Christians, parents, and churches, not by the educational elite. In many cases, young people themselves have promoted it. Yet some "experts" continue to fight against it. They flatly refuse to acknowledge that a human being can control his or her urges and drives. In fact, they claim, trying to do so will cause our children to self-destruct. But we teach our kids to control their appetites, their aggressions, their anger—why not their sex drive? No one in the history of the world has been seriously harmed by saying no to their sex drive. On the other hand, millions have ruined or seriously damaged the lives of others by not controlling their "need" for sex.

During the fall of 1995, an incredible event took place on the Washington Mall. Thirty thousand youth from all over the nation came to the capital to make a statement for virtue. These young people, mostly under eighteen, represented more than one hundred thousand youth who had signed virtue cards pledging to remain virgins until marriage. They drove stakes in the ground bearing these thousands of commitment cards. It was an impressive sight! The program was begun by Southern Baptist youth, picked up by Josh McDowell in the True Love Waits program, and was imitated by Lutheran and Catholic youth and many others. It was an event inspired by youth and promoted largely by them.

The tragedy is that, for the most part, it was ignored by the government, educators, and media. Why? Because it was out of step with the "in" wisdom-of-man philosophy. It dared to declare that sexual activity should be reserved for those who are mature enough to bear the responsibility for their behavior. Sexual activity, according to the wisdom of God, requires the marriage of two people of the opposite sex. And interestingly enough, all statistics still indicate that children function best in families including both a mother and father.

I am confident that God looks at the "wisdom of this age" sexologists and says "Foolishness!" Marriage, an institution created by God Himself, is still the safest and best way to invest one's sex drive. Not just for the propagation of the race, but also for enjoyment and fulfillment, as well as the health of our society. A recent survey indicated that married men of all ages had a higher sexual satisfaction and frequency level than single men—by three to one![2]

The wisdom of man is a foolish path to travel. God's plan for sexual satisfaction, which He calls *marriage,* is safer, more satisfying, and more enriching to both the individual and society.

THE UNHAPPY GAYS

Thanks to the medical and nutrition professions, the mortality rate in this country has been cut almost in half during the last one hundred years. At the turn of the century, the average man died at thirty-four, the average woman at thirty-seven (rates partially due to the catastrophic death rate of babies). Now it is about seventy-three for men and seventy-seven for women.

The big exception is gay men, whose life expectancy is between thirty-nine and forty-two. Health hazards are enormously greater among gays, even before AIDS is factored in (the average age of AIDS victims is twenty-nine). And the suicide rate among the gay community is much higher than in the heterosexual population. Statistically, the most unhappy and unhealthy lifestyle today is homosexuality, for both men and women.

When I pastored in San Diego, I counseled many homosexuals and quickly discovered it is definitely not a "gay" lifestyle. Our church was not far from the city park where many of the gays congregated. Many of these troubled souls found their way to my counseling room. Some of the most miserable people that came to me for counseling were angry, rejected, depressed, and often ill homosexuals.

Yet the "wisdom of this world" thinkers want to present homosexuality as an alternative lifestyle to impressionable young children. Some of the greatest conflicts between public educators and parents and between TV programmers and viewers have been over the "foolish" obsession with promoting a dangerous lifestyle that has ruined the lives of so many millions of people. In so doing they cheat millions of potentially normal individuals from enjoying a lifetime of marriage, family, and children, as God intended. But like so many of "the wisdom of this world" thinkers, they do not want to take responsibility for their actions or to be confronted with the results of their policies. They are convinced that without God they know what is best for mankind, even though their policies make it clear they have a warped view of human nature.

The tragedy of this kind of thinking is that liberal elitists who set our national policy have given up on changing homosexuals back to heterosexuals. Most psychiatrists have such a huge failure rate in this area they have concluded "Once gay, always gay." Nothing could be further from the truth! As we have seen, there are thousands of former gays who have converted to Christ and have been transformed by the power of the cross and today live a "straight" life, even enjoying marriage and fatherhood. Yet because the intellegencia of our day have lost hope, they transmit that loss of hope to the gay community.

During the twelve years we lived in Washington, D.C., my wife had her hair done in a shop employing several gay hairstylists. Though they recognized her as leading the largest women's group in the nation, one that had taken a strong stand against the militant policies of the gay and lesbian community, they saw her Christian grace and acceptance of them as individuals. Consequently, over the years she built a casual friendship with some of them. One came to work one day with both his arms in casts. In a "lover's quarrel" his partner got so angry at him he deliberately broke both his arms, which kept him from working for over three months.

The manager of the shop, a man in his early thirties, was "in between relationships," during which time he confided, "Mrs. LaHaye, I would love to have children. The worst thing about my lifestyle is that I will never be a father." When she suggested there was a way to get out of that lifestyle, he protested that it was impossible. "Everyone knows 'once gay always gay,'" he said. Yet as we have seen, that simply isn't true.

In my 1979 book, *The Unhappy Gays,* I referred to a homosexual named Frank who had been converted and was dedicating his life to leading homosexuals to the cross and out of the gay lifestyle. The last I heard of him, he had married a former lesbian who also had bent her knee to the cross. Today they have three children and a normal, fulfilling lifestyle. Frank was the founder of Exit Ministries that now has over 130 centers across the country, specializing in introducing homosexuals to the cross as a means of helping them come out of that lifestyle. It *is* possible to come out of that lifestyle, but it takes supernatural power, beginning with the cross.

It is a tragedy that the wisdom of this age offers no hope to homosexuals, for with all their treatments, medication, and other therapies, they are not able to turn many around. Consequently, they no longer offer that opportunity to gays. And that is the greatest tragedy of all! The temptation to remain in the homosexual lifestyle is so powerful that when a Ph.D. counselor or psychiatrist says to a gay, "There is no hope," then to that individual there is no hope—unless, of course, he is introduced to the gospel message. Then he can bow before the cross, his bag of sins and guilt will roll off him like the Pilgrim in John Bunyan's great allegory, and God will empower him with His Holy Spirit to come out of that lifestyle.

When Jesus told the woman who had five husbands, "Go and sin no more," He implied that with God's help she could overcome her sexual addiction—and so it is today, for there is power in the cross. Not only is that a divine promise, it is also a daily practice for multiplied thousands of former gays. The evidence is so over-whelming it is *foolishness* not to accept it.

TODAY'S FOOLISH AIDS POLICIES

Using the word *foolishness* to describe current AIDS treatment poli-cies is inadequate. A better word would be insanity. AIDS is the worst communicable disease to come on the world scene in a cen-tury, and it has reached epidemic proportions. There were no known AIDS patients in this country, until in 1983 the Center for Disease Control demonstrated that a Canadian homosexual flight attendant had introduced the disease into this nation. They traced his sexual promiscuity to twenty-three known infected cases.

Soon after that it became common knowledge that infected persons first became HIV positive, then in three to ten years they came down with full-blown AIDS. From that point, an agonizing death usually takes anywhere from weeks to three years. No rea-sonable person would wish the disease on his worst enemy, much less on himself.

Yet for reasons known only to the elite "wisdom of this age" thinkers, this rapidly spreading disease is not treated in the same way that TB, cholera, or other communicable diseases are handled. Consequently, over a quarter of a million people have died of AIDS; more than one million are afflicted with it; and three to five million are believed to be HIV carriers, waiting to get AIDS. And while billions of dollars have been spent on AIDS research, with only minimal success so far in retarding the disease, the medical profession is not hopeful of a cure anytime soon. Yet the thought of quarantine as a normal medical policy is never considered for homosexuals with AIDS. Although homosexuality is still the major cause for the spread of the disease, the practice is not outlawed or condemned but instead is presented in schools as a legitimate alternative lifestyle. Contact tracing to determine who is spreading the disease is so regulated, it is, for all practical purposes, useless. In some cases, liberal judges committed to the wisdom of this age have used the law to protect these carriers of HIV, allowing them to continue exposing healthy citizens to the virus.

A Christian doctor confided to me that he is forbidden by law to inform the wife of his AIDS patient of her husband's disease. While there is a kind of skewed logic behind this desire to protect the privacy rights of the AIDS-carrying husband, the "experts" condemn the wife to certain exposure. As my doctor friend said, "refusing to tell the wife is assigning her to certain, premature death." It is like knowing a murderer is stalking your house and refusing to call the police because you want to protect his privacy rights. Or as he said, "I violate the law if I warn her, but if I do not and she dies of AIDS, I will feel like an accomplice to her murder." So what did he do? "The best I could do under the circumstances was to get him to promise never to have sex with his wife unless he used a condom." Unfortunately, the AIDS-infecting agent is so small that it has proven capable of penetrating the condom.

And speaking of rights, what about a dentist's rights? One dentist, the father of three young children, decided he would not expose himself to an early death by contacting the disease, so he declined to treat a known AIDS patient. Instead, he recommended that he go to the nearby university clinic that had a complete department set up with special equipment for just such patients. The AIDS "victim" sued him for refusing to treat him, despite the fact that his office was unequipped for such treatment. His case is still in the courts.

The wisdom of this age jeopardizes healthy people to protect the *rights* of those who have contracted that disease by defying God's laws so that they may satisfy their own lusts. Current statistics indicate that sodomy, promiscuity, and dirty drug needles are still the overwhelming means by which AIDS is passed on. Only a tragic few are innocent victims of receiving the virus by contaminated blood or by contact with bleeding tissue.

It should be noted that those formulating the insane policies currently followed are not ignorant and unlearned people. They are some of the most educated people in our nation, such as judges, lawyers, doctors, medical professionals, and educators. Their one common denominator is their "wisdom of this world" thinking, that man can solve the problems of man without belief in God and an understanding of the fallen nature of mankind. As the writer of Proverbs once said, "There is a way that seems right to a man, but the ends thereof are the ways of death." Our official AIDS policy is a perfect illustration of that truth. One cannot help but wonder how many more millions will get infected with this incurable disease before the elite controllers of our society realize that their theories are not merely anti-God, they are antihuman and do not work. Instead of saving lives, they destroy them.

A NATION ADDICTED TO ALCOHOL

The greatest killer of innocent victims in America today is not AIDS, drugs, or even violence—it is alcohol-related traffic accidents and alcohol-related murders or violence. Drunken drivers, according to statistics published by Mothers Against Drunk Drivers (MADD), killed "300,274 persons in alcohol related traffic crashes alone between 1982 through 1995."[3] That is almost six times as many American service personnel as were killed during the entire Vietnam war. If you add to that the number of death-by-alcohol induced acts of violence during that same period it would be almost eight times greater than the Vietnam death toll.

And all those hit by drunken drivers were not killed! Many were paralyzed, lost limbs, or had their lives traumatically changed by the so-called respectable beverage of alcohol. In 1996, "about 1,058,990 were injured in alcohol-related crashes, an average of one person injured approximately every 30 seconds. About 30,000 people a year will suffer permanent work-related disabilities."[4] The economic costs of alcohol-related crashes are estimated to be $45 billion yearly. An additional $70.5 billion is lost in quality of life due to these crashes."[5] "Drunk driving is the nation's most frequently committed violent crime."[6]

It is impossible to estimate the number of divorces, abused mates and children, and other forms of human suffering perpetrated by drunkards or heavy drinking. Alcohol often changes a person's personality. Many times I have heard women say, "I love my husband when he is sober, but when he has been drinking, he turns into a different person, a person no one can love." "The battle for the bottle," as one woman described it, had cost her fifty-eight-year-old husband a relationship with his son and two daughters, and he became impotent at least twenty years before he should have—a high price to pay for his love for alcohol. If she had not been a Christian, she never would have stayed with him.

I often think of these unknown casualties of our nation's obsession with alcoholic beverages when I hear liberals in one accord decry the "evils of Prohibition." Whether it is movie or TV producers, educators or sociologists, they all "know" that the worst thing to happen in this century was when religious and conservative citizens banded together at the turn of the century to usher in the prohibition movement. They claim that prohibiting the sale of alcoholic beverages spawned gangsters that waged Chicago wars between Al Capone and the FBI's Elliott Ness. They would have the nation believe those dangerous times prove the need to open up the sale of alcohol to everyone above the age of eighteen.

The truth is, more people are killed by drunken drivers in one week than were killed in the crime wave of the entire prohibition period. Yet the elite "wisdom of this world" thinkers still make Prohibition the whipping boy of their false propaganda. They try to shame those of us who believe some kind of social curbs should be put on the nearly unrestricted use of alcohol today, never honestly admitting to the social havoc and human suffering it causes.

Just look at the beer commercials aimed at our nation's youth.

The most watched sport on TV today is football, and much of it sponsored by beer and alcohol companies who pay (for Superbowl commercials) 1.2 million dollars for 30 seconds to deceitfully portray their product as beneficial and enhancing. Never do they show the head-on collisions that take the lives of over 20,000 people each year. Never do they show the poor orphaned children whose parents were killed by a drunken driver.

Our whole national policy on alcohol can best be described as foolishness. So entrenched is alcohol in our society that it would be political suicide for any leader to suggest we make it illegal to sell that which makes otherwise law-abiding citizens into motorized murderers of the highways.

THE TIP OF THE ICEBERG

I am not campaigning for a return to Prohibition, which was a sincere attempt by right-thinking people to improve the quality of life in their generation. What I would suggest is a return to sanity in holding responsible those who produce harmful drugs and beverages. What would happen to the alcohol industry if the widow with four small children whose husband was killed by a drunk driver could sue the company that manufactured the beverage, the distributor, the bar or store owner where it was sold and the bartender or clerk who sold it? That possibility is ridiculed out of hand in today's climate. Better to let all of them go free while the widow and her little children suffer, so they can all be free to do the same to other potential sufferers. That is wisdom? Yes, the wisdom of this world.

But this is just the tip of the iceberg; there are many other social changes the "wisdom of man" thinkers wish to introduce into our society, from legalizing drugs to euthanasia, from abortion on demand even in the birth canal to eliminating all laws against pornography. And the list goes on—ever attacking the traditional values of what was once the greatest, freest, safest nation on earth.

It is impossible to have total freedom in a collective society without putting limits on that freedom. Driving your car on the freeway is a good example. Thousands of people can travel a freeway at the same time *if* they are all going the same way. Let just one of those drivers exercise his total freedom by turning around and heading the other way, and chaos results. Society holds him responsible for his driving by demanding that he obey the rules.

Why can't the beer and liquor companies be held responsible for their behavior, just as the cigarette companies are finally being held responsible for the huge number of premature deaths their products have caused?

My wife interviewed the mother of a seventeen-year-old girl who had undergone an abortion just after she had testified before congress. School officials urged her daughter to get an abortion without parental approval. It turned out the doctor did a poor job and left parts of the fetus in the young mother's womb, which caused a dangerous infection that almost took the girl's life. The parents were responsible to pay the $26,000 it took to save her life, and nothing can reverse the hysterectomy that was necessary, preventing the girl from ever having her own children. Yet Planned Parenthood and other abortion providers continue to pre-empt parental rights by giving approval to take the lives of the parents' unborn grandchildren. Such groups abuse their freedom because they are not held responsible for their actions.

Something is definitely wrong in this country, and most citizens realize it. But the liberal elitists who have the most control are determined to disregard history and the standards of God in the pursuit of their man-centered "wisdom of this world." The late Dr. Francis Schaeffer so aptly said, "All roads from secular humanism lead to chaos."

THE LAST BEST HOPE FOR MANKIND

On a hillside high above the five little cities that make up the Palm Springs area in California, someone has planted a large cross. At night it is lighted and can be seen for miles throughout the entire Coachella Valley. That cross is a landmark almost as eye catching as the mountain upon which it is located. Whenever I drive toward the main part of the city, I see that cross and remember what those who placed it there had in mind. It offers hope to all who pass by saying, "There is hope from the foolishness of those who follow man's wisdom. It is the cross on which Jesus Christ died for the sins of the whole world." Without that cross, this would be a hopeless world.

The choice you must make is whether you will recognize the hope that is still in that cross. Have you bent your knee before it and said, "Yes, Jesus Christ, I believe You died on that cross for my sins and am willing to receive You as my Savior and Lord today"? If you will—like Paul, Jim, Lenora and millions of others—you will see your greatest need fulfilled, a real life transformation.

THE MOST BASIC DESIRE IN MANKIND

If an objective poll were taken, I am confident that most people would admit that their greatest desire is to experience in full the emotions of love, joy, and peace. It is true that the hunger drive, self-preservation instinct, and the desire for sexual satisfaction are all powerful factors, but over the long haul of a lifetime, human contentment, peace, and the ability to love and be loved take precedence over everything else. Our founding fathers foresaw that when they inserted into the constitution the guarantee that everyone had a right to "life, liberty, and the pursuit of happiness."

They understood that everyone wants to be happy. But secularism cannot provide it. In fact, its ways and beliefs produce just the opposite. Man's wisdom that now controls the engines of influence in our society produces misery, poverty, crime, fear, hostility, and rebellion.

Paul saw that clearly when he wrote,

This I say, therefore, and testify in the Lord, that you should no longer walk as the rest of the Gentiles walk, in the futility of their mind, having their understanding darkened, being alienated from the life of God, because of the ignorance that is in them, because of the hardening of their heart; who, being past feeling, have given themselves over to licentiousness, to work all uncleanness with greediness. (Ephesians 4:17–19)

The "gentile mind" Paul is talking about is the Greek humanism of his day, which today has been fused with French skepticism, German rationalism, Enlightenment thinking, humanism, and Unitarianism, to produce modern-day secular humanism. This God-rejecting, man-centered, amoral philosophy (with its devotion for government-run socialism) is the official philosophy of almost all governments, systems of education, media, and the entertainment industry. We have already seen that they are shaping our culture today and leading western culture straight into Sodom and Gomorrah. In the process, they are making more people miserable and unhappy. As Paul said, man's ways are "foolishness" and cause men and women to "walk in the futility of their mind." Why? Because their mind is "alienated from the life of God."

They do not understand that in the wisdom of God, the world through wisdom did not know God. All the secular libraries of our day will never introduce man to God, for as Paul said, he is not learned by the writings of men but "by the foolishness of preaching." That is why the "thinkers" of our world are predominantly atheists; they start out with the assumption that God does not exist and unsurprisingly conclude that there is no God. The psalmist said, "The fool has said in his heart, 'There is no God'" (Psalm 53:1). He is a fool to begin with because he refuses to see the abundant signs of God all around him and concludes He does not exist. From then on his thinking is all downhill, and he develops theories that make mankind miserable.

When I attended Northwestern High School in Detroit, I had an English teacher I really liked. She was the first teacher who believed I was educable. How well I remember in our hot afternoon classes, she would try to rouse us from our mental lethargy by challenging us to "strike the pose of the thinker." She had in mind the stone image of the well-muscled Greek athlete/thinker in front of the Detroit Public library. What she didn't realize is that if he, or if all thinkers like him, thought until they turned green, they would never come to the knowledge of God. God is not thought up by man, or discovered in the books, microfiche, or videos of man. He is revealed in nature, in the Scriptures, in the life of His Son Jesus Christ, and by the transformation that occurs in the lives of those who bend their knees at the cross and receive Him as Savior and Lord.

Without that conversion experience, men and women will never find lasting happiness. They may find moments of excitement, joy, and happiness, but they will not find in man's wisdom the sustaining "love, joy, and peace" of God that will help them in the chamber of death and in the valley of life's turmoil. Instead, because of the hardening of their heart; who being past feeling, have given themselves over to licentiousness, to work all uncleanness with greediness" (Ephesians 4:18–19). Isn't that a picture of modern "wisdom of man" thinkers? They must be continually entertained, sedated by drugs, alcohol, and medication; their lusts can seldom be satisfied; and they end up with STDs, AIDS, or degenerative diseases long before they should. "Man's wisdom" may look good at twenty or thirty years of age, but how many enjoy real happiness into their fifth and sixth decades of life—particularly as their bodies begin to break down due to the harmful chemicals they have used through the years?

Just recently a doctor whose wife passed away after thirty-seven years of marriage confided in me that she had been a drinker all her life. She died twenty years prematurely and in great suffering with cirrhosis of the liver. Fortunately for her, she finally bent her knee at the cross, received Christ, and by His power overcame her lifetime addiction. Although she did outlive her doctor's prognosis by four years, even salvation did not undo the harmful effects on her body inflicted by her earlier years. At fifty-seven she died a painful death—but had she received Christ in her youth, she probably would have lived another twenty or thirty years. And this is man's wisdom?

A BETTER WAY TO FIND HAPPINESS

Jesus Christ promised that "when He, the Spirit of truth, has come, He will guide you into all truth" (John 16:13). Part of that truth is explained by Paul when he commanded Christians everywhere to "walk in the Spirit, and you shall not fulfill the lust of the flesh. The fruit [results] of the Spirit, is love, joy, peace" and six other strengths necessary for long-term happiness (Galatians 5:16, 22). Note carefully the promise of emotional contentment through the indwelling Holy Spirit—love, joy, and peace, the very emotions we yearn for most in life.

And the beautiful truth is, these emotions that can sustain us through the ups and downs of life have no ill side effects. You no doubt know that most drugs and intoxicants have harmful side effects, as do many prescription drugs. Not so the spiritual injection of "love, joy, and peace." They are ours, free for the taking, beginning the moment we bend our knees at the foot of the cross.

Doubtless you know of many people who cannot face the trials of life without a drink or a beer or their favorite crutch. Once we become Christians, the Holy Spirit is in us to provide the emotional stimulus for the everyday problems of life. Bill Kennedy, the prisoner whom I have been mentoring by phone, is a good case study. He has every reason to be angry at the injustice of being sentenced to twenty years in prison for something he did not do. He is the victim of hiring an in-house lawyer who he did not know was a "takeover specialist" who robbed him of his business, plunged it into bankruptcy, and then blamed him for the whole thing. The man even violated his lawyer-client privilege of confidentiality by secretly revealing to the government prosecutor his defense strategy. Instead of being upset and depressed because he had been so unfairly treated, Bill is using the time, while awaiting an appeal, to grow spiritually. He has been studying the Word of God about three hours a day and is so committed to God that he often encourages me. He has led so many men to Christ in prison that he has had up to twenty-four studying their Bibles and sharing their faith at a time.

Today as we talked, Bill described how he was able to encourage an overworked school administrator to "Commit your way to the LORD, trust also in Him, and He shall bring it to pass" (Psalm 37:5). When he finished, his friend thanked him and said, "If you can find that peace and joy in prison, I guess I can find it here at home." Then Bill laughed and said that when people understand and adopt the viewpoint of Paul, who learned that in "whatsoever

state [even prison] we are in, we can be content," they find that
same inner peace he had. Then he quoted Paul's words written
from prison (he was there for preaching the gospel):

> Rejoice in the Lord always. Again I will say, rejoice! Let
> your gentleness be known to all men. The Lord is at hand.
> Be anxious for nothing, but in everything by prayer and
> supplication, with thanksgiving, let your requests be made
> known to God; and the peace of God, which surpasses all
> understanding, will guard your hearts and minds through
> Christ Jesus. (Philippians 4:4–7)

Everyone wants peace, joy, and love. These inner emotions
produce happiness regardless of the circumstances. They are not
found through the futile wisdom of this age, but are abundant at
the foot of the cross through the power of God that alone can
transform your life.

MAN'S WISDOM COULD NEVER DO THIS

People are not being positively converted today by the wisdom of
this world. No one ever undergoes a positive lifestyle transformation by kneeling before a pile of philosophy or psychology text-
books. They are simply not in the life-transforming business,
mainly because they lack supernatural power.

On the other hand, the power of the message of the cross is
legendary. It has been transforming lives for two thousand years
now and knows no barriers, works in all cultures and nations, and
can still transform anyone willing to bow before it. Dr. Bill Bright
of Campus Crusade for Christ International gives some amazing
illustrations of this limitless, unending power.

I have known Bill for more than forty years. I remember when
he had only one full-time worker. Today Campus Crusade has
more than sixteen thousand workers all over the world who are
sharing the power of the cross with lost souls. Bill probably has
helped lead more people to Christ than anyone since the apostle
Paul. His *Jesus* film has been translated into more than four hun-

dred languages and has led multiplied millions to the Savior. Always they are presented the way to the cross to cleanse their sin and save their soul. Bill has seen countless lives transformed. Consider these exciting, but contrasting, experiences.

During the past fifty years I have seen many moving examples of people being changed by coming to the cross and experiencing God's pardon, peace, purpose, and power in their lives.

Probably none is more of a contrast than when, some years ago, I was invited by the warden to speak to the inmates of one of the most infamous high-security prisons in America: the Federal Penitentiary in Atlanta, Georgia.

It was a place where prisoners who had committed major crimes, such as murder, were incarcerated. Some of our Campus Crusade staff members had been working with hundreds of inmates, and several of them had become Christians. When I arrived at the penitentiary assembly room, several of the inmates rushed over to me, embraced me, and called me "brother." They told me they had heard my messages on tapes, read my books, and told how they had been helped by them and our staff. Before I spoke, several stood and gave testimony of how they had been forgiven by God through faith in Christ's death on the cross and His resurrection. One man spoke of how he had murdered five people. Another three. Others had committed similar crimes. They told of how they came to the prison full of hate and fear—and then they met Jesus and were transformed!

Tears streamed down my face as I listened to these testimonies of God's forgiveness, grace, goodness and love. Again and again different ones said, "I'm glad I'm here. If I had not been sent here, I would not know Christ and I would probably be dead because of my life of crime."

These prisoners—these men behind bars—had experienced the wonder of God's eternal pardon from their sins.

They had been born again. They had received peace of heart and mind. They were experiencing purpose and meaning for their lives. And they had been given power to be different, even in their prison cells.

As I sat there, my mind raced across the continent to Hollywood, California, where just two nights previously I was privileged to be a guest in a great gathering of Hollywood personalities, many of whom were the famous movie stars, producers, directors and entertainers of the world, gathered to honor one of their own. I sat between a man who for more than thirty years had been one of the great actors of our country, and the daughter of one of the founders of the Hollywood industry and presently the wife of a famous actor. I had hardly taken my seat when the woman began to tell me how miserable she was and how she was thinking about committing suicide. She said she had nothing to live for. Her little dog, the most prized, beloved possession she had, died the day before, and she was devastated. She lived in a palatial mansion. She was world famous. She had a great fortune at her disposal. And yet she felt she had nothing to live for. I was happy to share the most joyful news of Christ's love for her, and I saw with my own eyes a dramatic change in her countenance. She seemed overwhelmed to learn that God loved her and had a wonderful plan for her life. She asked if she could keep the evangelistic Four Spiritual Laws booklet which I had shared with her, stating that its content was so wonderful that she wanted to read it over and over again. Her countenance actually changed before my eyes.

I turned to the man on my left, known to most Americans. He was inebriated. I tried to initiate a conversation by speaking to him of my work with students, whereupon he responded angrily, saying "Why waste your time on students? They are just a bunch of hotheaded radicals. Why doesn't someone work with older people?" He began to sob, saying, "Why doesn't somebody work with people like me? I need help." I was able to help that dear man. Later he was baptized in one of the leading churches in southern California.

I was overwhelmed with the contrast. I thought of these people of wealth and fame and power in Hollywood, in the prisons of their own selfish desires and their own fleshly pursuits of materialism in their egocentric ways. They thought they were free, but they were actually in prison—a self-imposed prison. Sadly, this is true for most people throughout the world today.

Then I thought of the men in the federal penitentiary in Atlanta who would never see the light of day outside those gray, bleak prison walls, because of their life sentences. Yet, because of Christ they were free. They were free, happy, rejoicing and giving thanks to their Savior. Oh, what a contrast! God's pardon, peace, purpose and power are available to everyone, no matter where or who they are.

SPECIAL NOTE

The stories of life transformation contained in this book may seem overwhelming, but they really aren't. The truth is, they don't represent one one-thousandth of one percent of such stories that could be presented from our own generation. Add to that the millions like them since the days of Paul, Luke, and Barnabas. Everywhere the gospel message has gone, it has confronted suffering, sin, tragedy, and obsession. In every case where people have responded, it has elevated the individuals, the society, and the culture. Vital Christianity always has raised the level of peace, love, and joy where it has been embraced. Man's wisdom does just the opposite; it produces sin, crime, misery, and heartache.

Central to the message of the gospel is the cross. The cross of Christ is the only power that can transform the life of anyone who will bend their knees before it and receive the Savior which it represents.

ROOM AT THE CROSS

A Christian attorney invited me to help present a divorce-prevention seminar in St. Louis, along with a Christian psychologist and a Christian psychiatrist. I knew and trusted both of these mental-health professionals, for I had read their books and knew they based their concepts for helping people on the same biblical principles that I did. So I accepted the invitation. Besides, I am always charmed when a Christian tries to use the free-enterprise system to advance the kingdom of God.

To avoid any legal difficulties, he charged ten dollars to attend the seminar and wrote off the rest of the day's expenses against his legal firm's income. He felt it was worthwhile to offer his clients the same opportunity to save their life and marriage that had made all the difference in his own—a commitment to Jesus Christ.

This attorney handled many divorce cases each year. His wife, also an attorney, worked in his office and between them they prayed for each client and considered it more important to reconcile the couple and save the marriage whenever possible, rather than just to work out a good divorce settlement.

Frankly, I enjoyed the experience so much I have participated twice. The first time I accepted his offer, I received a call from the pastor of his church where the seminar was to be held asking me to stay over Saturday night and preach for him on Sunday. For a message that morning I was led to select 1 Corinthians 1:18—the core verse for this book—as the text for my sermon. I called it "The Power of the Cross" and it formed the embryonic basis of this book.

I was not prepared for what I encountered that Sunday. The seminar had not been conducted in the church auditorium on Saturday, so I was surprised when I saw its beautiful architecture. Instead of a big platform and choir loft, the church had a small platform in front of a beautiful brick wall. The choir sat in the congregation until it was time to sing, after which its members returned to sit with their families. That idea impressed me, but not nearly so much as the magnificent, hand-hewn, black wooden cross that hung on the wall. It was a simple cross, much like the one on which our Lord was crucified.

This unique cross was not empty. No, it was not a crucifix; instead, it was adorned with more than 250 silver plates, each about three by seven inches. On the plates were names! On the left crossbar were the names of Adam, Eve, Seth, Abel, Noah, Joseph, Moses, Ruth, Naomi, Caleb, Samuel, Elijah, Elisha, Isaiah, Jeremiah, Daniel, and many other Old Testament figures. A man in the church had printed all these names carefully in his home shop over a period of time. On the right crossbar were the names of the Twelve Apostles, the noted women of the New Testament, Luke, Mark, Paul, and many others, including Lydia, Onesimus, Philemon, Aquila, and Priscilla. Down the front of the cross he had printed out the names of the early Church fathers: Irenaeus, Papias, Justin Martyr, Clement, Eusebius, many Christian martyrs rarely heard of in today's church, Augustine, Hippolytus, John Calvin, John Knox, Wycliffe, Tyndale, many missionary martyrs, some moderns like D. L. Moody, John Wesley, Billy Sunday, Billy Graham, and many more.

At the bottom of this impressive array of Christian heroes of the faith I saw about thirty empty nameplates. I was instantly reminded of one of my favorite hymns. At the close of the service I led the congregation in that hymn as an invitation. After the service I told the pastor how much I loved that hymn and how often I had used it as an invitation hymn. "That is my favorite hymn too," he replied. "In fact, that is where I got the idea for this cross, shared it with the congregation, and one of the artisans in the church offered to make all the nameplates. We dedicated the cross the same day we dedicated the new church building."

Visualize that cross as you read the following inspired words:

Room at the Cross for You
The cross upon which Jesus died
Is a shelter in which we can hide;
And its grace so free is sufficient for me,
And deep is its fountain—as wide as the sea.

Tho millions have found Him a friend,
And have turned from the sins they have sinned,
The Savior still waits to open the gates,
To welcome a sinner before it's too late.

There's room at the cross for you,
There's room at the cross for you.
Tho millions have come, There's still room for one—
Yes, there's room at the cross for you!

This old song by Ira F. Stanphill is not merely an invitation hymn sung at the close of thousands of church services every Sunday, it is also a genuine offer from God Himself. If you have never bent your knee at the cross to receive Jesus Christ as your Lord and Savior, or if you are not sure you have done so, I would urge you to take the first step immediately. I can promise you this: You will get up from that experience a new person and will have the power to live the transformed life, in both this world and in the life to come.

One of those blank nameplates has room for your name! So don't leave it blank. Choose to invite Jesus Christ into your life right now, and start experiencing the overwhelming power of the cross.

Notes

CHAPTER THREE

1. In Muslim countries the symbol is the Red Crescent, adopted in 1906 at the insistence of the Ottoman Empire.

2. John Stott, *The Cross of Christ* (Downers Grove, Ill.: InterVarsity Press, 1986), 19–20.

3. Ibid., 43.

4. Ibid.

5. Stott, 45, quoting Justin Martyr, *First Apology,* chapter IV.

6. Ibid., 46, quoting Tertullian, *De Corona,* 94.

7. Ibid., 22, quoting Gregory, *Apostolic Tradition of St. Hippolytus,* XI .

8. Charles Colson, *A Dangerous Grace* (Dallas, Tex.: Word Publishing, 1994), 69–70.

9. Stott, 10.

CHAPTER FOUR

1. "The Love of God" by F. M. Lehman © 1917. Renewed 1945 by Nazarene Publishing House. All rights reserved.

CHAPTER FIVE

1. *Holman Bible Dictionary*, ed. Trent C. Butler (Nashville, Tenn.: Holman Bible Publishers, 1991), 321.

2. Associated Press reports, March 1997.

CHAPTER SIX

1. For overwhelming evidence of this, see the author's book, *Jesus, Who Is He?*

CHAPTER SEVEN

1. Bruce Corley, *The Road from Damascus* (Grand Rapids, Mich.: Wm. B. Eerdmans Publishing Company, 1997), 14.

2. Dave Hunt, *In Defense of the Faith* (Eugene, Ore.: Harvest House, 1996), 165–7.

3. Corley, 13.

4. From a pamphlet by Lord Lyttelton found in the Library of Congress.

5. Josh McDowell, *Evidence That Demands a Verdict* (Nashville, Tenn.: Thomas Nelson, 1979), 365–6.

CHAPTER TEN

1. Chuck W. Colson, *Born Again* (Old Tappan, N.J.: Fleming H. Revell Co., 1976), 129–130.

2. Pamela Constable, "The Soft Sell", *Washington Post, 16* February 1997, F4.

3. Larry Witham, *Washington Times,* "Study Says Reading Bible Cuts Inmates' Rate of Rearrest" 17 March 1997.

4. Telephone conversation with the Good News Jail and Prison Ministry (GNJPM).

CHAPTER ELEVEN

1. Josh McDowell, *More Than a Carpenter* (Wheaton, Ill.: Tyndale House Publishers, 1980), 126–8.
2. Ibid., 77.
3. Ibid., 128.
4. T. J. Simers, *Washington Times,* 17 April 1997, C1, C7.
5. From a personal letter by Dr. Adrian Rogers to the author.
6. From a personal letter by Luis Palau to the author.

CHAPTER TWELVE

1. Survey of Alumni of Teen Challenge of Chattanooga, by Dr. Roger D. Thompson, University of Tennessee, 1992–94.
2. Ibid.
3. Jay Strack, *Shake Off the Dust* (Nashville, Tenn.: Thomas Nelson, 1988), 18–28, selected portions.
4. Ibid., 29–30.
5. Ibid., 29.

CHAPTER THIRTEEN

1. Tim LaHaye, *How to Win over Depression* (Grand Rapids, Mich.: Zondervan, 1974), 67.
2. Ibid., 90–1.

CHAPTER FIFTEEN

1. John Bunyan, *The Pilgrims Progress and Explanatory Notes* (republished by Grace Abounding Ministries, Inc., 1986), 119–120.

CHAPTER SIXTEEN

1. Josh McDowell, *Evidence That Demands a Verdict* (Nashville, Tenn.: Thomas Nelson, 1979), 370.

CHAPTER SEVENTEEN

1. 1995 summary of statistics, MADD 1996.
2. Ibid.
3. Ibid.
4. Ibid.
5. Ibid.
6. Ibid.

EPILOGUE

1. "Room at the Cross for You" by Ira F. Stanphill, ©1946. Renewed 1974 by Singspiration.